D0118161

To Rich + Ruth,

YOUR GREEN ABODE

Tara Rae Miner

YOUR GREEN ABODE

a practical guide to a sustainable home

Tara Rae Miner

SKIPSTONE

© 2010 by Tara Rae Miner

All rights reserved. No part of this book may be reproduced or utilized in any form, or by any electronic, mechanical, or other means, without the prior written permission of the publisher.

Published by Skipstone, an imprint of The Mountaineers Books
Printed in the United States of America
First printing 2010
12 11 10 09   5 4 3 2 1

Copy Editor: Julie Van Pelt
Design: Heidi Smets
Cover illustration: © istock.com

ISBN (paperback): 978-1-59485-275-6
ISBN (e-book): 978-1-59485-298-5

Library of Congress Cataloging-in-Publication Data
Miner, Tara Rae, 1974-
  Your green abode : a practical guide to a sustainable home / by Tara Rae Miner.
      p. cm.
  Includes bibliographical references and index.
  ISBN 978-1-59485-275-6 (trade pbk.) — ISBN 978-1-59485-298-5 (ebook)
  1. Ecological houses. 2. Sustainable living. I. Title.
  TH4860.M56 2010
  640—dc22
                          2010015531

Skipstone books may be purchased for corporate, educational, or other promotional sales. For special discounts and information, contact our Sales Department at 800-553-4453 or mbooks@mountaineersbooks.org.

Skipstone
1001 SW Klickitat Way, Suite 201
Seattle, Washington 98134
206.223.6303
www.skipstonepress.org
www.mountaineersbooks.org

LIVE LIFE. MAKE RIPPLES.

FOR JASON AND SIGNE

CONTENTS

INTRODUCTION

When my husband and I purchased a 160-year-old schoolhouse in the rolling hills of western Massachusetts, greening it was the furthest thing from my mind. I quickly fell in love with its quirky characteristics, eleven-foot ceilings, and wavy, handmade glass windows. But before we had even closed the deal, I had already put together a mental checklist of what we would need to change. Step 1: remove hideous wallpaper. Step 2: remove hideous vinyl counter tops. Step 3: paint over hideous yellow walls.

Faced with a gamut of home remodeling choices, I'm guessing that you, like me, would probably rather invest your limited time and money in a couple of gallons of paint—make it look good—and get back to your busy life. A green house might conjure up images of that funky straw-bale thing a friend of a friend built on that creek outside of town or one of those hexagonal structures mildly reminiscent of extraterrestrial aircraft.

For some, a green building is the latest multibillion-dollar high-rise downtown. For others, it's a home you have to build from the ground up, complete with solar panels, radiant floor heat, low-E (low-emissivity) insulated windows, and sustainably harvested lumber. A green home is alternative crunchy or the latest hip thing. I certainly didn't think the concept could apply to my house in Massachusetts, a structure built well over a century before the word *green* was used to describe a lifestyle or building.

And yet the first premise of this book is that any home can be green. And I mean any—from your 400-square-foot loft on the Upper East Side to your 1970s-era suburban ranch, from your farmhouse on twenty acres to your sweet bungalow in the old part of town. You can make it green.

The second premise is that any shade of green is better than brown. In other words, every little bit helps. And perhaps this idea is the more important of the two.

This book is not intended to make folks feel guilty about their carbon-emitting, chemical-laden, resource-intensive homes (kidding!). Few of us are capable of a whole-house renovation, and I wouldn't suggest it anyway. The process of greening your home is a process of getting to know your home. If you rush, you'll not only make mistakes, you'll miss out on all the fun. My advice is to start small; do what interests you and what you can afford (or what might save you money, as many green upgrades do).

But of course it's not all about you. If you've picked up this book, I'd venture to guess that you have an interest in the welfare of our planet—our home in a bigger sense. If someone has given you this book as a kind hint, you might be surprised to know that residential homes are responsible for 17 percent of U.S. greenhouse gas emissions. That's right—green choices don't just involve coal-burning power plants and whether you drive or bike to the grocery store. Where we live, and how we live there, has a big impact on the climate and our extended environment. As global warming's dire predictions top the headlines every day, along with news of old-growth forests falling to the chainsaw and sprawl, along with scary statistics of the number of chemicals coursing through our bodies, along with…Doesn't it make you want to do something? The good news is you can. And what better place to start than under your very own roof?

This book can help, but let me clarify what it's not. It's not a book for aspiring green architects and designers. I'm not going to talk about your house's energy or crystals or even feng shui. I have never built a house, though I have changed the carbon footprint of one.

What I would like to offer you is some advice based on my own experience, both in home remodeling and in my own best attempts at green living—oh, and a little optimism too. I really do believe that there is something empowering about understanding the impact your personal choices have on the planet and being able to make better ones.

So if you've ever wondered how much energy you really save by screwing in a compact fluorescent bulb, here's where to look. Troubled by the list of undecipherable chemicals in your bathroom cleaning products, curious if there are better natural options? I've got some answers for you. Think cork is only appropriate for wine bottles or that compost comes in bags? I'm here to tell you different. Believe natural, eco, and green need be dull, muted, and drab? Time to reevaluate.

Your Green Abode is filled with advice on green living, green remodeling, and green gardening. It'll help you understand how much energy your house uses and how to spare both the planet and your budget. You'll learn how to keep the air and inhabitants inside your home healthier and how to save trees, water, and land simply by exercising your power of choice. Organizations and publications are mentioned throughout the book and in the Recommended Resources section at the end, to help you on your way.

Our homes reflect who we are. Isn't it about time yours stood for what you believe in?

PART 1

YOUR CARBON HOMEPRINT

You can't measure them in square footage, but the benefits of green changes you make to your home will extend well beyond its walls. This need not be a completely altruistic endeavor, though my money is on your heart being in the right place. Greening your home comes with many associated benefits that improve planetary health, including some that translate into money in the bank.

CHAPTER 1

GREEN HOME, GREEN PLANET:
BEST PRACTICES FOR A BETTER WORLD

Our concept of home was radically changed when, in 1968, astronauts on the Apollo 8 mission sent back images of Earth. For the first time we saw in its entirety our blue planet—eerily beautiful and completely isolated, a fragile sphere hanging in the vast expanse of outer space. It was a big wake-up call: we'd better make sure we took care of it, because there didn't appear to be any other place to go. Some say these pictures helped birth the environmental movement. For the purposes of this book, let's consider their impact this way: home = planet, planet = home. Taking care of one means taking care of the other.

Which brings us to the subject of climate change. I won't waste a lot of time giving you reams of data or go out of my way to convince you that (a) it's real and (b) we humans are the ones to blame. Nor will I go into detailed explanations of carbon dioxide (and other greenhouse gas) buildup and how drastically our emissions have increased since the Industrial Revolution. Many an expert has written thoroughly on this subject, and I'm not one of them. But I do want to make sure you're aware that you have an opportunity to combat the greatest threat to our planet and civilization right in your own home.

Reducing greenhouse gas emissions is not just about how many miles you drive in a week or flights you take in a year. In fact, in the grand scheme of our society's energy consumption, buildings are the largest users. That means that your home sweet home, the roof that provides shelter for you and your beloveds, can make a real difference in getting our planet back on track if you start taking steps to conserve energy. Or consider it this way: every dollar you save on your energy bills yields interest in the fight against global warming.

YOUR HOME'S ENERGY ISN'T JUST ABOUT FENG SHUI

Let's pause for a moment for a sample helping of statistics. These are not meant to shift you into complacency or, even worse, scare you into a state of helplessness. Their purpose is to sketch out the scope of our challenge as well as some tangible and rewarding opportunities we have to effect change.

YOU MEAN MY HOME IS RESPONSIBLE FOR ALL THAT?

Our homes, offices, and factories account for 40 percent of the energy that we use worldwide. In the United States alone, the heating, cooling, and lighting of buildings makes up roughly 36 percent of our energy consumption. According to the U.S. Department of Energy (DOE), buildings annually consume $20 billion more energy than would be necessary if they were greened.

Coal is our nation's largest energy source (accounting for more than half of our energy production). The coal industry also holds the dubious distinction of being the biggest polluter and the largest source of greenhouse gas emissions and mercury poisoning in the air and water (not to mention the devastating effects of mining the stuff; if you've not heard of mountaintop removal, take a look at parts of West Virginia on Google Earth).

Energy used in the home of a typical American household (two-car, single-family) accounts for about half of that family's entire greenhouse gas contributions and energy costs. While transportation is in the lead with 55 percent, household emissions are not far behind at 45 percent.

YOU MEAN MY HOME CAN MAKE THAT MUCH OF A DIFFERENCE?

Consider this: for every kWh of electricity you avoid using, you save more than 1.5 pounds of CO_2. If you replace that Ronnie Reagan-era 20-cubic-foot fridge with a modern energy-efficient model, you could save more than 500 kWh and almost 1,000 pounds of CO_2 emissions per year. Replacing just ten 75-watt incandescent bulbs with 23-watt compact fluorescents (CFLs) can save up to 1,400 pounds of CO_2 per year.

If you plant shade trees around your home and paint it a lighter color (or convince your landlord to do so) in lieu of or to augment your air conditioning, you can save 1,800–4,800 pounds of CO_2 per year.

We've already come a long way. Appliance standards that took effect in the early 1990s saved a whopping 88 billion kWh in 2000—about 28 million tons of CO_2. In 2010, the next generation of updates to these industry standards saved more than 250 billion kWh.

Imagine a movement. If the roughly 40 million households that live in climates with large heating needs boosted their furnace or boiler efficiencies from 70 to 90 percent, some 45 million tons of CO_2 would be eliminated every year.

Need more data? I've put together a useful Recommended Resources section at the end of the book. Talk, too, to your local utility and check out your state's energy conservation programs to get details on saving energy in your particular region.

CONSERVATION FIRST

What else might it take to make your home carbon-free, or at least carbon-light? Perhaps you're already dreaming of solar panels, a brand-new heat-reflecting roof, a state-of-the-art geothermal system—the envy of your neighbors. Pause for a moment and take a deep breath. Scan your bank statements and don't forget to find out how truly understanding your partner, friends, and children will be when you enter a more demanding relationship with your home. Now consider instead picking the low-hanging fruit.

By that I mean start with conservation. Before you get caught up with that sexy solar photovoltaic system, evaluate your home's energy efficiency. Though not quite as exciting at first glance, it's well worth your time and will pay dividends—financially, psychologically, and practically—in your quest for carbon neutrality.

Dan Chiras, author of *The Homeowner's Guide to Renewable Energy*, has studied energy efficiency for three decades. This expert equates saving energy with producing energy. To illustrate his point, he cites the following example: Say in your quest to conserve energy you add insulation to your attic, seal up your home's drafty leaks, and install storm windows. These direct actions will help you save big time on your utility bills. The energy you save also translates into a familiar commandment: love your neighbor as yourself. This is because the energy conserved through these upgrades is now available for other customers. And the utility company doesn't need to source new coal or oil or natural gas to meet their needs. Through saving energy you've essentially produced energy.

Chiras recommends combining efficiency with frugality, the latter of which might be a dirty word to those who believe the American way of life consists of limitless possibilities and zero sacrifice. But being frugal is actually a form of thoughtfulness. It's as simple as turning off a light when you leave the room (even if it is a CFL), taking shorter showers (even if you have a water-saving showerhead), or putting on a sweater and setting your thermostat below *tropical* when you're home and turning it down even further when you aren't (even though you've just blown insulation into your walls). You'll double the impact of your conservation measures, save money, and maybe even attain a sort of Zen-like state by more fully understanding the consequences of your actions.

Speaking of spiritual acts, Stephen and Rebekah Hren, in their ambitious *Carbon-Free Home*, recommend keeping an energy diary as a "consciousness-raising exercise." The process involves inventorying all of your appliances, measuring their power draw, taking notes on every time you turn them on and off, and, at the end of the week, tallying those numbers and multiplying the amount of time you used those appliances in hours by their watt numbers—giving you the total watt-hours you used that week. One simple way to do this is with a Kill A Watt meter, which tells you how much energy an individual appliance uses while it's plugged in. The

Energy Detective is a similar green gadget that monitors your home energy use in real time and predicts your energy bill long before it arrives—perhaps giving you a chance to lower it. Whatever method you choose, this energy-use inventory is a great way to see where you're wasting energy and where you might save it. Did you need to use that hairdryer for twenty minutes when ten might have done the trick?

Conservation is the first step in lightening your carbon homeprint—whether you're heading for that magic number zero or have less ambitious (but equally important) goals. Starting with conservation first means that when you're truly ready for that totally hot solar photovoltaic system, you'll find that you don't need one quite so big (and expensive) to get the job done.

There are many ways to conserve the energy your home uses, and they range from getting a professional energy audit to evaluating your home's energy efficiency to installing a programmable thermostat. But for those of you who are just about to embark on the joys of homeownership or are ready to make an upgrade from dorm room to apartment, you're in a lucky position. Your ability to reduce the size of your homeprint, before you even set foot inside it, is huge.

LOCATION, LOCATION, LOCATION

Prior to signing a lease or applying for a mortgage, consider first where you'll pedal your bike or use that bus pass. Where's the closest grocery store? Can you walk there? How about a hipster coffee shop, cute café, or hardware store (oh so necessary for all those home improvement needs)? Is there a nearby park or community center or school?

These may sound like particularly urban questions, but our country is not without suburban neighborhoods that are self-sufficient in roughly the same way. If you really must live out in the country, off the grid, and away from neighbors—unless you are planning on becoming a hermit and growing and procuring your own food à la hook, bullet, and dirty fingernails—your challenge to reduce your carbon homeprint will be much greater. I'm not saying you can't do it, but it won't come without sacrifice. Consider this statistic: an American "typically" drives more than 12,000 miles a year, which adds 148 million Btus (British thermal units—a measure of energy output) to each "typical" household (with two cars, each averaging 21 miles per gallon).

Since you'll park those cars in your home's garage, and so your car can be considered an extension of your home, that's a lot of Btus to make up for.

I'm not trying to be preachy or to discourage you if you already live in the hinterlands—when I lived in western Massachusetts, my commute to work was only 6 miles, but there was no bus service and the closest amenity was a nearby marsh. But I can't help but encourage those willing to consider living in a neighborhood where a car might not be necessary. The benefits of living "close in" are too numerous to count. Besides drastically reducing your total carbon output, you'll most likely be in better shape through all that walking, cycling, and running to catch the bus; you'll have a more lively social life through the other friendly people you meet out and about; you'll spend less time in the car and thus have more time in your day for your family or hobbies (like greening your home); and you'll contribute to a strong, vibrant neighborhood full of unique restaurants and local businesses. Thus, your green home will be surrounded by good company.

How does one find such a house, condo, or apartment? The easiest way is to grab a map and set out on foot. Take the time to explore a neighborhood, and note the

TIP

LIVING ON GREEN STREET

Have you always wanted to live a hardcore urban lifestyle but can't afford the higher housing costs that often go along with it? You may be in luck. The Natural Resources Defense Council and Chicago's Center for Neighborhood Technology teamed up to create a Fannie Mae–backed mortgage that takes location into account when determining a home-buyer's credit limit (as of 2010 the program is available in Seattle, Chicago, the Bay Area, and Los Angeles in Orange County).

The average American family spends 20 percent of its household budget on transportation. Based on the fact that folks who live in urban areas spend less on transportation, the Location Efficient Mortgage Program increases the amount you're able to borrow if you want to buy in one of those trendy, dense, public-transportation-happy urban areas. Visit the Natural Resources Defense Council website for more information.

distance from your job, schools, or other places you frequent. Talk to people. If you have neither the time nor resources to do this, you can exercise your fingers while surfing the web. One organization has made it easy for you: Walk Score is devoted to walkable neighborhoods in a serious way. Its website is full of neighborhood resources and ranks places from 0 to 100, from car dependent to walkers' paradise (a score above 90). New York City wins hands down, and the usual suspects like Seattle, Boston, San Francisco, and Portland, Oregon, have strong showings. But Kansas City and Milwaukee also rank among the best, proving you don't need to be coastal to be green.

LIKE IT OR NOT, YOU'RE ON THE GRID

How many of us give a thought to what happens when we switch on a light? In our modern society, this act is mostly taken for granted. Subconsciously we all recognize that we benefit from electricity, but we often don't know where it comes from and how it gets to our home. But we should. For most of us, the energy that powers our toasters or heats our showers comes via the grid.

Simply put, the grid is an interconnected network that transfers energy from suppliers to consumers. It can support electricity generation, electric power transmission, and electricity distribution. A grid can be a grid at many levels, from the local and regional to the national and continental—it can even be as quaint as a central generator linked to homes in a remote area. But let's think big and take on the more complex method of moving electricity around in a developed country like the United States.

Imagine the grid like a tree, where a lot of power from a central trunk flows out into progressively smaller branches (or lower-voltage lines) until it reaches our homes. Or, sans metaphor, electric power is generated at a big plant, which it leaves at a very high voltage as it connects to a transmission network and moves very long distances (often from state to state) until it reaches the substation of your local distribution company. Here voltage is decreased again as it enters smaller distribution lines. Once it reaches your home, power is decreased again so you can use it. This is the traditional centralized model of electricity distribution. Why is it important?

Because it's a very inefficient system. Moving that electricity great distances results in a huge amount of energy loss. In fact, only one-third of the original fuel-source energy reaches your home as electricity. The rest is lost, a victim of the process of converting that fuel to electricity and then distributing it. For this reason, CO_2 emissions per unit of energy for electricity are higher than for other fuel sources. Or put another way, the 100 million Btus of energy used per year by the average U.S. home requires 172 million Btus of energy—72 million Btus are lost to inefficiencies in transmission and refining. In natural-gas power plants, only 50 percent of the energy contained in the natural gas is converted to electrical energy. In coal power plants, only one-third of the energy embodied in those black rocks becomes electricity.

The good news is that the dinosaur-age grid that has shaped our conception and consumption of energy may be at the end of its epoch. Research and federal legislation are pushing us toward "smart grid" technologies. *Smart grid* is the buzz phrase on everyone's lips. It can mean a lot of things, but its most basic definition is bringing the modern technologies of the Internet and its limitless approaches to communication to our aging electricity infrastructure. It will allow utility operators to communicate better with different aspects of the grid, from transformers to home appliances. It has the potential to reduce all that energy that's lost in transit, thereby eliminating the burning of unnecessary fossil fuels. Like anything of modern appeal, it'll have gadgets too. So-called smart meters will allow consumers to track (and reduce) energy use at our homes through free web-based services.

The real challenge of the smart grid will be integrating renewable sources of energy; specifically, figuring out how to connect them to the grid (installing new transmission lines can be contentious) and how to deal with their intermittency (the sun isn't always shining, nor is the wind always blowing). Watch for new developments of this exciting new technology. In the meantime, don't forget to unplug your cell phone after it's finished charging.

GREEN ENERGY WITHOUT THE PERSONAL INFRASTRUCTURE

Do you have the desire to power your home with green energy but not the capacity (financial or otherwise) to invest in your own windmill? You don't have to feel left out. There are hundreds of utilities in forty-one states that can set your home up with energy powered by wind, sun, water, even landfill methane gas. Getting this green option may be as easy as visiting your local utility's website. You can also visit the Department of Energy's Green Power Network site to see whether a utility near you offers such a program. The cost, which will likely help support the development of renewable-energy projects as well as educating consumers (read "advertising") about their merits, is a little higher than traditional energy sources, but not much. For a typical apartment in New York City, the price of switching to 100 percent wind power is $10–$20 per month, or an average Gothamite's daily coffee budget. Keep in mind that energy sources, whether coal or wind, are inextricably commingled on the grid. So, though you may be purchasing and supporting wind energy or other renewable sources, that energy is not necessarily the same or only energy that reaches your light socket.

If there is no green energy provider nearby, don't fret—you need not be left in the dark. Renewable energy certificates, or RECs, can help you offset your home's carbon-intensive energy use. RECs are also known as green tags, tradable renewable certificates, or green certificates. Josh Dorfman, in his wonderfully titled book, *The Lazy Environmentalist*, provides a simple explanation of RECs with this anecdote: Let's say an energy company wants to buy the lowest-priced energy available (would you expect otherwise?). The choice is likely to be coal. If a wind company were to try to make itself as competitive as coal by lowering its prices, it would go out of business. So it creates an REC that equals the difference in cost between the two energy sources. Here's where you come in. When you purchase an REC, you help that company stay in business and lower its price to make it competitive with coal, and this in turn allows you to offset your "bad" home energy with that which is "good." Call it energy karma, or the power of subsidization.

RECs are not without their critics, especially among the climate-change policy experts. Simply put, a typical REC doesn't do anything to promote *new* renewable energy development or to lower existing CO_2 levels (and for this reason is insanely cheap). A $2 REC from a wind farm that's already been developed is nice for the wind farmer (and a great way to support wind power in general), but it doesn't change emissions levels. On the other hand, a "forward REC," as climate activist Auden Schendler calls it, would make a renewable development come online and thus would be much more expensive and would require a long-term commitment on the part of a corporation. In an article posted at the Climate Progress blog, Schendler recommends the companies Native Energy and Community Energy as "forward REC" brokers.

You can find out more about RECs, including a list of marketers, at the Department of Energy Green Power Network website or at Green-e.org, which also certifies companies that provide renewable energy.

WHEN TO LOOK FORWARD TO AN AUDIT

There may be one time and one time only in your life when you get to look forward to an audit, where shortcomings become opportunities, the first steps on your path toward a greener home. Knowledge is power, and there's nothing like a whole-house energy audit to give you the power you need to reduce your home's carbon footprint. It's something you should do before considering upgrades, purchases, or

TIP

ONLINE TOOLS THAT GIVE YOU AN EDGE

Energy Star (www.energystar.gov): Energy Star, a joint program of the Environmental Protection Agency and Department of Energy, promotes energy-efficient products and practices. If you thrive on competition and have five minutes and twelve months of utility bills, you can use the program's "Home Energy Yardstick" to compare your home's energy efficiency to similar homes across the country. Don't fret if the results are disappointing. You'll also get recommendations for energy-saving home improvements. To get started, go to the Energy Star website with basic information about your house in hand (zip code, age, square footage, number of occupants). If you've recycled your old bills, contact your utility for a twelve-month summary.

Home Energy Saver (http://hes.lbl.gov): This government program touts itself as the first web-based do-it-yourself energy audit tool. You can use it to estimate how much energy, money, and emissions can be saved by implementing green improvements. You'll receive instant initial estimates simply by entering your zip code. For example, based on my former New England zip code, Home Energy Saver gave me the difference between the energy cost (in dollars per year) of an average home and an energy-efficient home in my area: $833. I also got the difference in annual greenhouse gas emissions: 28,388 pounds of CO_2 versus 8,546 pounds. And that's just the beginning. By providing even more information, you can receive detailed results, increasingly tailored to your particular home—including simulation for a typical weather year, domestic water heating consumption, energy consumption for your appliances, and a list of recommendations ranked by payback time.

makeovers. And in the end, instead of paying delinquent back taxes, you actually get to save money.

Getting a home energy audit is usually pretty darn cheap, in many cases free. Your local utility is the first place to look. If you're a do-it-yourselfer, you can perform an audit on your own, but a professional will have the skills to perform many tests and to analyze information that you can't. He or she might serve as the best counselor you and your home ever had. Think about giving both approaches a try.

What better authority to start with than the U.S. government? Those bureaucrats have energy audit advice cornered. A visit to the Department of Energy's website is rewarding, yielding information on both do-it-yourself energy audits as well as what happens and how to prepare for a professional audit. For the handywomen and men out there, DOE advises focusing on air leaks, insulation, heating and cooling, and lighting…and then gives you dessert: financing and incentives and a weatherization assistance program. Look for problems with a simple but thorough walk-through of your home, pen and paper in hand. List all the troubles you find, and then prioritize them. Think of the satisfaction that will come with crossing off items on that list.

GOING WITH A PRO

My New England house benefited greatly from a **professional energy audit**. Our auditors gave us valuable insight and saved us both time and money. They used a blower-door test, determined our insulation situation, coordinated the contract for the blow-in insulation into our hollow wall cavities (which we received at a huge discount), installed an insulated box for our drop-down attic stairway, facilitated a zero-interest loan for an upgraded heating system, and even sealed and caulked ductwork and gaps. They did all this for free.

Preparing for a professional energy audit is not unlike preparing for any other audit. You'll need to do some groundwork first. DOE suggests making a list of problems like drafty rooms, condensation, or high heating bills. In fact, have a year's worth of utility bills to give to your auditor. Your utility company should be able to provide this financial and energy record if you don't have it. The information will help your auditor zero in on what to look for during the audit. A good auditor will not only examine your home from top to bottom, inside and out, he or she will also analyze its residents' behavior. According to DOE, a good analysis will include information about who is home during working hours, the average thermostat setting

TIP

A GOOD ENERGY AUDITOR IS NOT HARD TO FIND

Your state or local government or weatherization office might be able to help you find a local company or organization that conducts audits (like the nonprofit that performed mine). Your utility company may also offer its services. No matter who you choose, make sure to check references, contact the Better Business Bureau, and see that the vendor uses a calibrated blower door and does thermographic inspections. Online resources include:

- **Energy Star (www.energystar.gov):** Energy Star participates in Home Performance, a national program currently limited to specific regions of the country (go to the "Home Performance" page of the website). Contractors audit your home and make recommendations. You may be one of the lucky ones. I was. National Grid partners with Energy Star through a program called Mass Save to offer no-cost home energy assessments and a 75 percent rebate up to $2,000 to complete recommended improvements.

- **RESNET (www.natresnet.org):** The Residential Energy Services Network is a nonprofit that certifies and rates building energy performance. You can find the group's certified raters by state, including Green Raters, who have been trained to verify the green features of a home in addition to energy performance.

for summer and winter, the number of people living in the home, and whether or not every room is in use.

Make sure you're around when the auditor does the inspection. Not only will you be able to ask questions, you'll get to marvel at the equipment, which may include a calibrated blower door, infrared camera, furnace-efficiency meter, surface thermometer, and thermographic scanner.

DIY

First on the do-it-yourselfer's list should be the **air leaks**, a.k.a. drafts. Cold in the winter? Suffering from high heating bills? Drafts are most certainly to blame. DOE estimates that reducing the flow of this cold air can result in energy savings of 5 to 30 percent per year. Likely culprits include gaps at baseboards, junctures of the walls and ceiling, switch plates, fireplace dampers, attic hatches, pipes and wires, and, of course, doors and windows. If you can see broad daylight around a door or window frame, or if you can rattle them, you've got an air leak. Time to caulk and weather-strip.

All this checking for gaps and leaks, wandering around the house and searching for problems might feel a little uninspiring. Still dreaming of solar panels, windmills, and the latest green gadgets and new technologies? None of these things can match the power of the unsexy caulk gun. The Natural Resources Defense Council claims that all those gaps around your windows and doors are equivalent to having a 3-by-3-foot hole in the wall. According to a study funded in part by the ClimateWorks Foundation, improving the energy efficiency of existing U.S. buildings by 2030 could limit greenhouse gas emissions more than a major increase in wind or solar power. Take heart and get in touch with your itchy trigger finger!

And don't forget to check the outside of your home for gaps as well. Likely culprits include meeting places: at corners, between siding and chimneys, and between the foundation and siding. Check your doors and windows on the outside too. When you find those holes, caulk and weather-strip.

Once you've tackled all the gaps and holes in your home, check your **insulation**. In the context of an energy audit, this means figuring out what kind you have and where you have it. Heat loss through the ceiling and walls can be huge if insulation levels are below the recommended minimum. Or consider this statistic: each year the amount of energy lost through uninsulated homes in the United States is equivalent to the amount of oil delivered through the Trans-Alaska Pipeline.

When your home was built, the builder most likely installed the amount of insulation recommended at that time. For my family's nineteenth-century home, that meant zero. We were quite surprised when our energy auditor pointed out the 4 inches of air space between the clapboard siding and our interior walls! Even if your house does have insulation, it might not be adequate to do battle with today's energy prices. Too, there are many more options on the market now, including eco-friendly ones.

The three main places to check for insulation include your attic, walls, and basement. If the attic is insulated, check to make sure that the hatch is too. Get out the caulk gun again and seal up any openings around chimneys, pipes, and ductwork. The feds also recommend looking for a vapor barrier under the insulation (like tar paper or a plastic sheet). If it's not there, consider painting your interior ceilings with a vapor-barrier paint. Otherwise, large of amounts of moisture will potentially pass through the ceiling, reducing the effectiveness of your insulation and causing structural damage to your home. Along similar lines, make sure that the attic vents aren't blocked with insulation. You want good air circulation up there. If your attic isn't insulated at all, your job is easy: insulate it with modern-day recommended levels.

Checking the insulation in your walls can be a bit trickier. Do-it-yourselfers will not be able to tell if all the wall cavities are 100 percent evenly insulated—only a professional thermographic inspection can do this—but you can get a pretty good idea of what's in there. One way is to remove the cover plate of an outlet and use a screwdriver to probe around inside and feel for resistance, which indicates the presence of insulation. (*Very important note:* Before you start mucking around those

TIP

TAKING ON THE DRAFT

If you're having a tough time finding gaps and leaks, the Department of Energy suggests conducting a "basic building pressurization test." Professionals have a special blower door just for this purpose, but you can do it yourself too for less technical, though no less useful, results. Here's how:

- Step 1: Close all exterior doors, windows, and fireplace flues.
- Step 2: Turn off all combustion appliances, such as gas-burning furnaces and water heaters.
- Step 3: Turn on all exhaust fans (found in your kitchen and bathroom), or you can also use a big window fan to suck the air out of the rooms.

Diligently following these steps increases the infiltration, or air flow, through your home's cracks and leaks, making them much easier to find. Buy some incense sticks and light one up and walk through the house, pausing at possible problem areas. Air on the move will cause the smoke to waver. If you dislike earthy aromas, you can alternatively get your hand damp. Drafts will make said hand feel chilly.

electrical wires, make sure to turn off your circuit breaker. Double-check that no power is surging in your particular outlet by plugging in a radio or lamp.) Another option is to drill a small hole in the wall, maybe in that messy closet or behind a piece of furniture (renters probably shouldn't venture into drilling territory unless they are really good at patching holes or have an ecominded landlord's permission).

If you have a basement and it's unheated, insulate under the living-area flooring. If your basement is heated, make sure the foundation walls are insulated. Your water heater, hot-water pipes, and furnace ducts should all be snuggly wrapped and warm if they're at all exposed to the elements.

What's the point of plugging all the gaps and insulating your home if your **heating and cooling equipment** are lame ducks? Check your sources of warmth or coldness every year, or as often as recommended by the manufacturer. If your furnace is the forced-air type, you'll need to check your filters too—probably about once a month if your heat is consistently blasting in the depths of winter—and replace them when they look like they need it. If the ductwork associated with your heating unit has dirty streaks, you've got leaks. Seal them up with mastic tape. No matter whether you like doing it yourself or not, have a professional check and clean out the gunk from your equipment every year. If you can, replace the entire system if it's teenaged. The newer energy-efficient units will save you tons of energy and money.

Finally, **light bulbs**. You've likely heard many a spiel on the virtues of compact fluorescents, but they can't be touted enough. I think they're such a good investment I handed them out as wedding favors. DOE recommends replacing your incandescent bulbs with CFLs for heavy-usage sockets. But why not replace as many as you can? According to DOE, lighting accounts for about 10 percent of your electricity bill. If all Americans switched out their incandescents for CFLs, we'd eliminate emissions from eighty coal-fired power plants. A CFL bulb uses a fraction of the energy of a regular bulb, produces 70 percent less heat, lasts ten times longer, and will save you on average of $30 or more over its lifetime. Plus, your utility company may offer rebates or other incentives for switching. You don't need a professional to figure this one out, though the Environmental Defense Fund has a great guide to find out which CFL is better and which is best for you.

A word about mercury: a CFL contains it, about 5 milligrams, and mercury is highly toxic—but the largest source of mercury pollution in the United States is from coal-fired power plants, and using CFLs will reduce that. Do take precautions if you break a bulb: ventilate and vacate the room for about fifteen minutes and, afterward, as you're cleaning up, avoid contact with the heavy metal (use paper, stiff cardboard, tape, and gloves). Seal up all the materials in a plastic bag or lidded glass jar. Vacuums or brooms can spread the mercury to other parts of the house so avoid using them. Find out the proper way to dispose of both intact and broken CFLs in your community—in many places it is illegal to throw them out with the garbage. For collection sites, visit the U.S. Environmental Protection Agency's (EPA) online list of recycling options by state, or go to the Earth911 website; LampRecycle.org lists regulations on CFL recycling in your state; and some retailers, like IKEA, take back CFLs free of charge. Finally, in the future, look for advances in light-emitting diodes (LEDs), a promising mercury-free alternative to CFLs.

KEEPING WARM, STAYING COOL

As discussed above concerning energy audits, insulating, in combination with sealing all of those gaps and cracks in your home, will have *the* biggest impact on your energy bills and carbon homeprint. No other single act comes close. Simply put, insulation regulates your home's temperature—keeping it warm in the winter (like when you put on a coat) and cool in the summer (like your freezer). When you don't have adequate insulation, you're wasting money and energy, heating and cooling the great outdoors.

When should you insulate? Obviously, if your home's energy audit determines that you don't have enough, or any, you need insulation. But also consider adding it if (a) you find yourself too hot or too cold in the winter or summer (a common-sense indicator); (b) you're remodeling (which can often be the easiest time to add it); (c) your house was built before 1981 (which means it's old); or (d) if your house wasn't built with energy efficiency in mind (which means most of us should consider adding insulation). Where should you insulate? The walls are an obvious choice. But don't forget the attic and the floor above a crawl space (80 percent of the cold air here will find its way up into your living quarters), the foundation, and exposed hot water pipes.

Adding insulation can be a complicated affair. There are many different kinds, each with advantages and disadvantages. A lot depends on the specifics of your home— for instance, unless you have an open wall cavity, it's pretty much impossible to add

TIP

R-VALUE: RESISTING THE FLOW

When you start looking at insulation, you'll hear all about R-value. For our purposes, and to keep things accessible, R-value is the measure of an insulation's resistance to heat flow and depends on the material, plus its thickness and density. The higher the number, the greater an insulation's resistive power (there is no ultimate high-end number because R-value is additive, not a set range). Adding more insulation increases overall R-value. And making sure that it's properly installed (i.e., not compressed) is key to insulation's R-value and thus effectiveness.

What's the magic number for you? That depends on where you live—Minnesota versus Florida, for example—what kind of heating and cooling system you have, and where in your house you plan to insulate.

Department of Energy to the rescue: Visit the agency's website and find the insulation fact sheet or the zip-code insulation program (www.ornl.gov/~roofs/Zip/ZipHome .html). Plug in the type of house you live in, type of heating you use, and your zip code. The handy-dandy calculator will give you a recommendation for different parts of your home—the attic, wall cavity, floor, crawl space, basement wall, and so on. Then match your magic numbers to the insulation type that meets your needs.

rigid or batt insulation. Some types of insulation are better than others (see "R-Value: Resisting the Flow" in this chapter). Some are greener than others, although, according to certain experts, all will offset nongreen attributes by the energy they saved in the long run—any insulation is better than none. And, of course, some are more expensive than others. You'll have to decide what works best for you. That said, let's outline some basic types.

You're probably familiar with the pink fluffy stuff. It's a type of **batt insulation (R-value 2.9–3.8)** and fits between the studs of your walls. The pink stuff is actually fiberglass, which unfortunately is filled with lung-irritating chemicals. Greener batt alternatives include formaldehyde-free versions (see the Greenguard Environmental Institute for certified versions) and cotton, which includes post-industrial denim (Bonded Logic is one brand).

Loose-fill cellulose (R-value 3.1–3.7) is sprayed into closed-up walls and other difficult to access places—the greenest option is made of recycled newsprint and treated with natural chemicals (borax) to make it fire resistant.

A hard-hitting R-value insulation, **spray-in foams (R-value 3.6–6.2)**, expand to fill the tiniest of spaces. Unfortunately, many use chlorofluorocarbons and are toxic. You can try a soy-based foam instead or other nontoxic brands, including Icynene and BioBased products.

Finally, **rigid foam board (R-value 3.9–7)** receives the highest marks for R-value, though it's the most expensive per inch. It's good for tight spaces. Unfortunately, it often also contains the dreaded formaldehyde. You can avoid this by choosing polyisocyanurate or extruded polystyrene.

Stephen and Rebekah Hren have put together the best chart I've seen comparing insulation types, including R-values, pros and cons, and ease of installation. You'll find it in their book, *The Carbon-Free Home*. It's worth perusing before you decide on insulation for your abode.

WINDOWS: EFFICIENCY WITH A VIEW

Windows are the soul of any home. They let in light, set a mood, allow fresh air, and make us feel connected to the world around us. We all need windows, but, as your chilly feet may be telling you (or perhaps your sweaty brow), too many are drafty in the winter and during the warmer months can induce a saunalike atmosphere. Indeed, next to insulation, windows have the greatest impact on energy use besides heating and air conditioning. How can you make them more efficient? Should you replace them?

I don't have straightforward answers to these questions. In fact, I'm going to give you contradictory, though valuable, information. Many, if not most, energy experts will recommend *emphatically* that if you have the financial wherewithal you should upgrade your old windows with something new. They have good reasons. Facts, even. But others, including myself, don't believe replacement windows are always or necessarily the best option. After much deliberation, I chose not to replace but to restore my windows (see "Out with the Old?" in this chapter). And there's a third option: many smaller, inexpensive measures you can take to dramatically increase the energy efficiency of your existing glass panes besides complete, often expensive, restoration or replacement. But before we go there, let's start with an overview.

WINDOW MECHANICS 101

There are three ways windows gain and lose heat: conduction, radiation, and air leakage. Conduction via the glass or frame. Radiation into the house via the sun and out of the house via room-temperature objects (you, your furniture, interior walls). And air leakage via the windows themselves, through and around them. These properties can actually be measured (and this information, usually displayed on a sticker, is vital when choosing new windows) in the following ways.

U-value: U-value is essentially the inverse of R-value (discussed above). It's a measurement of the heat flow (nonsolar) *through* a material. The lower the number, the better. According to *Green Remodeling* authors David Johnston and Kim Master, the best windows you can buy today have U-values of around 0.20.

Solar heat gain coefficient (SHGC): This is essentially a measurement of the sunlight that passes through your window and is released as heat in your home. What you want in SHGC depends on where you live. The lower the SHGC, the less heat is transmitted and the more shade is provided—low SHGC is good for warm climates. The Natural Resources Defense Council suggests that folks who have high air conditioning bills seek out windows with a SHGC of 0.35 or lower. On the other hand, the higher the SHGC, the more effective the window is at providing solar heat— good for the cold winters in northern climes.

Air leakage: According to DOE, air leakage is "the rate of air infiltration around a window, door, or skylight in the presence of a specific pressure difference across it." The pressure differences concept might seem tricky, as well as the way it's expressed: in units of cubic feet per minute per square foot of frame area (cfm/ft^2). But we can simplify it. If your window has a low air leakage rating, it's tight. High, and you're leaking a lot of air. Dan Chiras, author of *The Homeowner's Guide to Renewable Energy*, suggests looking for windows with air leakage rates of 0.3 cfm/ft^2 or less.

WHY UPGRADE?

Chiras explains in his book that if "your windows are old and leaky or were manufactured with aluminum or steel frames, or God forbid, are the single pane variety,

TIP

LET THERE BE LIGHT (OR NOT)

All this talk of windows' role in losing or trapping heat could make you forget one of the reasons we actually put windows in walls in the first place—to let in light! Windows—especially well-placed windows—as well as skylights, can provide significant amounts of natural daylight, thereby reducing electricity usage (with a potential 60 to 70 percent reduction). The concept is called daylighting.

Think about how your daily activities and furniture arrangement might coordinate with the free light provided by windows in your home. If you're considering adding a window or two, pick the south side. Windows here will allow more sunlight in the winter but less in the summer (which means less unwanted heat). North-facing windows can work too, providing consistent natural light, sans glare, with little heat gain in June, July, and August. Windows on the east and west sides of your home will give you good light in the morning and evening, but they'll heat up your home in the summer.

And this leads us back to the issue of heating, in this case solar heating, or passive solar design—another great characteristic of a well-placed window. If your window is efficient, you can use that light streaming in as heat—in most climates you want to minimize this heat in the summer and maximize it in the winter. With modern-day windows you can pick various glazings to accentuate this, even tuning them to different exposures and orientations of your home. Southern windows work best for solar heating in climates where heating costs dominate your bills. In warmer climates, use north-facing windows and shade your south-facing windows. You can pick glazings with low SHGCs to reduce your solar heat gain even more and thus your need for AC—trading one acronym for another.

you should consider a complete upgrade." I might add: if you can afford them. New windows cost a lot—about $8,000 to $10,000 or more if you've got a lot of windows, with a payback period of about ten to twelve years to recoup your investment. Granted, you'll feel more comfortable immediately and you won't be sending all that wasted energy out the window. Too, with rising energy costs, you could see a return on your investment much sooner.

Modern double- or triple-pane windows have a lot going for them. The very best can have up to four times the insulation value as their counterparts from the 1970s. Window technology has come a long way, possessing a basic anatomy that leads to energy efficiency. This includes new and improved frame materials—made up of wood composite, vinyl, and fiberglass—which reduces heat transfer and increases insulation. These frames are filled with two or more panes of low-E glass with air or a gas-filled space between them—again for better insulation. And warm edge spacers—made of steel, foam, fiberglass, or vinyl—keep the glass panes the right distance apart, reduce heat flow, and prevent condensation.

Those are the basics. A lot of factors make up the specifics. For instance, depending on which of the cardinal directions your window faces or your climate, you'll want different types of glazing or glass—of which there are many, from heat-absorbing tints to double- or triple-glazed glass to reflective and spectrally selective coatings. All of these technologies can be combined, giving you infinitely more options.

Stripped to their bare bones, however, your most important energy-efficient technologies to consider are as follows.

Low-E (or low-emissivity) coatings: These coatings are transparent, made up of tin or silver oxide, and are placed on the window glass to help retard heat flow (while allowing sunlight to pass through). They not only keep heat inside your home during the winter, they keep it out during the summer.

Low-conductivity gasses: These are used to fill the space between the panes of glass, with the idea that they conduct heat even less than air. Argon is the most commonly used (it has an insulating value 40 percent higher than air). But the highest-performance windows bring out the Superman stuff, using krypton, which has an insulating value 1.4 times that of air.

If this feels a bit overwhelming, help is available. The National Fenestration Rating Council's Certified Products Directory is an extensive online database that details the organization's energy-efficient certification for windows as well as for doors and skylights. Energy Star also has criteria for windows, doors, and skylights that receive its seal of approval. Their ratings are tailored to four climate zones (northern, north/central, south/central, and southern) and are based on heat gain and loss in cold weather and heat gain in warm weather.

GOOD-AS-NEW GREEN RETROFITS

If replacing windows is a nonstarter (i.e., too expensive or you don't own them), there are many ways to make your existing windows more energy-efficient. Short of complete restoration, here are few less ambitious but highly effective options.

Caulking and weather stripping: We've extolled the virtues of these simple yet profound acts earlier in the chapter. According to DOE, most energy gurus agree that caulking and weather stripping will pay for themselves in just one year. There are many different types of caulk, from water-based to butyl rubber. Consider those with fewer or zero volatile organic compounds (VOCs, discussed at length in chapter 4). AFM Safecoat is one of many green brands. You have many choices in the realm of weather stripping as well, from felt to foam to tape to vinyl to rubber. I used a bronze V-shaped weather stripping in my windows. Metals (such as bronze, copper, stainless steel, and aluminum) are relatively inexpensive, classy, and long lasting. DOE has a great chart on its website that compares different types according to best uses, cost, advantages, and disadvantages.

Shades: According to DOE, "window shades can be one of the simplest and most effective window treatments for saving energy." But they must be properly installed. This means they should be hung as close as possible to the glass, with the sides close to the wall, which creates a sealed air space. To work with that magical and free solar heat, lower shades in the summer. In the winter, raise them up on the south side of the house. You can get specialty shades, like quilted roller and special Roman shades that have sealed edges and fiber batting. There are also high-efficiency dual shades, which are reflective on one side and absorb heat on the other. You can switch them around with the seasons—the reflective side should face outward when it's cold and inward when its warm.

Blinds: By design, blinds aren't much good at reducing heat loss in the winter because of all those openings between the slats. But those slats offer lots of flexibility—adjustable light and ventilation—when it comes to reducing summer heat. DOE states that when reflective blinds are closed all the way on a hot sunny window, they can reduce heat gain by about 45 percent.

Drapes: Like shades and blinds, drapes can minimize heat loss or gain through your windows. The same principles apply: close them during the summer on windows that receive direct sunlight; in the winter, keep the drapes closed day and night on those windows that don't receive direct sunlight. The simple act of closing drapes in winter can reduce heat loss from a room by up to 10 percent.

To make drapes as effective as possible, hang them as close to the window as you can, let them fall on the floor or windowsill, and add a cornice to the top of the drape or place them against the ceiling. Then seal the sides and bottom to the wall (Velcro or magnetic tape will do the trick). Following this recipe can reduce heat loss by 25 percent. Also try layering two drapes to create a tighter air space and to make a room cozier—the interior drape will remain about as warm as the inside of your home.

Insulating window panels: Also known as pop-in shutters, these are usually made of a core of rigid foam insulation that can be pushed or clipped into the interior of a window. The edges seal tightly against the frame. This is an inexpensive option with a lot of bang for the buck—panels typically have an R-value between 3.8 and 7, according to DOE.

Awnings: Do you live in a hot place? DOE claims an awning can reduce solar heat gain in the summer by 65 percent on south-facing windows and 77 percent on west-facing windows. Awnings are made from synthetic fabrics that are resistant to mildew and fading—choose one that's light-colored to reflect more sunlight—and they come in different styles, such as Venetian, hood, and hip. Retractable awnings will give you flexibility in the winter, when you want to let more warm sun in.

Storm windows: These have been used to improve a window's energy efficiency for centuries, and they're still a good bet if you want to reduce air movement in and out of your windows. If you don't have the money or inclination to replace your old glass with something modern, you should definitely consider storm windows.

There are interior and exterior varieties, cheap plastic sheets and triple-track glass with low-E coatings, polycarbonate plastic and laminated glass, and it seems like everything in between. Which one is right for you depends on your budget, and on visibility and longevity issues, with glass generally being clearer and lasting longer but also being more expensive and fragile. You have your choice of frames too, with wood, aluminum, and vinyl the most common. Each has its strengths and weaknesses: aluminum is strong but poor at insulating; wood insulates well but weathers with age and is subject to swelling and contracting with humidity (which makes an exact fit hard to achieve); and vinyl or polyvinyl chloride (PVC) frames hold up well against sunlight but often warp when it's very hot and crack when it's very cold. The manufacturing of PVC is also a pretty toxic process (see chapter 4).

If you're an apartment dweller, you may want to consider interior storm windows, which are easier to install and remove, require less maintenance on your part since they aren't subject to the exterior elements, and can actually be more effective at lessening air infiltration since they hug the window tightly. A good fit is important, whether you go with interior or exterior storm windows: they should align as perfectly as possible with your window and be well sealed with our hero, caulk.

When temperatures begin to drop in late fall, many of us resort to clear plastic film, tape, and a hairdryer to construct a poor man's storm window of sorts. It's a popular option because it's cheap and it works. Problem is, it also looks cheap and can do a lot to impair your wintry view. There is a slightly more upscale option: Plexiglas. Though Dan Chiras and the Hrens might disagree on the subject of replacement windows, they are all big fans of Plexiglas, whether used as a removable insert or to permanently seal up an often-closed window.

LOVE THE ONES YOU'RE WITH

Finally, back to the controversial subject of whether to upgrade or not upgrade your windows. Perhaps you've already made up your mind. You see the definite advantages of new windows and have your heart set on low-E. If you think modern windows are right for your home, go for it. You'll certainly lower your carbon homeprint. For those of you who are hesitant for whatever reason, consider the following information and opinions.

As I revealed earlier, I decided to not replace my old, wood, single-pane windows. Instead, I went for the complete restoration route, combined with weather stripping and storm windows. The decision was primarily based on the historic quality of my windows—I felt modern windows would look out of place in my old converted schoolhouse—but there are other good reasons you might want to keep the windows you already have (and, of course, boost their efficiency).

Rebekah and Stephen Hren report in *The Carbon-Free Home* that there has been "much ballyhoo" over replacing single-pane windows with double panes in order to reduce the transfer of heat. They claim the insulative difference between them is quite small (from R-value 1 to R-value 2 generally). They complain about the sticker shock. They criticize the fact that many are made of vinyl, "a product that lasts only about 20 years before severely cracking when exposed to ultraviolet light, compared to wood or metal windows that can last 200 years or more when properly cared for." The Hrens also point out that the seal around that double-pane glass is made of synthetic rubber, which also breaks down after about twenty years, resulting in all that argon gas between the glass dissipating, further resulting in condensation and foggy windows.

Renters beware. You have no excuse not to save energy, though you may have made plenty in the past. "If only I owned my house, I'd go ...." (fill in the blank: solar, geothermal, off the grid). In the meantime, while you've been dreaming (or complaining), energy has been leaking from your living space, much of it easily preventable. Applying weather stripping, insulating plastic, and blinds to windows that aren't yours is easy, cheap, and just might convince your landlord to tackle bigger projects. Here's a handful of tips to consider, for both owners and renters alike (and see the rest of the chapter for details):

- **Start with the light bulb:** Replace all those incandescents. *Grid* magazine, out of Philly, claims that switching only ten of them for CFLs in a one-bedroom apartment will save you the equivalent of one month's electric bill per year. In the coming years, look for increasingly available (and hopefully more affordable) LEDs, or light-emitting diodes. They use about one-tenth the energy of incandescents and half that of CFLs; and they last about 60,000 hours, compared to 1,500 for incandescents and 10,000 for CFLs.

- **Install a programmable thermostat:** This will take the thinking out of turning down the heat at night and while you're away. Even if your landlord won't do it, consider ponying up the cash yourself. Thermostats are pretty darn cheap and will save you money in heating bills: an Energy Star model can save you $150 a year. Consider, too, setting your average temperature lower (and bundling up in sweaters) in the winter and higher in the summer. The U.S. Green Building Council recommends setting your thermostat to 78° F in the summer and 68° F in the winter—when away from the house or sleeping, try 62° F or lower. You'll save an average of 121 pounds of CO_2 a year for every degree you adjust your thermostat.

- **Use programmable or smart power strips:** These can help you eliminate the dreaded vampire load—the energy sucked by devices when they're turned off but still plugged in (think computer, cell phone, BlackBerry, charger, game console; really, any electrical device, even if it's on standby). Programmable power strips let you schedule your energy use, while smart power strips actually know when your gadgets are turned off and adjust energy output accordingly. DOE says that about three-quarters of the electricity that powers consumer electronics is used while the products are turned off—costing about $1 billion annually. We now have about twenty such products in every household (compared to three in 1980). Worldwide, they suck up 15 percent of household electricity demand; this amount is predicted to triple over the next thirty years, requiring the equivalent of 560 new coal-fired power plants or 230 nuclear plants. Make sure off means off.

- **Cool off:** If you can get permission, plant strategically placed trees to cool your home or building or install a ceiling fan. A fan will keep you cooler in the summer (while using less air conditioning) and warmer in the winter (while using less heat)—remember, warm air rises. Of course, you'll save even more energy by using an Energy Star model; the same goes if you purchase your own AC unit.

- **Use sun shields, blinds, and insulating curtains:** These all help regulate temperature, both hot and cool. This kind of décor will help make those windows your landlord won't upgrade or renovate more efficient.
- **Seal up leaks and drafts:** Put that lowly caulk gun to use. If you can, apply weather stripping to windows and exterior doors. In the winter, you can also get out the hairdryer to help seal a layer of insulating plastic over window frames. Another inexpensive option for both the homeowner and renter is rope caulk, recommended by carbon-free home gurus Stephen and Rebekah Hren. It's cheap (about $5 for 90 feet, which covers about six windows), doesn't require a caulk gun, doesn't harden, and is easily removable—simply apply to your sashes in the fall, remove in the spring, and save for next winter.

- **Change your furnace's air filter:** If you have access to your furnace, and your landlord's permission, this fix will increase efficiency, improve indoor air quality, and save you money. It will take only minutes and cost less than $20.
- **Insulate your water heater and exposed pipes that connect to it**: You'll need permission from your landlord, but this is another inexpensive fix that cuts down on energy use, benefiting your own space, other apartments in your building, and the planet.
- **Buy green power:** Even if your landlord doesn't do green, you still can by working directly with your utility provider.
- **Practice good habits:** Inventorying the amount of power you use, turning off lights, thinking about how you can save energy (so it doesn't need to be produced), keeping an energy diary—these actions aren't limited to homeowners, and their combined holistic effect will perhaps have the biggest impact of any energy-saving measure you can make.

To quote the Hrens at length: "In our opinion, replacing a functioning window that could potentially last many decades if not several centuries with a window that will be defunct in 20 years is planned obsolescence designed to sell as much product as possible. It is inherently energy inefficient and not viable in the long run." And this from a couple who have transformed a 1930s conventional home into a carbon-free residence.

Yes, many old windows are inefficient, leak, and produce drafts. But the truth, at least the truth according to the Hrens, is that all windows—even the fancy sealed and double-pane variety—will produce a draft when it's chilly outside. This is because glass is so excellent at radiating—it absorbs heat from inside and sends it where it's cold, outside, producing a draft. The Hrens claim that the air gap in double-pane windows does nothing to stop this, which is why the difference in R-value isn't that great, even though the difference in cost is. They advocate the much more economic approach of storm windows, sealing, and weather stripping in the quest toward carbon neutrality.

What's the right decision for your home? So much is dependent on your particular circumstances that it's a very personal choice. There's no doubt that whatever steps you take, you'll certainly do better than your current leaky windows. And for that the planet will thank you.

SMALL IS BEAUTIFUL

Save energy, save money. Energy conservation is a pretty simple concept, and simplifying your life is another way to achieve its rewards. Small is not only beautiful; it's a way to conserve energy. Perhaps the age of the 5,000-square-foot McMansion will soon be over—it doesn't take a genius to figure out that the larger your home, the more resources you burn through to keep it maintained, lit, warm, and cool, not to mention the natural resources that went into its construction.

Here's where families, college students, and those with roomies can score major energy conservation points. And here's also where those who bought or rent minimal square footage should celebrate rather than complain about their lack of closet space. Because whether you're cohousing with a coed in a tiny flat or own what real estate agents call a "quaint cottage," you're saving in more ways than one. Small spaces use fewer resources, and resources shared among many go further. That means you need less energy for heat and light, you save money on bills, and you all live with less stuff.

JOY OF THE COMMONS

A word to those of you who live in a shared building: Hallways, stairways, and other common areas in your condo complex or apartment can save oodles of energy (and maybe improve your team-building skills). When it comes to shrinking your carbon footprint, you may think first about your individual living space and, of course, there are both opportunities and limitations for those of us who don't own outright. But you shouldn't forget areas you share with neighbors.

Your first step is to get involved. If you have a chance to meddle in the management of your building or complex, take it. Join a committee, try to influence the rules and bylaws of your condo association, get proactive, tap into your community. You may not want to spend your free time sitting through onerous meetings or debating the value of turning down the building's water heater with a grumpy neighbor who insists on scalding showers, but think of your ecoheavenly rewards. The potential to have a real impact is as big as your building and the number of people living in it. And who knows what large-scale green options these conversations can lead to?

Even if you're living under a monarchy, don't be dissuaded. Landlords are people too, and competition among them for your lease can be fierce. Let yours know that

TIP

HOUSING FOR THE INTENTIONAL

You might believe that intentional communities faded away in the haze of the sixties or, rather, that these days they're hidden behind locked gates. But there's a breed of this sort of development that is very modern, affordable, and übergreen. It might have a shared garden and eating space and contain houses powered by solar panels, with connecting walkways lit by efficient bulbs.

This is today's cohousing community, and there are reportedly one hundred from Massachusetts to Washington State. They're filled with like-minded folks who often govern by consensus. Most contain a common house where meals are shared, sometimes also with a shared laundry room, kids' playroom, workroom, guest room, and library. Some communities are geared toward the older crowd and retirees, but others are integrated and sport a mix of ages, incomes, and family sizes.

Some people see these developments as an antidote to large subdivisions and a reliance on cars. And indeed some are more intentionally eco than others, embracing alternative energy solutions, green insulation, and Energy Star appliances. But all have a significantly reduced impact on our planet because they share resources. To find out more, visit the Cohousing Association of the United States (www.cohousing.org) or the Fellowship for Intentional Communities (www.directory.ic.org).

green initiatives are important to you (and hopefully to your neighbors too). Said royalty might be inclined to fund green improvements if you do the math or offer your own labor free of charge. Paint a pretty (and accurate) picture: a green building has a higher property value, will save your landlord money in the long run, will retain tenants, and will attract new renters.

If you're not so lucky in the landlord department, you can always move—this being a free country, as they say. One fantastic resource that might aid you in your quest for an ecorental is GreenRenter.com. Initially started in Portland, Oregon, the website has expanded to other areas of the country. It allows you to find, and list, green commercial and residential buildings. The organization deems a building green if it meets criteria in at least one of seven categories: energy, water, building materials, operations, building surroundings, certifications and awards, and other innovative green features.

Back to the here and now, to the hallway you walk through every day, the laundry room, the rec room—the modern-day commons. If you've got the support of your neighbors, landlord, condo association, or other governing body, it's pretty easy to make the green changes we've talked about in this chapter. You can collect data to understand your building's energy use. You can hire a professional to conduct a whole-building energy audit. You can (and should) replace all incandescent lighting with CFLs or increasingly available LEDs. Consider putting in timers and motion-sensitive lighting in areas that don't require a constant glow. And if you feel a breeze instead of the warmth of community in your shared spaces, applying weather stripping, caulking, or plastic glazing to leaky windows or doors is cheap and fairly easy—it'll lower your landlord's utility bills too. Installing sun shields, blinds, and ceiling fans will keep you cool and might also help mellow out an irate neighbor.

All of this goes to show that even if you can't pursue every green measure a homeowner can, you might be able to have a larger impact by virtue of sharing the good, green life with others, who will perhaps pass on the same gift.

MAKING IT ALL ADD UP

Many of the worthwhile energy-saving upgrades you can make aren't cheap. Experts will say they'll pay for themselves in "x" number of years, and if you're accustomed to focusing on the long view this news brings a satisfactory feeling. But most of us aren't made out of money, and paying that extra amount up front can be difficult. Good thing help is available in the form of regular rebates and tax incentives from state and federal governments, usually a percentage of the purchase price and often with a cap. Tax breaks change from year to year, so do your research before you buy new appliances or invest in upgrades (e.g., things like solar water heating or biomass stoves). But do look into what's available—credits are often in the hundreds of dollars, sometimes in the thousands. And that can really add up. Visit Energy Star's website to find out the latest.

Your savings aren't limited to deductions on IRS forms. To give folks a nudge toward buying energy-efficient products, many Energy Star partners offer sales-tax exemptions, credits, or rebates. Go to Energy Star's website, enter your zip code, and find out if there are any special offers where you live. The list of products is extensive, including everything from appliances to ceiling fans, from furnaces to cordless phones, from insulation to CFL bulbs, and from printers to heat pumps.

A similar incentive search engine can be found at the Database of State Incentives for Renewables and Energy (DSIRE) website. There you can find information on state, local, utility, and even federal incentives that push energy efficiency and renewable energy.

Finally, financial assistance for your home's energy upgrades is available for lower-income folks. If you qualify, the Low-Income Home Energy Assistance Program will pay a portion of your energy bills and help you find a weatherization assistance program. Additional help can be found through DOE's Weatherization Assistance Program which has been around for about three decades. According to the agency's website, the program has helped 6.2 million low-income households.

OUT WITH THE OLD?

The single-pane, double-hung windows in my nineteenth-century home were beautiful. Each piece of glass (twelve in each window) was handmade and possessed its own personality—showing off waves, pockmarks, and, in the right light, a rainbow of colors. They belonged to the house.

Were they inefficient? No doubt. Ice built up on the storm windows on cold winter days. Were they difficult to move? You bet, especially in the summer when humidity swelled the wood. To make matters worse, layer upon layer of paint (most of it likely lead-based) cracked and chipped from the muntinbars.

But I just couldn't replace them with modern, vinyl, energy-efficient, low-E, double-pane, argon-gas windows. I decided to professionally restore my old windows instead. Did I fall victim to soothsayers from *This Old House*? Do I deserve a special place in energy-hog hell? Perhaps not. Though many energy experts won't agree with me.

One woman who does is Jade Mortimer, owner of Heartwood Building and Restoration. Heartwood specializes in the restoration of historic wood windows and in energy-efficient upgrades to wood windows and sashes, including invisible epoxy repair, wood repair and preservation, salvaged glass replacement, sash chains, and modern weather stripping. (Full disclosure: Mortimer restored the old wood windows in our former house in Massachusetts.)

Why and when should homeowners keep their original windows?

Homeowners should always consider keeping their old wood windows because they are repairable, often made of tight-grained, old-growth wood that is more stable than the farmed wood sold today, and they can be made more energy efficient. Old windows employ the best joinery available, mortise and tenon, which allows for expansion and contraction and normal stressing of the building. And there is no better balance system than the rope—or chain—and pulley system. Your window size and design fit and complement the architecture of your home.

If you are considering replacing an old wood window because you consider it energy inefficient, I would suggest you first look into weather stripping and storm windows. If you are considering replacing a window because it is slightly rotted, that can be repaired—but if more than half the window is rotted, and it's not historically significant, it may be time to consider replacing it with a good quality new window.

How do you define "old wood window?" How old are we talking about, and is there a decade in window evolution when quality went down and restoration doesn't make sense?

There was a time when most manufacturers, builders, and mom-and-pop stores took great pride in the quality of their products and customer service. That was true about windows until the big spending boom of the late forties and early fifties—with a car in every driveway, a chicken in every pot. Mass marketing of home building products became a big deal and quality began to go the way of the Edsel. There are exceptions, but I would say most windows built in the 1950s and on will be more difficult to restore if there is a significant amount of rot in the wood.

Most affordable energy-efficient windows are made of vinyl. Are there tradeoffs?

PVC—polyvinyl chloride—windows contain dioxins that are known carcinogens and are stabilized by metals such as lead and cadmium. Contrary to popular belief and marketing, vinyl windows are not maintenance free, and the frame does not have the insulating value of old-growth wood. A vinyl window cannot be repaired; it must be replaced. And the embodied energy involved in the manufacture and transportation of a new vinyl window and disposal of the original window far exceeds that of restoring an old window.

What about new wood windows that contain insulating glass?

New wood windows are made of lumber that has been farm grown—forced to grow faster, not unlike adding hormones and other chemicals to a cow's diet—and [are] inferior to old-growth wood. Mass-produced wood windows—the majority of replacement windows—are made of finger-jointed smaller pieces of this inferior wood, which is glued and stapled together and often clad with vinyl or aluminum. Also, the seal on double-glazed windows often fails, releasing the air and/or gas that offers the insulating value. A vacuum is created, causing fogging between the panes, and the only solution is replacement.

Can old wood windows be energy efficient?

Absolutely! An old window that is upgraded with spring-bronze and/or silicone weather stripping with the addition of a storm window will offer the same or better insulating value as a double-glazed window and will last much longer for less money.

Are there any drawbacks to keeping original windows? What inconveniences might a person need to accept?

People today have been convinced that maintenance is a dirty word and may consider painting a window every five to ten years an inconvenience. Part of our social interaction used to come from being out in our yards or working on our homes—think barn raising or painting one's house. The neighbors would stop by to chat or to lend a hand or share supportive compliments on those newly restored windows.

Describe the process you use to restore an old window.

The window sash is removed and transported to an off-site shop. A storm window or a temporary panel can offer a closure in the meantime. All paint, glass, and hardware is removed down to bare wood. Repairs are made where necessary. A linseed oil conditioner is applied to all wood surfaces, and glass is reinstalled with a traditional linseed oil glazing putty; salvaged glass is available for those panes that are cracked or broken. One coat of oil primer and two coats of finish paint are applied. Then the sash is reinstalled with new weather stripping and new or old hardware.

What measures can homeowners and renters take on their own to increase their windows' efficiency?

Adding spring-bronze weather stripping, which has been known to last one hundred-plus years, and a good-quality storm window. Curtains, blinds, and shades will also add to comfort levels and energy efficiency in all climates and seasons.

What got you interested in window restoration?

Circa 1996, I was one of many contractors submitting a bid to restore the oldest house in Provincetown, Massachusetts [1746]. I was the only contractor who agreed that the windows could be salvaged and restored and was awarded the contract. It just so happened that a window restoration conference in Washington DC was scheduled for the next month. I boarded a plane with a half-rotted windowsill under my arm. My hunch that it could be restored was confirmed and thus my adventure into window preservation began.

CHAPTER 2

SAVE TIME, USE LESS ENERGY:
GETTING THE MOST OUT OF YOUR APPLIANCES

There was a time not so long along when the modern appliance was designed and marketed with the classic American housewife in mind. In 1950s ads you'd see a smartly coiffed mother patiently awaiting the 5:30 PM arrival of her briefcase-toting husband. Her hair was styled and lipstick applied, dinner set and on the table, dishes washed and kitchen gleaming, children scrubbed and dressed in freshly laundered clothing—this moment brought to you by GE or Maytag or Whirlpool. Today, thankfully, a more equal distribution of household chores makes appliances everyone's purview. And thank goodness we have them. After my daughter was born, I gained a whole new appreciation for laborsaving devices such as the washing machine and dishwasher, and so did my very tired husband.

We've come a long way since the days of June Cleaver, and I'm not just talking about men with laundry baskets. We also have a lot more appliances and electrical gadgets, all of which use a whole lot of energy. Our plugged-in lives pose a challenge in the quest to make our homes more energy efficient. Appliances, lighting, and water heating make up about half of a typical household's electricity consumption.

With challenges come opportunities, however, and there are many ways to lighten the carbon load of our mechanized servants. Replacing older, inefficient models with shiny new energy-saving heroes is one step. Energy Star appliances promise to use 10 to 50 percent less energy and water than other models. They also often qualify for rebates, tax exemptions, or credits—see the Energy Star website for information on freezers and refrigerators, room air conditioners and air cleaners, heating and cooling systems, water heaters, home electronics and lighting, dehumidifiers and office equipment.

You'll hear a lot about Energy Star in this book. Environmental groups praise the program for giving the public major incentives to buy energy-efficient products and subsequently reduce the amount of CO_2 belched out by power plants. In recent years, however, Energy Star's rating system has not kept pace with technological advances as the market as a whole has shifted toward greater efficiency. For some products, this has resulted in grade inflation—in some cases more than half of the contenders have received the coveted star, making the value of the rating questionable. A recent audit turned up other irregularities, and those in charge have taken this as a wake-up call to make the program more robust. Officials say that ideally Energy Star would only reward the top 25 percent of models in a category, and in the future they promise to get tougher with the times.

So, how much energy does that twentieth-century fridge really use? When should you replace that old top-loading washing machine? How much money can you really save by replacing your dinosaurs with energy-efficient models? Or, if you don't have the bucks to replace your appliances or are renting your refrigerator along with your apartment, what practical steps can you take to make your existing machines more efficient? Let's take a look at what I'll call the major appliances—the ones that take up the most space and use the most energy but that you'd have a hard time doing without.

THE REFRIGERATOR

Though some hardcore folks keep their food cold in a cooler, chest freezer, or root cellar, 99.5 percent of American homes have a refrigerator. Fridges come in all shapes, sizes, colors, and vintages, and, of course, efficiencies. Many say the fridge is the most ravenous appliance in terms of energy consumption. Energy gurus Amory and L. Hunter Lovins, together with Paul Hawken, claim that a typical fridge eats up so much energy that the coal used to generate it would fill it top to bottom each year. Others, like Pascale Maslin, founder of Energy Efficiency Experts, think otherwise: "If I was to examine my life and ask what would reduce my carbon footprint, I would say stop eating meat," Maslin said in a 2009 *New York Times* article. "That's much more significant than unplugging your fridge."

Whether or not your fridge is really the scariest energy beast in your home, there's no doubt that if yours is dated, upgrading will save you both money and carbon output. Energy Star touts some compelling statistics. A fridge made before 1993 could be costing you more than $100 a year to operate, while an Energy Star model might cost you half that. Though it may hold retro appeal, a seventies-era fridge uses four times as much energy and costs $200 more a year to run than a newer Energy Star unit.

Replacing an old appliance with a new one doesn't *always* make sense if you're looking to reduce your carbon impact—if you consider the embodied energy it takes

TIP

ENERGYGUIDE: BECOMING A YELLOW-LABEL SHOPPER

Those bright yellow tags you see on many appliances, including clothes washers, dishwashers, refrigerators, freezers, water heaters, air conditioners, and heat pumps, are meant to do more than just catch your eye. They're actually required by federal law. The Federal Trade Commission (FTC), the nation's consumer protection agency, designed them to help you to compare energy uses, key features, and costs of different models. See www.ftc.gov/bcp/edu/pubs/consumer/homes/rea14.shtm for a quick tutorial in interpreting the tag.

to manufacture and transport that product (something many energy experts don't do). Sometimes it's just best to let your appliance finish out its days before putting it out to pasture. But this is rarely the case with a fridge. Thanks to huge improvements in insulation and compressors, today's modern fridge is just plain better and, in terms of carbon savings, will outperform its predecessor before you know it.

If you take the steps to recycle your old fridge, you'll lighten your impact on the planet even more. An average ten-year-old fridge contains more than 120 pounds of recyclable steel, and the energy saved by recycling it equals about 290 kilowatt-hours—or enough energy to run a new efficient fridge for eight months. Check with the appliance retailer, your local electric utility, your local waste management division, or your local scrap-metal recycler for recycling programs—some may even offer rebates and cash incentives (renters, use this as a bargaining chip with your landlords). This goes for the afterlife of all your old appliances. Recycle them, or consider finding them a new job in a needy home.

BUYING NEW, COOL, AND GREEN

If you do decide to go shopping, I'd suggest not only spending time on the Energy Star website first, where you can research different models, but cross-referencing what you find with Consumer Reports, which will allow you to compare performance features, reliability, and cost. Consumer Reports has also developed a GreenerChoices website, which ranks energy and water usage among models. Once you're in the store, you can also check out the bright yellow EnergyGuide label, which will give you in no uncertain terms a particular model's energy use, compare that to similar models, and estimate the annual operating cost.

Besides considering Energy Star models (which are required by the feds to be 20 percent more efficient than models that don't carry this badge of honor), there are other simple steps you can take to make sure the fridge you buy is a good one:

I **Go for the top:** Choosing a model with the freezer on top, as opposed to bottom or side-by-side units, will save you 10 to 25 percent more energy.
I **Size is important:** Generally, though not always, the bigger the fridge the more energy it consumes (a small fridge with poor-quality compressors and minimal insulation is the exception). Energy Star says the most efficient models are usually 16–20 cubic feet.

- **Skip the frills:** If you want to pay $75 to $250 more and use 14 to 20 percent more energy, by all means purchase a model with an automatic ice-maker and/or a through-the-door dispenser. Otherwise, keep it simple.

GETTING GOOD MILEAGE WITH THE OLD

Are you renting, strapped for cash, or both? You don't need to buy your way to energy efficiency. There is much you can *do* to make your existing refrigerator a little friendlier to the planet. Follow these best practices to help green your fresh food storage:

- **Keep it cold, but not too cold:** Energy Star recommends setting the temperature between 35° F and 38° F. As counterintuitive as it may seem, don't let things get too frosty. If you have a manual or partial automatic defrost fridge or freezer, get rid of the icy buildup as regularly as you can. It'll help prevent your refrigerator's compressor from running longer—and wasting energy—to maintain the cold.
- **Speaking of cold:** The fridge itself should be kept in a cool place. That means not setting it up against an oven or dishwasher or in direct sunlight. For every degree above 70 surrounding your fridge, it'll use 2.5 percent more energy to keep itself cold.
- **Let it flow:** Let air circulate behind your fridge by leaving a few inches between it and the wall. Refrigerators produce heat, and putting them in well-ventilated spaces keeps that heat from getting trapped and requiring more cooling.
- **Clean the coils:** If you have an older model, Energy Star recommends that you clean the condenser coils regularly. Writing in the *New York Times* in 2009, Steve Kurutz advised that if you have furry friends, do this every three months. Although the folks at the Lawrence Berkeley National Laboratory say it's an energy myth that cleaning the coils saves a measurable amount of energy, I can't help but think it'll at least help keep your old model humming a little smoother.
- **Seal 'er up:** Don't let even the tiniest bit of cold air escape. Make sure the seals around the door are airtight—if they're cracked or broken, replace them.
- **Fill 'er up:** A full fridge is an efficient fridge. And if you lose power, it'll hold its cool temperature twice as long as it would if it were half full.

- **Use glass:** Glass stays colder longer than plastic (which in turn helps your fridge stay colder). It's also a good idea to let your foods cool on the countertop so the fridge has less work to do to get them colder.
- **Close the door:** Don't get caught staring into the depths of your fridge. Think about what you want to eat before opening the door, and don't open it too often. This will limit the run time of your compressor, which will in turn save you energy. A whopping 50–120 kilowatt-hours a year are wasted by a typical household's open fridge door. That equals three 100-watt bulbs burning all year.

A NOTE ON THE FREEZER

For those of you who are into long-term food storage—big hunks of meat or bags of frozen peas, for example—please don't keep using grandpa's vintage venison freezer in your garage. The older the freezer, the higher your energy bills.

If you're into eating locally (made easier by storing summer's bounty in the winter), using an old freezer might negate the benefits of your hundred-mile diet. If your freezer was born before 1993, you'll be paying an extra $35 a year on your utility bill (twice that if it dates to the eighties). As you might expect, a new Energy Star freezer is about 10 percent more efficient than a regular model. A chest freezer will save you 10 to 25 percent more than an upright.

Follow an energy-saving routine similar to that for your fridge: keep the temperature appropriate (0° F); don't expose the freezer to temperature extremes (a basement location is a good option); allow air to circulate around it; take good care of the seals; and think before you open the door.

THE DISHWASHER

A woman by the name of Josephine Cochrane invented the dishwasher in 1886, apparently because she was tired of having her fine china chipped by the servants. Since it's more likely that you have a dishwasher than servants in your home, you might be wondering if it's energy-efficient and cost-effective to use it...or if it's better to forgo the luxury of having a machine clean your plates and, due to that lack of servants, become a dishwasher yourself.

Your laborsaving appliances may soon be saving you a little mental energy too. Technological advances on the horizon (Whirlpool says it will have a million smart clothes dryers on the market in 2011) will allow your dishwasher and washing machine to have a conversation with each other, and with the electricity grid as well—a feat that could allow energy savings of 30 to 50 percent for each of your machines and stave off the construction of new power plants to meet peak electricity demand.

These futuristic features will involve demand-response appliances that are connected to smart utility meters and an interactive grid. This setup will allow utility companies to charge more when energy usage is particularly high (making it more expensive to run your dishwasher at 5:00 PM, for example), thereby encouraging you to use your appliances at nonpeak times of day. Another example: You'd like to cook your dinner when you get home from work. The demand-response system will allow your stove to tell (via your home's power lines or a wireless network) your washing machine to delay the clothes wash, and your washing machine to advise your dishwasher to begin after it has finished its job. Or set up a monthly utilities budget and watch your appliances modify their behavior to meet it!

The answer is, if you have a dishwasher, don't feel guilty about employing it—especially if it's a newer, energy-efficient one. But even if it's not, you can take a few steps that will allow it to save more water and energy than your own two hands. According to one recent study, the average dishwasher uses only half the energy, one-sixth of the water, and less soap than washing by hand. Or, to look at it another way, your typical dishwasher uses about 15 gallons of water per load, while your typical dishwashing servant uses about 5 gallons per minute.

Do you already have an energy-efficient dishwasher? Then there's not much of a reason to don those rubber gloves. These models use just 4 gallons per cycle, saving up to 5,000 gallons per year compared to washing by hand—and $40 in energy costs and 230 hours of your time (according to Environmental Protection Agency). It looks like Ms. Cochrane's invention ended up being good for more than just washing china.

A SPARKLING CLEAN NEW MACHINE

If you're in the market for a new dishwasher, there's more good news brought to you by Energy Star: rated dishwashers use 41 percent less energy than the federal minimum standard; they can save you up to $30 a year in utility costs (if your current model was made before 1994); and because they use less hot water than even new conventional models, they'll save you about $90 over their lifespan.

Hot water usage is key to energy savings too. Up to 80 percent of the energy required by a dishwasher goes to heat the water. And don't underestimate the difference a few gallons of water can make. Say you and your family or roommates run the dishwasher every other day. The difference between using a dishwasher that sucks up 3.5 gallons per load (very efficient) and 12 (so-so) can add up to 1,500 gallons in a year.

GREENWASHING TIPS

Don't fret if you don't have the means or desire to replace the dishwasher taking up space in your kitchen. As with the refrigerator, you can make it more planet-friendly. Follow these tips to green your machine, whether it's an efficient model or not:

▌ **Scrape, don't rinse:** Many dishwasher users are guilty of using gallons of water rinsing their dishes before loading them. Why waste water and do what your dishwasher is about to do for you?
▌ **Run only a full load:** This goes without saying. Your dishwasher will use the same amount of energy to heat the water whether it's half full or full, so get the most out of that energy.
▌ **Let your dishes air-dry:** Turn off whatever drying cycle your dishwasher has (if it won't let you, simply open the door when it's done washing). You can save $25 a year on your electricity bill and reduce your dishwasher's energy usage by 15 to 50 percent. Drying with air costs neither kilowatts nor dollars.
▌ **Avoid prerinse and rinse-hold cycles:** Doing so saves water by the gallon. While you're thinking about which cycles to avoid, it might become obvious which ones to embrace: energy-saver, light wash, air-dry—essentially the shortest applicable cycle that will get your dishes clean.
▌ **Mind the temperature:** Turn down your water heater to 120° F or lower. You'll save energy and still get your dishes clean.

Finally, a word to those of you who don't have a dishwasher: you can save water and energy too. Just be a little more conscientious about your habits. Stop up the drain or fill a basin to avoid running and running and running water. Better yet, use two basins. One for washing, one for rinsing. If it's not too soapy, you can even use the rinse water again to quench the thirst of your houseplants.

THE STOVE

Before we leave the kitchen and its food-related matters, let's take a brief look at the stove. Energy Star doesn't rate this appliance, but that doesn't mean you don't have choices when it comes to cooking carbon-light. If your cooking elements are failing you despite your best efforts to become a better chef, you might be in the market for something new.

If you like cooking with gas for its even temperature, make sure you buy a range with electronic ignition (as opposed to the older models with pilot lights). It'll use about 30 percent less energy. Make sure, too, that your cooktop has a ventilation fan above it that sucks the combustion products outside—they're not good to breathe.

If you prefer electric, by far the best option is induction elements—which transfer electromagnetic energy directly to the pan and, as a result, use half as much energy as standard coils. These elements also throw out less heat into the kitchen than both conventional gas and electric designs. And they cook your food about 50 percent faster. There is a catch—they only work with ferrous metal cookware, such as cast iron, stainless steel, and enameled iron.

For all your baking needs, a convection oven is the best bet. Because hot air is continuously circulated around your food, it cooks quicker, more evenly, and at lower temperatures. The end result is about 20 percent in energy savings.

THE WASHER

A typical American household washes 400 loads of laundry a year. Perhaps we can all breathe a collective sigh of relief that the washboard has mostly been relegated to

PROTECTING YOUR RIGHT TO USE A CLOTHESPIN

Have you ever come face-to-face with covenants or regulations that ban you from showing off your skivvies in your backyard? Can't get enough of the way your sheets smell after they've been flapping in the breeze? Check out the Project Laundry List website (www.laundrylist.org). The organization's mission is to make "air-drying and cold-water washing acceptable and desirable as simple and effective ways to save energy." The group does this through art, education, and advocacy, and the website is chock-full of resources, including laundry tips, clothes clips, a library, and opportunities for you to get involved. As the group boldly states, "all citizens nation-wide should have the legal right to hang out their laundry."

a musical instrument. But although the modern washing machine has saved us time and sore backs, it's not without consequences for the planet. The folks at the online environmental magazine *Grist* have compiled a full load of scary statistics: 35 billion loads washed every year in the United States; 76,000 gigawatt-hours of annual energy consumption; 16,000 annual gallons of water used by an average American household; and 13 million annual metric tons of greenhouse gas emissions from American washers and dryers. That's a whole lot of gigawatts, gallons, and greenhouse gases to keep our clothes clean. But don't worry. I won't be asking you to stop regularly changing your socks to reduce your carbon footprint. There are fresh ways to clean clothes without dirtying the earth.

Whether you rent or own it, if you can only do one thing, *wash your clothes in cold water.* Ninety percent of the energy used by a washing machine is used to heat the water. If you use cold water, the only energy you use is to run the machine. Treehugger.com reports that using the hot/warm cycle on a top-loading machine with an electric water heater for every load of laundry for one year is the same as burning 182 gallons of gasoline or driving about 3,600 miles in an average car (that gets 19.8 miles per gallon). If you use the hot/cold cycle with the same machine, you'll burn just over 2,400 pounds of CO_2 a year, which equals a roundtrip cross-country flight. Contrast that with cold/cold: you'll use about 0.24 kilowatt-hour, about 0.41 pound of CO_2 per load, about 162 pounds of CO_2 per year, which equals about 8 gallons of gas, or 164 miles of driving. With a choice between 3,600 miles and 164, you don't need a roadmap to figure out which way to go here.

There are other energy-saving detours you can make. Since your washer will use the same amount of energy regardless, make sure you only wash a full load. Avoid super-hot cycles like "sanitary" (see above). If you can choose your spin option, choose the highest speed available to fling out as much moisture as possible and thus reduce your drying time.

FRONT-LOADERS

If you've been to a Laundromat, you know what a front-loading washer looks like. There's a reason why a smart business owner will install multiples of this machine over its top-loading cousin. Front-loaders are by far more energy efficient, and they're easier on clothes too—which translates into both money saved and satisfied customers.

If it's time to replace your home machine, and you've got extra money to spend up front, buy a front-loader. You'll make up for that initial extra cost by saving up to $120 a year on utilities, which can add up to $1,560 over a washer's average thirteen-year lifespan. Because there is no central agitator, there's more room to wash more clothes per load. You'll also use one-third to one-half the energy of a top-loader, and you'll save on water too: 40 gallons per load for an old top-loader versus 16 to 25 gallons for a new front-loader. You'll also spin out more of that water after the rinse cycle, which will reduce drying time. And you'll spend less on detergent—maybe less on clothing too, since your shirts and slacks will last longer through tumbled front-loaded washings (rather than the agitated top-loaded method).

Your front-loader purchase will be that much smarter if it also has the Energy Star label (though Energy Star does rate some new top-loading machines that use less water and energy than older top-loaders). Buy Energy Star models over a nonqualified washer and save on water (18 more gallons a load), energy (over 40 percent), and utility bills ($50 a year).

PEDAL PUSHERS MAKE A COMEBACK

It's worth mentioning that there are options beyond front-loading, beyond the energy-saving ubiquity of Energy Star, even beyond your old-fashioned washboard, laundry plunger, or wringer. You can clean your clothes with pedal power. Alex Gadsden, inventor of the Cyclean machine, has developed a washing machine that's good for the planet and your cardio workout too. And in her book, *The Human-Powered Home*, Tamara Dean provides plans for a pedal-powered washing machine as well as host of other devices for housework, cooking, and gardening. If you're truly committed, ecologically and physically, check them out.

THE DRYER

On to the other half of the laundry agenda: the dryer. On this front, I have less to report. Because a dryer is a dryer is a dryer. They're all pretty similar, so much so that Energy Star doesn't rate them—though gas-powered dryers are a bit more efficient, all dryers use about the same amount of energy. And as it turns out, unfortunately, that's a lot: about 800 kilowatt-hours a year.

In their book, *The Carbon-Free Home*, Rebekah and Stephen Hren call dryers a "colossal waste of energy" and add that, "simply put, you should not use this machine." If your climate allows, this is certainly a viable option. Use sunshine or the heat already circulating through your home and dry your clothes on a permanent clothesline, retractable clothesline, or drying rack. These incredibly simple, elegant, and essentially free alternatives also have a powerful impact. According to the folks at Project Laundry List, dryers use 10 to 15 percent of domestic energy in the United States.

If, however, you live in a frequently wet and/or humid environment (or in tight urban quarters), you might be loath to give up your dryer, or your access to a dryer. Since every little bit counts, consider these small steps to decrease the heat:

I **Check the settings:** Use the moisture-sensing option if your machine has it. It'll automatically and sensibly turn off the dryer when your clothes are dry.

I **Keep it clean:** Clean the lint filter after each load to increase air circulation and efficiency.

I **Go halfway:** Try letting the sun dry your laundry as much as possible, then finish up in the dryer as necessary.

WASTE NOT, WANT NOT: GREENING YOUR HOT WATER

Right after heating and cooling, hot water is a typical home's biggest energy expense. The EPA reports that the average household spends $400 to $600 a year on it. And for all that money spent, you won't get a lot of well-used energy in return. That old tank buried behind boxes in your basement is most likely losing a ton: only 43 percent of a water heater's energy goes toward heating the water you actually use; 31 percent is lost to standby heating (keeping the water in the tank hot). I'm talking about a clunky, more-than-a-decade-old hot water heater, the kind many of us— 27 million households—own. Seeing as a water heater only lasts about ten to fifteen years, we'll have no choice but to upgrade soon. Here's an opportunity to start thinking about energy-efficient options now, before that hot water runs out.

Conserve before you buy: Before we get to the new showroom models, let's return to our mantra of conservation. Maybe your budget won't allow for a big piece of new hardware, or maybe your landlord won't pony up for the building. There's still a lot you and your fellow tenants can do. If you're hardcore, shorten your showers. Or if you don't have the self-control, reduce your use automatically, and thus your heater's workload, by installing a low-flow showerhead.

Dial it down: Next, try turning down the temperature. This isn't as scary as it sounds—you won't be left with dirty dishes or suffer through washing your hair in lukewarm water. Many hot water heaters are preset to 140° F, which is too hot for most domestic uses. Ever have to mix your hot water with cold to get just the right temperature? You're wasting the electricity that was used to heat the hot water in the first place. You probably won't even notice the difference if you turn down the thermostat to 120° F (115° F may feel just fine), and you'll also save roughly 10 percent of the energy it takes to heat your water. Or to look at it from a financial perspective, for every 10° F you lower the temperature, you'll save 3 to 5 percent on your water-heating costs. Don't forget to turn your thermostat to the lowest possible setting when you're away on vacation. There's no sense in heating water for nobody to use.

Last but not least, insulate: See chapter 1 for an extensive review on the merits of insulation in general. Dressing up your older water heater in a blanket (most newer heaters are already well clothed) is perhaps one of the easiest do-it-yourself energy saving actions you can perform. It's cheap too: a home-improvement store will likely have one on the shelf for around $25. Swaddling your pipes in conjunction with the tank will save you roughly another 10 percent. This is easier said than done, because of the nature of pipes winding this way and that and disappearing into walls and crawl spaces, but at the very least you should insulate exposed pipes—they sell pipe-sleeve insulation, the thicker the better, just for this purpose.

ABOUT TO RUN OUT OF HOT WATER?

Let's say you've been conserving and insulating for a few years, but recently your water heater started giving signs that it's heading for the grave. Now's your chance (or your landlord's chance if you can convert her) to purchase a modern energy-efficient model. Energy Star recently gave its coveted blessing to five different types of water heaters; some only came on the market in 2009. There seems to be a model for everyone, in every situation (for solar water-heating options, see chapter 3).

First, a slight but significant shift up from the status quo. Do you or your landlord have a gas water heater? Are you pretty much satisfied with it, in terms of delivery of hot water and maintenance? Do you have a little extra cash to spend but not much? Then Energy Star recommends a **high-efficiency gas storage water heater**. You'll trade a little money spent up front (recouped in about two and a half years) for an approximately 7.5 percent increase in efficiency and a 7 percent reduction in your water-heating bills—about $30 a year or $360 over the course of its thirteen years of life. What's more, the planet gets a break too. If everyone who planned on purchasing a gas water heater in 2009 opted for a high-efficiency model, about 1 billion pounds of CO_2 would be kept out of atmosphere. All of this results from some simple improvements in the basic water heater design: better insulation, heat traps, and burners.

If you have a couple teenagers in the house and/or for other reasons often run out of hot water—and want to take advantage of newer technology—think about a **gas condensing water heater**. Yes, you'll pay more up front, but you'll decrease the money spent on hot water by about 30 percent, saving roughly $100 each year. That savings is compounded by regular federal tax credits (30 percent of the cost up to $1500 in 2010) as well as potential local rebates. Energy Star boasts that if only 5 percent of prospective gas water heater buyers purchased one of its qualified gas condensing models, consumers would save $25 million every year, and the effect would be equivalent to taking 17,000 cars off the road.

Plus you get lots and lots and lots of hot water—you won't have to worry about running out in the morning if you're the last person in the shower line. New technological design helps the tank heat up almost as quickly as it's filled up. Like regular gas water heaters, condensing models produce waste combustion gasses. Unlike their conventional counterparts, they don't vent them directly outside but capture them and use them to heat the water more before finally releasing them.

Many a homeowner or utility-paying renter has suffered through the high cost of running an electric hot water heater. Though a good electric tank is more efficient than a good gas tank (90 percent versus 60 percent; the remaining percentages are what's wasted in the process of heating the water), electricity is much more expensive in most parts of the country and, more importantly when considering your energy budget, is a much less efficient form of energy because energy is lost when electricity is transmitted through the grid.

So who among the electric water-heating crew wouldn't jump at the chance to cut his or her bill by about 50 percent? Or to save roughly $300 a year?

Takers should consider an **electric heat pump water heater**. If all who were planning on buying a new electric water heater did, the planetary savings would be significant: Energy Star says that in 2009 buyers could have kept 19.6 billion pounds of CO_2 out of the atmosphere by choosing an electric heat pump over a conventional tank—a feat equivalent to taking 1.6 million cars off the road.

Heat pumps operate using a technology that Energy Star describes as a "refrigerator working in reverse." While your fridge expels hot air from its chilly interior to the outside, a heat pump takes warm air from outside the water tank and brings it inside to heat the water—essentially moving heat around instead of wasting more energy creating it. There are drawbacks to this more efficient method: heat pumps need to be housed indoors at a temperature between 40° F and 90° F (they don't operate as well in the cold); they're claustrophobic (requiring about 1,000 cubic feet of air space around them); and they're a bit frigid themselves (they actually cool the air around them). Energy Star recommends putting them in a space with extra heat, like a furnace room—this seems like a good option for an apartment building to me. Electric heat pump water heaters are also more expensive up front, but their payback time is better than most—about three years—and they qualify for tax credits and rebates at all levels.

With water heaters, thinking outside the box means getting rid of the tank. This isn't really revolutionary so much as it's common sense. Do you use hot water all the time, every hour of the day? Of course not. So why feed energy to a standard tanked-up water heater so that it can keep water hot 24/7? **Tankless water heaters** possess a logic that's beautiful in its simplicity: they only heat water when you need it. This design can reduce your hot water energy consumption from 10 to 40 percent. The Department of Energy reports that for homes using 40 gallons or fewer of hot water daily, a tankless water heater can be 24 to 34 percent more efficient than a storage tank model. What's more, the water's always hot and continuously so.

You can get your tankless in electric or gas, but Energy Star only rates the gas models, which receive rave reviews. They will save an average family $100 per year on gas bills (or reduce them by 30 percent), last for two decades (far longer than their tank competitors), and are eligible for big tax federal credits (30 percent of the cost up to $1500 in 2010). All models eliminate the risk of tank leaks and water damage and save space, since they're small and attach to a wall—some can even be mounted outdoors.

Here's how gas models work in a nutshell: you turn on hot water to fill the tub; cold water flows to the water heater; the gas burner is activated, which heats a heat exchanger, which the cold water encircles, leaving to fill the tub at the determined warmed-up temperature. The leftover combustion gases are vented outside.

Installing this system is trickier than just replacing one tank with another. You might need to beef up your natural gas line or install new venting or electrical service—professional installation is recommended. A professional will also give you advice on the best size for your home or building. This work and planning on the front end could be a little stressful, but I'd predict that that stress will melt like an ice cube as you're enjoying your "on-demand," *almost* guilt-free hot water. I say almost…please remember that the energy used to heat the water still likely comes from an environmentally insensitive source: coal, gas, nuclear (even hydroelectric in many situations). So enjoy, but keep that shower as short as possible.

CHAPTER 3

INDIE ENERGY:
GREEN ALTERNATIVES FOR YOUR HOME

There's no denying that the future looks green. On bad days I like to remind myself of this fact—days when another depressing climate-change statistic is unveiled, another species is pushed closer to the brink, another ice sheet the size of a state slides into the ocean. It's hard to see beyond the present, but look back a few decades, even within our grandparents' lifetime, and think of the technological and social changes they witnessed: from telegram to telephone to Internet; from horse and buggy to automobile; from typewriter to personal computer; from oil lamps to electricity. Our lives today will seem just as antiquated in twenty years, maybe even fewer—our houses, apartments, and duplexes prehistoric, and the way we use energy…ancient.

I can't say exactly how all of these transformations will occur, but I do believe that, in terms of energy, a new spirit of independence will blossom—or perhaps *spark* is a better word. The foundation is already there, in the forms of sun and wind, photosynthesis and fire. We can have a more personal relationship with these as sources of our energy.

Biofuels, solar systems, wind turbines—these energy forms are currently available to those who wish to green their home or building. All signs point toward technology and availability changing rapidly. As it stands, powering your home with independent energy is an option for many of us right now and hopefully for more of us in the future. Seeing where your energy comes from, having a part in its production, can only encourage conservation. Having a stake in the heat behind your hot water might cause you to use that water more carefully.

LET IT GROW: BIODIESEL FOR THE FURNACE

I was surprised when I first moved to the Northeast from my native Oregon and learned that so many people there heat their homes with oil. In fact, 6.5 million households in the region do so. In 2006, Northeasterners burned through 4.1 billion gallons, which was 82 percent of total home fuel oil sales. Living for most of my life in a primarily hydropowered state with its relatively inexpensive (subsidized)—though by no means environmentally benign, just ask the salmon—electricity and within the larger western United States, with its abundant natural gas (not without its ecological costs either), I had never much considered home heating oil. And yet 8.5 million American households keep warm in the winter by burning oil—my Massachusetts home was one of them. For every gallon of oil we burned, 23.39 pounds of CO_2 were released into the atmosphere. Our method of keeping warm in the winter also released other greenhouse gasses and contributed to mercury deposition and ozone destruction. Short of installing a brand-new alternative heating system, a financial impossibility for most of us, what can we do to lessen our carbon homeprint?

Enter biodiesel, sometimes known as bioheat, which the Department of Energy says is the fastest growing alternative energy source on the market. Biodiesel is a vegetable oil that is chemically reacted with alcohol. Or think of it as a manufactured fuel oil or a renewable substitute for diesel fuel. About any vegetable oil will do, according to Greg Pahl, author of *Natural Home Heating*, including "soy bean oil, corn, canola, cottonseed, peanut, sunflower, mustard seed, and more." You can also use animal fat or recycled cooking oil.

On some progressive-city buses, or greener individuals' automobiles, you may have noticed a bumper sticker identifying biodiesel as the fuel powering that vehicle. In truth, it's primarily used as a transportation fuel, though it's growing in popularity as a replacement for fossil fuels in home furnaces. In Massachusetts, for example, all home heating diesel in the commonwealth was required to be 2 percent biofuel by July 2010 and 5 percent by 2013. Sure, this is a small percentage, but considering how much heating oil is burned in the state—777.1 million gallons in 2006 by 975,000 homes—the impact is certainly large. Massachusetts isn't alone. Pennsylvania passed a law in 2008 requiring that biodiesel be phased in to the fuel supply as more biofuel is produced in the state.

Is mixing oil with vegetables in your furnace something you should think about for your abode? Consider this: biodiesel is low polluting (especially compared to burning oil or natural gas), it's renewable and biodegradable, and it can be locally produced, thus providing a benefit to local farms. Biodiesel is energy efficient; it takes about the same amount of energy to produce 1 gallon of biodiesel as it does to make 1 gallon of petroleum diesel, but the energy going into making the biodiesel is renewable energy, not fossil fuel. It can even be considered a zero-emission fuel, since growing its sources (plants) reabsorbs roughly the same amount of CO_2 that's released when it's burned. At the UK Biodiesel Expo 2006, a fellow by the name of Andrew Robertson presented research suggesting that the use of B20 biodiesel (more on that below), could cut Britain's household CO_2 emissions by 1.5 million tons each year.

A cautionary note: The rosy glow of biofuels (and their carbon neutrality) is dampened if deforestation happens as a result of planting a biofuel crop. And their eco-value becomes even more questionable with a product like ethanol, which is made from corn, soybeans, and other food crops. Today, massive subsidization programs promote this biofuel, which may reduce carbon emissions but also threatens food security, especially for the world's poor (because food crops become more valuable as fuel). The intensive industrial farming practiced to grow this fuel also damages the environment. All biofuels don't burn clean. For your home, go local and small-scale if you can. Know your bio.

Are you wondering how to get started? If you've got a furnace, you've pretty much got all the technology you need. One of the virtues of biodiesel is that it will burn in virtually any oil-fired furnace; there's no complicated transition process or expensive adaptations. That said, a word of caution. When my husband called our home fuel oil supplier, he was told that using biodiesel could void the warranty on our brand-new furnace. Burn veggie oil? What kind of hippie nonsense is that? But worried suppliers aren't entirely off the mark. There are some very good reasons to be careful if you decide to pour biodiesel in your furnace. Biodiesel can thicken at cold temperatures—I have a friend whose biodiesel-fueled car often has trouble starting in the below-freezing temperatures of a Northeast winter—though anti-gelling agents mixed in will help.

Biodiesel also has the potential to eat at rubber parts and corrode copper or brass fittings in older furnaces. Because of its tendency to stir up the leftover oil sludge and varnishes in your tank, it can also clog fuel filters or burner heads. One way around this is to gradually introduce a blend of biodiesel so that the varnish comes off more slowly—all the while closely observing how your furnace handles each increase of the bioblend and decrease of petroleum. Eventually the solvency of the biofuel will clean out the tank entirely, making it much more efficient.

In fact, though it is possible to burn 100 percent biodiesel, or B100, with some modifications in your tank, 20 percent biodiesel, or B20, is widely recommended as doable for most existing furnaces. The National Biodiesel Board states that "although biodiesel (B100) can be used, blends of over 20% biodiesel with diesel fuel (B20) should be evaluated on a case by case basis until further experience is available."

The issue then becomes how to get the stuff. And therein lies two of biodiesel's biggest problems: cost and supply. Biodiesel is generally at least as expensive as regular home heating oil. In the fall of 2009, a local western Massachusetts energy company sold it for $3.50 a gallon, while a gallon of conventional heating oil went for $2.29.

Biodiesel is also hard to come by in some areas, but a large cadre of folks are working to change that. The National Biodiesel Board's website has gallons of practical information, including a search function that allows you to find the closest supplier in your area. For other resources, blogs, and forums, visit the online magazines *Biodiesel Now* and *Biodiesel Magazine*, check out the online biofuels library of the Journey to Forever nonprofit, or join the 5,000-member-strong Alternative Fuels Furnace Yahoo Group.

DIESEL FUEL, BIOFUEL, SAME DIFFERENCE

When you think about breaking new ground and fueling your furnace with B20—a 20 percent biodiesel and 80 percent fuel oil formula—consider first the inventor of the diesel engine. Rudolf Diesel imagined a more efficient source of power than the steam engines prevalent in the late 1800s. Diesel researched injecting fuel into the pressurized chamber above a piston, with the resulting explosion forcing the piston down and creating an opportunity to harness energy. He experimented with many different fuels and in 1893 patented his internal combustion technology.

The talking picture show debuted at the 1900 Exposition Universelle in Paris, and the diesel engine debuted alongside it—powered by peanut oil. Diesel recognized that a wide variety of vegetable oils could be used for this purpose. His biofuel-powered engine tripled the efficiency of steam power. The story may have continued but for Diesel's untimely and somewhat mysterious death in 1913 and the adoption of fossil fuels as the primary source for internal combustion engines.

FEELING THE HEAT: FEEDING YOUR STOVE WITH WOOD, PELLETS, OR CORN

When it comes to setting a mood, nothing beats a toasty fire. Sitting in front of a heating vent just isn't the same. Burning is embedded in our psyches by our ancestors—no wonder people are drawn to a flickering flame. Fire has kept our caves, huts, yurts, cabins, and other shelters warm for a long time. Today, there are many different ways to ignite a flame and a few to make it burn green.

YE OLDE LOG

Wood is traditional and appealing—at least to me—for its back-to-basic qualities, the healthy physical labor involved in gathering, cording, and splitting it, the fresh-cut smell, and the visible warmth as it burns. Wood is also a local resource: you get your heat from the landscape you live in. And it's potentially renewable too, with proper woodlot or forest management. You can heat your entire house with wood—a cord of it produces

as much heat as 200 gallons of heating oil. Today's best woodstoves are roughly 75 percent efficient, meaning 75 percent of the energy embedded in the wood becomes heat when burned.

But there are drawbacks. Burning wood releases CO_2 and other particulates. Because of this, it's generally not appropriate for urban areas and even some rural areas: where cleaner-burning hardwoods are available, it can be great; but in valleys prone to inversion (in my experience, Montana's Missoula Valley is a prime example), not so hot. If you've got an old woodstove or it's not properly vented, you're potentially breathing polluted indoor air as well. Another drawback is that you need to keep feeding the fire to keep the heat on—certainly not an option when you're at work all day. And the romance of cutting, splitting, and stacking wood that I spoke of earlier, well, that can get a little old after a while, at the very least tiring and time-consuming.

If wood is right for you and your locale, though, burning it will probably feel a whole lot better than burning politically tainted and environmentally destructive oil or gas or electricity from far-away unknown sources.

If you're determined to use it as a primary source of heat, choose a **woodstove over a fireplace**. Dan Chiras, author of *The Homeowner's Guide to Renewable Energy*, laments that "fireplaces are one of the least efficient heating technologies humans have ever invented." They're only 10 to 20 percent efficient and can lose more heat than they provide, because warm air from the room is drawn into the fireplace and up the chimney and is often replaced by colder air. A woodstove, on the other hand, instead of sucking air in and blowing it out the chimney, heats the air in the space you're living in.

Think about upgrading if you're currently splitting and stacking cords of wood to shove in an older woodstove. Today's **modern woodstoves** must meet standards set by the Clean Air Act, which means they produce minimal smoke and ash and, as a bonus, require less firewood to keep your home warm. The Environmental Protection Agency's certified stoves (visit the EPA's Burn Wise website for a list) produce only 2 to 7 grams of smoke per hour—while an older uncertified stove will likely belch out 15 to 30 grams in the same amount of time.

Keep in mind that concern about air pollution from woodstoves is rising, and local governments in places like Butte, Montana, and the Puget Sound region of Washington State provide cash incentives to help owners of old woodstoves switch to newer, certified woodstoves or pellet or gas stoves.

You have three types of stoves to choose from for your soon-to-be toasty firelit abode: radiant, circulating, and combustion. **Radiant stoves** do what their name implies. They heat the rooms in your home primarily by radiating heat off of a single layer of metal. The heat from the stove sets up a convection current in the room: the stove heats the air, hot air rises, and cool air flows by the stove and is heated, perpetuating a cycle that continues as long as you're feeding the fire logs. Most new stoves are radiant and, due to their spare use of a single layer of metal, they are generally less expensive than a circulating model, even though they reach the same efficiency of 70 to 80 percent.

Why shell out the extra bucks then? **Circulating stoves** cost more because more material is used to build them. They are double walled, a feature that prevents the stove's surface from getting too hot and makes them a safer bet for curious children. These stoves work a little differently too. Air is pulled into the space inside the outer shell and is then circulated through the room. If you can, whether you're trending toward radiant or circulating, purchase a model that allows you to control the air intake, which gives you control of the rate the fire burns and your room's temperature.

Finally, there are **combustion stoves**. They sound great at first, promising the heat-kick of a woodstove with the gentle ambience of a fire. Unlike other stoves, you can leave the door open and watch the wood burn. This, unfortunately, results in reduced efficiency of 50 to 60 percent, as too much hot air is sucked up the chimney. Get a radiant or circulating stove with a window and you'll have just about the same experience without the heat loss.

Two different features will increase a stove's efficiency: **catalytic converters and baffles**. With the former, a catalyst, such as palladium or platinum, grabs gasses that haven't completely burned and sends them over the fire again. This produces more heat and increases a stove's efficiency by 10 to 25 percent. Catalytic converters, however, are short lived, lasting only three to six years. In contrast, baffles last the life of the stove because they are a structural design element. As with a catalytic converter, unburned gasses are forced back over the fire and ignite before they have a chance to escape through the chimney. Again, you get more heat and an increase in efficiency of 10 to 25 percent.

A HOT BY-PRODUCT: PELLETS

Efficiency is key to a green home, of course. For super-efficient heating, you may want to consider wood of a different form altogether: pellets. What by all accounts looks like something you should be feeding a bunny, pellets are actually dry, compressed sawdust—waste from sawmills that's converted into a clean-burning fuel. Recycling a waste product is certainly green, but understand that pellets are usually a waste product of agroforestry and extensive logging operations. You have to be comfortable with that, comfortable really with the contradictions we often face when making decisions of this sort. Using pellets, like other energy decisions, has its pros and cons.

The pros: Pellet stoves burn more cleanly than most woodstoves, and since you feed pellets at a consistent rate you get a more precise and consistent heat, which is aided by a fan that distributes it evenly around a room. Pellet stoves are more efficient—75 to 90 percent of the fuel (pellets) is converted to heat. The stoves operate automatically, so you can heat your home if you're away.

The cons: Sometimes there are pellet shortages. The bags that the pellets are sold in are themselves plastic. If you're trying to heat a 1,600-square-foot home almost exclusively with your pellet stove during a typical winter in a chilly northern part of the country, you might burn through a 40-pound plastic bag of pellets in a day, and more than 120 bags in an average winter. One of the reasons pellets are stored in plastic is that they have to stay dry—get them wet and they'll turn to mush. You can't heat with mush, nor can you heat with a pellet stove if you lose power unless you purchase a battery backup. These stoves require electricity to operate, about 100 kilowatt-hours per month, which adds about 170 pounds of CO_2 annually to the atmosphere depending on your electricity source. Even though a pellet stove is more efficient than a woodstove, the savings might not be so great if you consider the energy embodied in the manufacturing of pellets and the transportation of the pellets from the sawmill to your doorstep—you can get regionally sourced pellets in some parts of the country, but your likelihood of finding locally cut wood is probably greater. Finally, if you're digging your pocketbook out of your purse, be prepared to pay more for both pellets and a pellet stove than you would for wood or a woodstove.

CORN-FED HEAT

Money was in short supply during the Great Depression, and the value of corn was low. So folks burned it to keep warm. Ever since, when the cost of corn has dipped, the popularity of burning it has risen. Today, when the price falls below $2 per bushel (about two buckets full), it's the cheapest fuel source around. And since North America produces about 300 million tons of corn each year, there's plenty to go around.

The first safety-certified corn-burning stove came into being in 1986. Today's corn-burning appliances are not unlike pellet stoves; they have an auger that feeds the fire-dried corn in carefully controlled amounts. Besides stoves, corn-burning implements come as fireplace inserts, furnaces, and boilers. Combustion is hot, hot, hot in these appliances, allowing the corn to burn cleanly, with low emissions. In fuel-burning competition, corn takes out wood and gives pellets a good running in the Btu category. One pound of dry corn produces 7,000 Btus, while wood produces 800 and pellets 9,000.

Corn is by no means a wonder fuel, however. Like wood and pellets, it has its disadvantages. Though corn is grown everywhere, it's really most plentiful and cheap in the Midwest. So if you're not a flatlander, you may be paying out in dollars and carbon emissions to ship it to your home. Storage is a problem too; corn must be kept dry and free from rodents, and, since it's cheapest by the ton, you need some amount of space to store it.

Corn is like any other plant: it absorbs CO_2 as it grows, and with most of these appliances it burns so efficiently that the CO_2 released is fairly negligible—especially if it's raised organically and with no-till farming methods. Consider, though, that vast swaths of land (73 million acres) in this country (some of it once habitat for wildlife) are given over to chemically intensive, pesticide-laden, industrial-style farming—with corn being the number-one product produced. And there are other moral issues. Is it right to burn a food crop in a world where so many are hungry? It might be more difficult than you think to find untainted corn to heat your home.

In the consideration of alternative fuels, it's hard to stay away from the cliché of "there are no easy choices." Perhaps there are lesser and greater degrees of bad environmental consequences of burning oil, wood, pellets, corn, or whatever new fuel source is on the horizon. That's the burden of being one of billions of humans in the twenty-first century—and a size X-Large carbon footprint American at that. Do the best you can with what's available where you live—both resource- and budgetwise. If you have no choice but the status quo, even if it's an ugly old oil-burning furnace, remember that conservation can have as big an impact as any new device you might buy.

TODAY'S FORECAST: SUNNY WITH LOTS OF HOT WATER

At the end of chapter 2, I gave you options for greening your hot water using conventional means. To eliminate energy-using guilt even more, choose solar-heated water instead. Unlike electricity from gas, coal, or oil, that from sunshine is completely renewable and, once you get your system set up, free for the taking. Using the sun to heat water is also the most efficient use of solar energy. Solar water panels transfer 70 percent of the sun's energy into heat, while photovoltaics are only 20 percent efficient at translating sunlight into electricity.

If you've always dreamed of solar, your best investment is to mix sun with water. Sustainable-home gurus Rebekah and Stephen Hren advise in their *Carbon-Free Home* that "if you have a south- or west-facing sunny roof that gets five hours of sun a day, you need to seriously consider a solar hot-water heater."

A backup auxiliary gas or electric water heater for cloudy days is generally recommended for your solar system. (If you aren't storing that solar-heated water somewhere, or running it through an on-demand tankless heater, you won't have hot water at night either.) According to Energy Star, this setup (with the program's qualified models) will cut your water heating bills in half each year—to about $190 for solar/gas-storage and $250 for a solar/electric tank. Visit the Department of Energy's Energy Savers website to estimate a solar water heater's annual operating cost for your home.

Though solar hot water systems are no doubt spendy—and, in terms of energy cost savings, they take roughly ten years to pay for themselves—federal tax credits and other rebates will speed up that payback time. The Database of State Incentives for Renewable Energy can help you locate these deals.

Energy Star recommends using a contractor certified by the North American Board of Certified Energy Practitioners, who ideally will be able to help assess your home's potential for solar (is your roof substantial enough, do you get enough sun?), recommend a system, install that system, and then do periodic maintenance. In other words, choose someone you don't mind having a relationship with—your solar hot water system will potentially be with you for twenty years.

Speaking of relationships, don't forget the one you have with the environment. Feel good about giving back to your lovable planet—with solar you can potentially cut your CO_2 hot water emissions in half. If you've got an electric heater, your impact will be quite significant: adding a solar system will keep about 4,000 pounds of CO_2 out of the atmosphere. This is like not driving your car for a month.

Ready to sign up? There are a few things to consider. A trusted professional will walk you through the complexities and help you make good choices for your home, condo, or apartment building. Nevertheless, self-education is a good thing.

Solar water heaters come in many different designs, but they all can be categorized according to which of three types of collectors they use:

- **Batch collector:** In this model, the water you use in your house is the very same water that's been heated by the sun. There are an almost infinite number of ways to do this—water is heated and stored within dark tanks or tubes or roof-mounted insulated glass boxes. This system won't work in cold climates, primarily because it won't work with a closed-loop circulation system (see below)—or, since this is the water you'll be using, there's no antifreeze in the water to keep it from freezing.
- **Flat-plate collector:** Simply put, copper tubes are attached to flat absorber plates, which are fitted within an insulated box covered with tempered glass. These plates are usually set up to contain 40 gallons of water, and Energy Star says two plates will provide for about half the hot water needs for a family of four.
- **Evacuated-tube collector:** This type generally costs twice as much per square foot as a flat-plate collector, but it has significant benefits: improved efficiency; the ability to overcome an overcast day; and functionality in temperatures as low as −40° F. Evacuated-tube collectors work like a thermos, heating a vacuum area between two glass tubes—one enveloping the other, the smaller holding water or heat-transfer fluid—and thus losing very little heat.

And there are two types of circulation systems, which can be either active or passive:

- **Direct circulation system:** Water passes through solar collectors where it's heated by the sun and then is either stored in a tank, goes through a tankless water heater, or is immediately used. This is a good system for climates with endless summers and rare winters.
- **Closed-loop (or indirect) circulation system:** This is good for the frostbitten. A nonfreezing liquid is used to transfer the sun's heat to your water. The sun heats the fluid in the collectors; the fluid passes through a heat exchanger in a tank, where heat is transferred to your water; the nonfreezing liquid heads back to the collectors.

- **Active system:** Either direct or indirect systems can be active. In an active system, water is moved from the solar collectors to the storage tank via electric pumps and other machinery.
- **Passive system:** Most passive systems, which use convection to move water around, are direct.

BEYOND SOLAR HOT WATER: IS PHOTOVOLTAIC RIGHT FOR YOU?

Light from the sun travels on average 93 million miles before striking the surface of our planet. About half of this solar energy is absorbed by the land and sea, while the other half is reflected and radiated back into space. Sunlight powers wind-driven currents over the ocean and creates heat on land. It makes possible the process of photosynthesis, which in turn supports the existence of life. Shining with a lot of untapped potential, solar energy is capable of doing much, much more for energy-hungry humans. About 3,850 zettajoules (ZJ) is free for the taking every year. In 2004, the whole wide world used only 0.471 ZJ. Or, to look at it another way, 5,000 times the amount of energy used on Earth hits the Earth each and every day. With the worst effects of climate change all but inevitable, it's time to move out of the dark ages of energy production and consumption and into the sun's light.

We've already covered the desirable qualities of a solar hot water system. Now let's look at photovoltaic, or PV, cells and panels, which right now at least are the most popular method of turning the sun's light into electricity (solar shingles and other integrated systems are currently available but very expensive).

Since 2002, PV production has been doubling every two years, making it the fastest-growing energy technology in the world. This, despite the fact that PV is also currently the most expensive alternative energy option on the block. Solar panel costs vary but average between $20,000 and $40,000 for a typical home. Most energy experts predict that, depending on your energy usage, it will take you on average five to ten years to recoup your investment (state and federal rebates might help shorten this time frame). Still, there's just something irresistibly sexy about solar energy. PV boldly signals your high ecostatus to your neighbors. If you're a landlord with panels on your rooftop, you're an automatic green hero to your renters and the envy of other building owners.

How PVs turn sun into electricity is complicated, but, essentially, sunlight hits a piece of silicon and sets electrons into a frenzied movement, creating an electric current. A PV module or panel is a set of PV cells that are connected together. Several panels on the roof plus a sunny day and you have a lot of crazed electrons creating a lot of electricity. Use a converter to turn this DC current into AC power and next thing you know you'll be in collusion with the sun when you hit a light switch.

If you haven't figured it out by now, the key ingredient is sunlight. If you don't have it, solar is a no go. You must have unobstructed south-facing exposure to achieve any sort of efficiency with a solar system.

Say you've got enough sun. Now you need to consider what sort of system to chose. There are three basic types: grid-connected, grid-connected with battery backup, and stand-alone (off-grid). Grid-connected is by far the cheapest and easiest option and most likely the best choice for remodeling an existing home. Having a battery backup is possible, but batteries are expensive—raising the price of the entire system by 30 to 40 percent—and they require a safe, climate-controlled environment for storage. If you have a stand-alone system, however, batteries are required to provide power during the night, on cloudy days, or sometimes during times of high usage.

The next point of business is size. Determining the right-size system for your home, condo complex, or building is tricky. Most experts suggest getting the help of a trusted professional installer. (A good place to look is the online Find Solar directory.) The installer may ask you about your appliances—how much you use them and how much power they consume. You can also consult tables that show standard energy use for those appliances. The pro might suggest that you size your system for your greatest energy use and lowest solar input. Here's where you have an opportunity to be proactive. Before you start calculating that energy use, before you even consider a PV system, get efficient. For every dollar you spend on efficiency you'll save $3 to $5 on your system because you'll be able to size it more appropriately, and size it smaller. This can mean anything from retrofitting and upgrading appliances to eliminating phantom loads.

Electricity primarily powered by a PV system is, hands down, a very good thing for the planet. Nonetheless, like anything else, it is not without its drawbacks. First off, if you coughed when I brought up the cost of a typical PV system, it was not without good reason. That's a lot of money. And that's probably solar's greatest drawback. It's hard to imagine a lot of people converting when faced with those numbers. At current prices, you'll be paying more per watt powered by your home's PV system than you will for a watt from the grid—or paying more for a greener, cleaner energy. If you can afford to do that, you should.

Secondly, remember that solar power is not always available by the hour. Darkness, clouds, pollution—all can affect efficiency (and even if you store that sun in a battery for use during these conditions, you'll lose a certain amount of energy).

Just the same, it's hard not to be impressed by solar energy's greatest asset: its endless abundance. There's a whole lot of sun going around. If, as a society, we can figure out how to maximize it to its fullest potential, we may be able to make solar energy an option for everyone. In the meantime, don't get too jealous over your neighbor's panels.

Those of you who want more information—maybe so you can create and install a system yourself?—may want to head to Build It Solar online, where you'll find free plans for hundreds of solar projects, design specs, ideas, tools and even an experimental section for backyard inventors.

CATCH THE WIND: RAISING A TURBINE AT HOME

Personal windmills are not a revolutionary concept. From small Midwest farmers to the intrepid Dutch, people have harnessed the wind for centuries. Today, small wind energy is a highly dynamic and evolving industry—thirty manufacturers sell 102 different turbines in the United States, and the number of companies promises to keep growing. You might find your very own windmill an irresistible prospect, but chances are that it *probably* won't be right for your home.

The biggest reason for this is simply that the wind may not blow enough where you live. The National Renewable Energy Laboratory online can help you identify how well the wind blows in your state and area. Most conventional thinking on personal wind energy suggests that your home should sit on 1 acre or more—that would mean 10 percent of the population, or about 21 million people, meet this prerequisite.

It's less expensive to buy a kilowatt of wind energy from a large turbine through your utility than it is to produce it with your own smaller windmill. But a strong environmental case can be made for harnessing the wind at home if you can. Local

Almost everyone has heard of it at this point—selling energy back to the utility, spinning your meter backward. These ideas are a part of "net metering," a system that provides a great incentive to generate your own electricity.

Net metering happens when a private party—say you—generates excess electricity from a renewable source, like solar or wind, and feeds the electricity back into the electric utility's distribution grid. Literally or figuratively, depending on your utility provider, the power meter on your house spins backward.

Though federal legislation establishes the broad outlines of how net metering works, individual states control the specifics of how it may affect you and your solar panel or windmill. It's worth investigating your state's net-metering policy *before* calculating the costs and benefits of an alternative energy system. States differ in placing caps on important details like how much energy can be sold back, whether you can roll over your credit for energy produced from one month to the next, whether the utility will actually buy the energy for cash or just give you credit against your own future energy use, and just how much you'll be paid per watt.

Selling power back to your utility can be a serious incentive to go solar. Solar cells generate more power during sunny daylight hours and less power at night. It used to be that the only solution to this problem was to invest in a battery array and store your daytime power for later use. This added to the cost of already expensive solar systems. With net metering, you may be able to use the grid as a sort of free storage area, feeding your excess power back into the grid for credit against future electricity usage, or in some states for cash.

Consumers considering net metering should contact their electric utility to learn how it works in their state. The Network for New Energy Choices ranks state net-metering policies. Look online to see what grade your state earns.

power eliminates the inefficiencies associated with its transmission and also helps us think more about our energy consumption because we can see where the power comes from. The American Wind Energy Association (AWEA) reports on its website that, over its life, a small residential wind turbine can offset 1.2 tons of air pollutants and 200 tons of greenhouse gases.

Be prepared to do more than just put up a pole with blades that spin. Home wind turbines are made up of those iconic blades (also known as a rotor); a shaft that connects to the rotor and spins when the blades turn; a generator that produces electricity from the spinning shaft; and, in most cases, apart from the turbine, a tower, charge controllers, and a metering device. (Because of this complexity, professional installation is recommended.)

Just like photovoltaic solar systems, there are three types of wind power systems: grid-connected, grid-connected with battery backup, and off-grid. And like solar, installing a wind system also means first meeting specific site and budgetary requirements. With wind, you oftentimes must also meet zoning requirements and sometimes those of your unhappy neighbors. Though some folks find windmills aesthetically pleasing, others think them an eyesore wrapped in noise pollution.

Today's small home windmill typically stands 80 to 140 feet high, or at least 30 feet above ground level *or* the level of any nearby structure; and the turbines range from 8 to 70 feet in diameter, giving 50 to 4,000 square feet of "swept area." That's a big presence in any neighborhood. It's also large on the power-generating front: bigger turbines can reach up to 8,000 kilowatt-hours per month if wind speed averages 10 miles per hour.

An installed residential wind system will cost between $6,000 and $22,000, with savings coming through reduced future utility costs. On its website AWEA says that a turbine will typically lower your electricity bill by 50 to 90 percent, noting that what you save "in the long run will depend on [the system's] cost, the amount of electricity you use, the average wind speed at your site, and other factors."

Conserving energy as a first step will help you size your system correctly, and a smaller system is less expensive to install. Getting the size right is important because there are no do-overs: if you've underestimated your energy needs, you can't put longer blades on your windmill or build your tower higher or, in most cases because of space constraints, add another turbine. So calculate carefully. Your pocketbook may be aided by state and federal rebates and incentives. Skystream, a residential wind turbine manufacturer, has an online database that can help you find local rebates.

City dwellers are taking advantage of the wind, too, by installing windmills way up high, on building rooftops. San Francisco has three small wind turbines already in place, one at the zoo. Like their country cousins, urban windmills are not without their controversies—neighbors worry about aesthetics, noise, and the potential for structural damage to the building (turbines generate vibrations, and the vibrations are transferred down the tower to the building). Too, the wind is so turbulent and gusty in an urban environment, it's difficult to harness, and thus a windmill is unable to reach its peak output.

Small wind power seems to have mixed potential. "Wind-electric systems are not easy, simple, cheap, or perfectly reliable," writes Ian Woofenden in *Home Power Magazine*. "But if you do your homework, buy quality equipment, and get the help you need, you can end up with a long-lasting and satisfying system." I can't come up with a better summary myself.

Sam Newman and Natalie Mims work at the Rocky Mountain Institute (RMI), an entrepreneurial nonprofit think-and-do tank established in 1982 by Amory and L. Hunter Lovins. Today, RMI has approximately ninety full-time staff, an annual budget of nearly $15 million, and a global reach; it works in the areas of energy, mobility, and vehicle efficiency and energy resource use, security, and the built environment.

Natalie Mims is a senior consultant in RMI's Energy and Resources core practice. She spends much of her time focused on overcoming barriers to energy efficiency and contributes to consulting projects on greenhouse gas strategies for electric utilities and regulatory analysis of electric utility systems.

In addition to research work for RMI's Solar Value Chain and Next-Generation Utility efforts (a proposed low-carbon utility system), Sam Newman contributes to consulting projects in the areas of electric utility strategy, industrial process efficiency, and corporate greenhouse gas strategy. His particular areas of focus include the photovoltaic industry and data-center energy consumption.

What are the best choices an individual can make to reduce the carbon footprint of his or her home?

Natalie: Making sure your HVAC (heating, ventilating, air conditioning) and water-heating systems and your refrigerator are efficient. Monitoring plug loads, ensuring that you have proper insulation and that your heating and cooling systems are sized appropriately. And, most importantly, behavioral choices: turning off lights, turning off your computer, and thinking about how you consume energy.

Sam: Besides what Natalie just mentioned, making sure your building envelope is tight, that you use Energy Star lighting, and that you take into account transportation. When you use carbon as a metric, a lot of things end up coming back to it. Recycling cuts carbon, because of the energy embodied in producing an aluminum can. So does gardening, because your food doesn't travel thousands of miles.

What's the biggest impact homeowners and renters can make on America's energy consumption as a whole?

Natalie: In addition to taking efficiency measures in your household, as discussed...

Sam: Engaging in more advocacy work. Talking to your neighbors about what you've done—efficiency isn't as noticeable as solar panels.

When RMI considers energy consumption, we consider four different end-use sectors: (1) residential buildings, (2) commercial buildings, (3) industrial buildings and their machinery, and (4) transportation. Residential buildings account for about 22 percent of total energy-use consumption, so our homes impact about a quarter of the pie. We can extend this impact by considering commuting miles from our homes, which is tied to the transportation piece, or by buying less from Walmart, which affects the industry sector.

What alternative energy choices do you currently see as the most suitable for individual homes?

Sam: Photovoltaic systems [PV] and solar hot water. There are huge opportunities for PV systems, especially in places like Arizona, New Mexico, California, and Hawaii, but also in the Midwest, where PV is only about 25 percent less efficient than in sunny states, and upstate New York, which is about 25 percent less effective than the Midwest. So PV can be pretty applicable to most people. Germany has sun resources comparable to the rainy Olympic Peninsula [in Washington State], but it's leaps and bounds beyond most other countries in terms of PV use.

The up-front cost of a PV system can be prohibitive—averaging about $20,000 to $40,000 for a typical home—but there are ways around this. One Block Off the Grid is a cool organization that pools together people who want PV and then uses that demand to negotiate cheaper prices for a system. The organization also provides homeowners with recommendations and cost estimates for their particular homes. Some companies have also started to help reduce the up-front cost. For example, SolarCity and SunEdison will install a residential PV system at low or no up-front cost. They then arrange the financing, and the homeowner pays for the PV system through a monthly payment. Since the monthly payment is lower than the cost of utility electricity saved by the PV system, it offers value to the homeowner.

Solar hot water is good technology and a rewarding investment—it's more cost effective than PV.

Natalie: Especially if you have electric hot water.

Sam: This is not necessarily an energy source, but as electric vehicles become increasingly available, you'll have battery capacities in more homes. Car batteries will have power to supply a home for a day or so.

What are the biggest impediments to developing a sustainable power system within the United States? How do you think the energy grid will change and how will this affect how we use energy in our homes?

Natalie: As the energy grid becomes the smart grid, there'll be better communication between you as a consumer and your utility. The smart grid means a lot of things to a lot of people. We think about it as a bundle of enabling technologies that will allow consumers to monitor their energy consumption more accurately—and modify it based on that information—and the utility to see, in real time, demand. This will allow the utility to more accurately plan on energy efficiency as a resource because they will actually see if consumers reduce demand at a certain time of the day because of price or information.

Sam: In addition, the smart grid will potentially help utilities manage increasing amounts of variable wind and solar electricity generation without sacrificing grid reliability.

Natalie: Utilities can slow or speed up the shift to a sustainable power system. So it's not exactly fair to say that they are impediments—it's more the business structure in which they operate. As a publicly traded company with shareholders, in a regulatory structure that rewards it for capital expenditures, they are acting rationally. In most states, utilities make more money the more electricity they sell—the exception is

California and a few other states that have decoupled profits from sales. We need to reduce the incentive to sell electricity.

Sam: Utilities still have gas and coal plants for backup for when the wind doesn't blow. We need to find appropriate ways to deal with the variability of wind and solar. Maybe it's improving battery technology. Maybe it's developing new ways to get a coal plant back up and running more quickly as backup—it currently takes an hour—so that we burn less coal.

Natalie: It requires a paradigm shift. Utilities need to move away from centralized generation, like nuclear and coal, to a variety of distributed sources. From turning on one switch one time, to turning on fifteen switches fifteen different times. This is a big shift and will require changes in behavior, to think that maybe we can do things differently, and it will still be reliable and secure, and the lights will still stay on.

Sam: In some ways, utilities might be the biggest impediment. They own the systems; they need to pay off debts so they need to make money. But they could also be the biggest enablers—in terms of capital and of people who know how to operate the system. They have a relationship with every American.

PART 2

A PERSONAL CLEAN AIR ACT FOR YOUR HOME

It all feels pretty overwhelming. Acid rain over the Appalachians. Smog in Los Angeles. Superfund sites galore and PCBs poisoning rivers. What can one person do? The same question can be asked of another environment—the one that exists in your home. And the answer? A lot. One person—you—can improve air quality and ban chemicals in your home and the little plot of land called your yard. Doing so will not only reap health benefits for you and your family. Because of the interconnectedness of all things (not necessarily karmic but certainly ecological), your clean home will help clean up the planet. Which means maybe your impact on those enormous pollution problems is bigger than you think.

CHAPTER 4

ABC, VOC...
REWRITING THE ALPHABET ON
COMMON HOUSEHOLD CHEMICALS

Hot, humid weather, forest fires, smog—all can produce air quality advisory warnings urging you to stay indoors and limit outdoor exercise. For most folks, the idea of pollution conjures up brown fields, toxic sludge ponds, factory smokestacks, and oil spills. For sure, our industrial-revolutionized world has altered the state of the air we breathe, the water we drink, and the land on which we grow our food.

Few of us realize, though, that despite those advisories, it really won't do us much good to stay inside. That's because the air you breathe indoors is potentially worse for you than the breezy outdoors. Technically, the concept is known as indoor air quality, or IAQ, and the Environmental Protection Agency warns that it can be ten times more polluted than the air outside your windows. Why? Primarily for two reasons: (1) the fumes and contaminants wafting out of our innumerable modern-day products and devices; and (2) energy-efficient construction (or even, to a certain extent, greened up older homes) that keeps warm or cool air from escaping but ironically also keeps pollution entrapped as well.

This pollution can mostly be summed up in three more letters: VOC, which is short for volatile organic compounds. According to the EPA, VOCs are produced by a thousands-long list that includes items such as paint and paint strippers, varnishes and waxes, cleaning supplies of all sorts, glues and adhesives, craft and hobby supplies, pesticides and office equipment, and furniture and building materials. Conventional dry-cleaned clothing (which, because the process uses the cancer-causing chemical perchloroethylene, comes back to your home dirtier than when it left), synthetic air fresheners and fragrances (whose "fresh" scent should be more accurately identified as toxic), and even candles (choose natural beeswax or soy varieties to avoid carbon emissions) all add to pollution levels in your home.

One EPA study concluded that a dozen common organic pollutants are two to five times higher inside than out. During an activity like paint stripping, and even for several hours just afterward, pollution levels are often one thousand times higher. Combustion products such as gas stovetops and woodstoves will also pollute your indoor air if they aren't properly vented, as will cars left idling in attached garages.

You don't have to be agoraphobic to experience the effects of bad IAQ—statistically speaking, we all spend about 90 percent of our time indoors. No wonder, then, that pollution levels in the home are blamed for myriad health problems. In fact, it's hard to think of a symptom that *isn't* connected to indoor air pollution: nausea; kidney, liver, and central nervous system damage; headache; allergic skin reactions; fatigue; dizziness; nose, throat, and eye irritation; conjunctival irritation; dyspnea; emesis; epistaxis; asthma; and cancer. Which brings the concept of home as a place of safety and comfort into question.

Yet it doesn't have to be this way. Simple acts can help you breathe easier. In fact, it's just a two-step process: ventilate and eliminate. Bring in fresh air and get rid of as many of those products or problems that are compromising your breathing space in the first place.

Ventilate: Ventilation is as simple as opening your windows on a regular basis—especially if there's a temperature difference between the outside world and the inside or if the weather is windy. This free exercise will help dilute dirty air and even blow some pollutants outside. Other fairly easy moves include regularly changing the filter on your heating system (preferably a HEPA, or high-efficiency particulate arresting, filter) and installing bathroom and kitchen fans. Folks with newer, tighter homes may want to consider a whole-house ventilation system, which can be added to your current furnace or cooling setup or purchased as an entirely new system. The Air Conditioning Contractors of America has a zip-code search function on its website that will help you find a professional who specializes in IAQ and ventilation.

Eliminate: The best approach to weeding out offending products is self-taught. Though it might require time and research on your part, you'll end up with long-lasting results that are seamlessly integrated into your home life. I've always started with this question: what chemicals are used and is there a natural alternative? Answers have led me to ban chemical cleaning products, conventional dry cleaning

---

TIP

PSYCHO IS RIGHT! WHY VINYL SHOWER CURTAINS AREN'T FIT FOR CIVIL SOCIETY

Who knew getting clean could be so dirty? According to the Center for Health, Environment and Justice, polyvinyl chloride—a.k.a. vinyl or PVC—shower curtains release over one hundred different VOCs after they're unwrapped and hung, some lingering for up to twenty-eight days. The strong plastic fumes associated with that new curtain smell are laced with phthalates, which can mess with your body's hormones and have also been linked to cancer and reproductive diseases.

Thank goodness there are healthier alternatives: hemp, cotton (preferably organic), and linen are natural water barriers; and polyester and nylon, though synthetic and not without their chemical and petroleum associates, are still a much better option than vinyl. I even steer clear of newer "PVC-free" plastic varieties—natural materials are certainly better for the environment anyhow. For a more permanent though considerably more expensive solution, you could even consider a glass door. Either way, avoid vinyl, because showering wasn't meant to be a psychotic experience.

(there are greener methods), chemical- and petroleum-based paint, air fresheners and room deodorizers, pesticides, perfumes, colognes, formaldehyde-containing plywood or particleboard furniture, chlorine-based dishwashing detergent, and mothballs—all of these are major clean-air offenders. I also vacuum my rugs regularly, dust with a damp cloth to avoid wafting contaminates back into the air, and make sure make sure my furnace is serviced at least once a year. What resonates with you? Achieving clean air at home is more intuitive than you might think.

There are, however, major chemical offenders that everyone should consider. What follows are some of the worst of the worst, and you should be armed with good information about them as you work on sparkling up your IAQ.

CHEMICAL MADNESS

Chemicals are an all too prevalent part of our modern existence, in more senses than one. They're not only found in products ranging from beauty supplies to medical equipment to clothing and food, they've become integrated into the fabric of our bodies. Scientists estimate that every living person on this planet carries at least seven hundred contaminants in his or her body—most of these we know virtually nothing about. Our homes and offices, where we spend most of our time, are major exposure routes.

Take **formaldehyde**. You may recall news headlines about folks being exposed to this toxic chemical in the wake of Hurricane Katrina. The FEMA-supplied trailers off-gassed formaldehyde in too-high amounts, sickening many people instead of giving them safe shelter, and the government was subsequently sharply criticized.

Yet people are exposed to formaldehyde every day. It's commonly found in pressed wood or particleboard (as a gaseous by-product of the glue), which in turn is found in cabinets, desks, bookcases, and other furniture items, where it potentially off-gasses for months or even years. Other sources of formaldehyde include antibacterial soaps, beauty supplies, paints, permanent-press clothing, and unvented fuel-burning appliances.

The effects of this exposure aren't good. Formaldehyde is a recognized probable human carcinogen by the EPA and is a suspected toxin to the liver and reproductive system. The American Lung Association warns that exposure can cause eye, nose, and throat irritation (including nosebleeds), headaches and dizziness, nausea and vomiting, and coughing and skin rashes.

Try your best to avoid these maladies. Stay away from high-VOC paint (see "The Surface of Things: Paint, Wallpaper, and Wood Stains" in this chapter). If purchasing new furniture, avoid pressed-wood or particleboard—though new formaldehyde-free pressed-wood products are becoming more widely available. Consider other materials such as metal, environmentally certified solid wood, or bamboo. My husband and I made sure our daughter's nursery was formaldehyde-free, supplying it with an antique dresser, Amish-built solid-wood changing table, solid wood rocker with hemp fabric free from stain guards and flame retardants, and a maple wood crib. Secondhand stores are a great option for finding all-wood furniture and giving it a second life. If you're already stuck with a product you suspect might be busily off-gassing, say a bookcase with particleboard backing, try sealing it to help mitigate this process—AFM Safecoat carries some great options just for this purpose.

Perhaps even more ubiquitous and thus even harder to avoid are **phthalates**. The list of phthalate-containing items is long and so is the history of these industrial chemicals. Phthalates were invented in the 1930s and, as the chemical industry today produces billions of pounds of them a year, they have since gone on to find their way into our lives via cosmetics and food wraps, building materials and toys, medical products, flooring, garden hoses, plastic bags, and—what I'd like to focus on here—polyvinyl chloride (PVC) plastic, a.k.a. the worst plastic of them all.

When it comes to PVC, phthalates' job is to add softness and flexibility. PVC plastic is as common as its progenitor. Greenpeace has put together an extensive compilation of what everyday products contain this insidious material. It will astound you. Thankfully, the group also provides a database of safe alternatives to PVC. Check it out. Briefly, I'll mention that in the home you should look out for PVC in your flooring, wallpaper, window frames, blinds, pipes, and shower curtains. It's got the number 3 recycling code or the word *vinyl*.

Why all the fuss? First let's look at phthalates in general. Animal studies have shown that exposure to this endocrine disrupter can cause a range of problems: developmental toxicity in the male reproductive system, lower sperm mobility, abdominal obesity and insulin resistance in men, and birth defects, among other serious concerns.

And PVC? In addition to the baggage of the added phthalates, the production of PVC creates toxic dioxins, a cancer-causing, immune-system-damaging industrial by-product that's wrapped up in our food chain, especially in fatty foods like dairy products and meat, and thus in our bodies as well. This plastic is difficult to recycle, so off to the landfill it goes, where it continues to leach out more dioxins into our environment, perpetuating its polluting cycle. Break up this chain of toxicity by avoiding vinyl whenever and wherever you can.

Ubiquity seems to be a common theme with the not-so-friendly chemicals bound up in our consumer goods and spread throughout our homes. Case in point, **polybrominated diphenyl ethers (PBDEs)**, a toxic class of chemicals found in flame retardants that co-opt the quality of your sleep, play, and communication modes. Beginning in the 1970s, PBDEs were added to upholstered furniture, mattress pads, carpet padding, and electronics. Today, you'll find them primarily in polyurethane foam products, items such as couches and upholstered chairs, futons, pillows (including nursing pillows!), mattresses, and children's car seats. They're also lurking in televisions and their remote controls, computers, printers, photo-copiers, hairdryers, cell phones, curtains and drapes, lighting, wiring, and other building materials.

This prevalence is cause for concern. Nena Baker, author of *The Body Toxic*, reports that studies of PBDEs' effects on animals showed thyroid hormone disruption, behavioral changes, permanent learning and memory impairment, delayed puberty onset, decreased sperm count, hearing loss, and fetal malformations. Particularly alarming is the chemicals' ability to accumulate in our bodies and store themselves in our fatty tissues and bodily fluids, such as in blood and breast milk. In fact, PBDEs exist in the body of nearly every American.

Children, as is often the case, are the most vulnerable and receive the greatest exposure. The nonprofit Environmental Working Group (EWG) conducted tests that showed high concentrations of PBDEs in kids, higher even than in their mothers. It makes sense, because they directly ingest more of the flame retardants. The chemicals that are released from the television or couch stick to kids' hands, toys, and other appealing objects, which, as any parent knows, will inevitably end up in kids' mouths. Another route of exposure is household dust. Dust, which some researchers call an indoor-pollution archive, is a sink for all household contaminants, including VOCs, metals, fungal spores, pet dander, and PBDEs—which mix with the dust as foam furniture breaks down or electronic products off-gas chemicals. Infants and toddlers, who spend much of their time on floors and carpets, where dust gathers, end up ingesting this toxic potpourri in surprising amounts (about twice as much as adults).

It's pretty much impossible to avoid PBDEs altogether, but this shouldn't depress you. Aside from urging your congresspeople to enact tougher regulations, there is a lot you can do to reduce your exposure. The type of PBDE used in foam products (i.e., mattresses and couches) was withdrawn from the U.S. market in 2005 because of safety concerns, so you shouldn't have to worry about new foam purchases. I say *shouldn't* because these materials may still have fire-retarding chemicals, some poorly studied, whose ill effects we've yet to discover. A better bet is to purchase less flammable materials such as leather, wool, or cotton. Wool is naturally fire resistant. And latex can be a great alternative to polyurethane foam, with the additional benefits of being resistant to dust mites, mildew, and fire. When it came time to replace our saggy old mattress, my husband and I opted for latex, with a protective organic wool/cotton cover.

What about the old foam products already present in your home? The EWG suggests taking these precautions: Replace any foam items that have a ripped cover or are damaged in any way. If you can't get rid of them, do your best to keep the covers intact. Don't be afraid to resort to tape and consider vacuuming more frequently. (You'll have more success removing contaminants if your vacuum has a HEPA filter.) Resist the temptation to reupholster your old foam furniture, no matter how ghastly the print. The process could release PBDEs or other fire retardants. Take extraordinary caution (HEPA vacuum and mop) when removing old carpet, as the padding could very well have PBDEs. And ask questions when you buy. Manufacturers should be able to tell you what type of fire retardants they are using—the brominated fire retardants (a family that PBDEs belong to) are the ones you should make every effort to avoid.

PBDEs, in a form known as deca (containing ten bromines), are still alive and well in electronics, kitchen appliances, and the electronic components, fabrics, and plastic in your car—there are currently no federal restrictions, though they've recently been banned in the enlightened states of Maine, Washington, and Oregon and will be phased out completely in the United States by 2014. Despite this, they will persist in our environment. Know where they live in your home, and keep infants and toddlers from mouthing them. Some manufacturers have pledged to phase out *all* brominated fire retardants; if you're in the market for a shiny new piece of equipment, consider patronizing Acer, Apple, Eizo Nanao, LG Electronics, Lenovo,

Panasonic, Microsoft, Nokia, Philips, Samsung, Sharp, Sony-Ericsson, and Toshiba—and visit EWG's website to see if more companies have joined their ranks.

While we're talking about the dangers of treated fabric materials and cookware, we shouldn't ignore **perfluorinated chemicals**, which are used to resist stains, grease, and water. They've been around since the fifties. Though you might not have heard of them, I'm sure you're familiar with some of their major brand names: Teflon, Scotchgard, Stainmaster, and Gore-Tex. Their use, according to Nena Baker, has led to "worldwide contamination of people and places." These chemicals are very persistent and can hang around in our bodies for years. If you're pregnant, exposure may lower your baby's birth weight. Your choice is pretty clear here. Avoid nonstick cookware and decline stain-resistant treatments on your clothes, shoes, and upholstery.

The EPA cites **methylene chloride** and **benzene** as chemicals you should use with caution and avoid if possible. Methylene chloride is found in aerosol spray paint, paint strippers, and adhesive removers. It has exhibited the tendency to cause cancer in animals and to convert to carbon monoxide in the body, causing symptoms similar to carbon monoxide exposure (headache, dizziness, nausea). Of course, if you're going to use products that contain this chemical, read the labels, follow the suggested precautions, and do your work outside if possible, or at least ventilate your work area indoors. I'd suggest not using such products at all.

Benzene is a *known* human carcinogen, so avoid it too. You'll find it in tobacco smoke, fuels, paint supplies, and car emissions. The EPA advises ventilating while painting as well as discarding unused paint supplies that won't be used right away. But as I'll discuss next, you have another choice: you can avoid toxic paint entirely.

THE SURFACE OF THINGS: PAINT, WALLPAPER, AND WOOD STAINS

We all like a change of scenery once in a while. And this applies to the indoors as much as the outside world. Who hasn't enjoyed a weekend spent rearranging furniture in a room or applying a fresh coat of paint to drab walls? Once you're finished, it almost feels like you're living in a new place.

But have you ever noticed how quickly a headache comes on once you start dipping that roller in the paint tray? Or how you have an urge to open a window after sanding and applying a new wood stain to your old wood floors? That's because while you're brightening your home environment you're also submersing yourself in some nasty chemicals. As beautiful as those new colors may be, they're transforming your indoor air quality in some not so pretty ways. Luckily, you have better options. Dip that paintbrush in an ecopalette of colors instead.

PICKING YOUR PAINT

Let's start with paint. Maybe your landlord offered a discount on rent if you agreed to spend the weekend improving your apartment. Or you've got a new baby on the way and want to turn that dark spare room into a sweet and vibrant nursery. Modern paint has, thank goodness, made a huge leap in terms of its impact on our well-being. You won't find paint with lead on the shelves anymore—that has been banned since 1978. Unfortunately, the same can't be said for volatile organic compounds. That gallon of color is full of hazardous chemicals and solvents, including formaldehyde, toluene, xylene, and other carcinogens and neurotoxins. And that's not all. The EPA says that VOCs in paint cause 9 percent of the airborne pollutants that create ground-level ozone. Another startling fact: if exposed to sunlight, some paint VOCs react with nitrous oxide and create smog. What's more, the disposal of those half-used cans pollutes landfills and groundwater. Like all toxic issues, what's bad for your health is bad for the environment too.

Though, unlike lead, paint VOCs haven't been banned, paint companies have responded to customers' health concerns, and there are several different routes you can take to greening your brush.

First and foremost, you should **avoid oil-based paint** whenever possible. Not only does this paint contain petroleum-based solvents, it's very high in VOCs. You'll substantially reduce your exposure to VOCs if you **buy latex paint**, which uses water as the principal solvent. Latex paint gets even better when you search for the low- and no-VOC versions.

Low- and no-VOC paint have very low levels of heavy metals and formaldehyde. Zero-VOC paint must have no more than 5 grams per liter of volatile organic compounds. I've painted with both versions and the difference in air quality was palpable. Be aware, though, that many of these paints may still have chemical-based pigments, biocides (to extend shelf life), and fungicides (to prevent mildew growth). The chemically sensitive among us may still have a hard time with them and may

You don't have to sacrifice style to get a substantially greener color. There are more low- and zero-VOC and natural paints and stains on the market than you can shake a paint stick at. Here are just a few of the zero-VOC and nontoxic options. Check out what your local paint store or online green retailer have as well.

- Mythic Paint: Zero-VOC, zero carcinogens, nontoxic, low odor, stylish colors.
- Yolo Colorhouse: Green Seal certified, zero-VOC, no reproductive toxins, no phthalates, no mutagens, and no ozone-depleting compounds.
- Benjamin Moore's Natura line and Olympic: Big-name paint brands that offer zero-VOC formulas, probably available at your local hardware store.
- BioShield: Paints, stains, thinners, and waxes mostly made of natural materials like bee and tree waxes, citrus-peel extracts, and essential oils; their Kinder Paint is even safer, created specifically for the baby's nursery.
- Green Planet Paints: Zero-VOC *and* non-petroluem-based, a step further than comparable brands; uses plant-based binders, mineral pigments, and minimal additives instead.

- Real Milk Paint Company and Old Fashioned Milk Paint Company: Both use milk protein, lime, and natural pigments to produce beautiful colors without VOCs or chemical headaches; the products are powdered, just add water.
- AFM Safecoat: Zero-VOC stains, sealers, finishes, and paint, also free of nasty ingredients like heavy metals, formaldehyde, solvents, and scary preservatives; an added bonus—you can use Safecoat products to seal surfaces and reduce off-gassing. The company is a recipient of the Scientific Certification Systems' Indoor Air Quality Gold Certification.
- Do-it-yourself: Check out Lynn Edwards and Julia Lawless's *Natural Paint Book: A Complete Guide to Natural Paints, Recipes, and Finishes*. You'll find fun and surprising recipes with ingredients like lemon juice, skim milk, borax, lime, cellulose glue, beeswax, tea, egg yolk, and vinegar.

want to search out brands that advertise a low-biocide and no-fungicide option. Keep in mind that exterior paint is usually always more chemically intense and often has fungicides—see if you can find brands that utilize zinc oxide for this purpose.

One step further on the green paint path will lead you to natural and **milk-based paints and whitewash**. Paint au naturel is created from earthy materials such as citrus, balsam, clay, chalk, and talcum. This water-based paint is smell-free, petroleum-free, biocide-free, and extremely low in VOCs. It comes in a rainbow of colors. Milk paint has been around for a very long time—you'll find it in cave paintings, Egyptian tombs, Renaissance art, and American Colonial homes. Its base is milk protein, or casein, and lime; and its color originates in earth pigments, like lime or clay. There's no odor to this paint, which comes as a powder you simply add water to (a process that gives it a fun arts and crafts feel). Whitewash has a straightforward recipe of lime and water and sometimes casein.

Natural-home expert Annie Bond says in *Home Enlightenment* that both milk paint and whitewash allow the surface beneath them to breath, thereby reducing rot and mold. And both have a high alkaline content, which acts like a natural insect repellent and disinfectant. The simplicity of these paints—both in terms of color and composition—allows for easy breathing.

PASTING IT UP

Some folks prefer complexity, though, and I hear that wallpaper is making a stylish comeback—for many people it never lost its patterned appeal. My husband and I spent quite a bit of time stripping all the wallpapered surfaces in our New England home, applying monochromatic, low-toxicity paint instead. We might not have done so if I'd known at the time of the many beautiful and natural wallpaper options on the market. The list seems almost endless: bamboo, rice papers, flax, cork, raffia, arrowroot, jute, and recycled paper. You'll also find grasscloths from honeysuckle vines, sisal coverings from recycled sisal carpets, and hemp mixed with cellulose, plant skins, and cottons.

This plethora of green options gives you no excuse to paste up conventional wallpaper, which is made of toxic glues and chemicals and, more often than not, is of the vinyl variety. As of this writing, these companies were creating beautiful, low-toxicity or natural wallpaper: Mod Green Pod, Ecofix, Twenty2, Phillip Jeffries, JaDecor Natural Wallcovering, and American Clay.

STAINING THE GRAIN

I'll briefly mention floor finishes here, because if you're looking to improve a wood floor's luster, sand out scratches, or brighten boards, you should know that there are low-chemical means to these ends. Take care to avoid commonly used solvent-based polyurethane finishes, which contain known toxic carcinogens, or petroleum-based waxes and polishes.

For a nontoxic alternative, try water-based polyurethane, which won't inundate you with strong odors. You may need to apply more coats than with a higher-toxicity product, but most of the time you can sleep in your house the same night. Some people prefer drying oils, like tung oil, or hardwax oils (Osmo is one popular virtually solvent-free brand sold by green retailers).

When we stripped the paint and refinished our old, wide-board pine floors—and a couple old doors as well—we had good results with Velvit Oil, a low-toxicity soybean-based oil. Many brands offer sample-size containers, allowing you to try a few colors, odors, and finishes before you commit.

IT'S NOT ABOUT THE SHAG

More often than not, carpeting is not your friend. In fact, the conventional variety is decidedly unfriendly, and its ugliness isn't limited to the shag vintage from decades ago. Sure, wall-to-wall carpeting may make a room feel cozy and warm, but there are enormous tradeoffs to the comfort it provides. These include a penchant for hosting dust, bacteria, mold, mildew, allergens, and a variety of VOCs in your living quarters. Here's more on what you should avoid and why, and some options for a healthier long-term carpet relationship.

WALL-TO-WALL CARE

Let's start with the carpet that's already beneath your feet. Maybe you covet wood flooring but got stuck with synthetic petroleum-based fiber (the composition of most carpeting). If you're a renter, or for any other reason are bound to your current floor covering, the best thing you can do is take off your shoes before entering your

home—and insist that everyone else does as well. Your carpet welcomes whatever your shoes have picked up off the streets, creating a sink for noxious pesticides, fertilizers, road oil, and lead. If you've got an infant scooching around, this is obviously a cause for concern. Remember, too, that toxic dust in your home gets trapped in carpeting. Vacuum often and with a HEPA filter if you can. Being a clean freak will help make your current carpeted situation more tolerable.

THE CASE AGAINST CARPET

If however, you have a choice of whether or not to carpet your floors, I strongly advise you against it. Besides the nasty chemicals that get trapped in the fiber from the outside world, carpeting lays claim to toxins of its very own. From its production in the factory to the moment it's affixed to your floor, your brand-new carpet is busy off-gassing VOCs from as many as 120 chemicals—and can do so for one to three months. Some of the worst offenders include benzene, toluene (a chemical that can cause eye, liver, kidney, and nervous system damage), and formaldehyde, which can all be found in the adhesives; also antimicrobial and fungicidal pesticides applied to the fiber and 4-phenylcyclohexene in the latex binders.

Speaking of formaldehyde, many carpets are tacked or glued onto particleboard subflooring—particleboard, as we've discussed, is one of the worst offenders in terms of emitting this dangerous chemical.

And the list of carpet offenses continues: in conventional carpeting there are chemicals in the fiber bonding materials, chemicals in the antistatic and stain-resistant treatments, and chemicals in the fire retardants. With this many chemicals you might think carpeting would at least last a long time—embalmed on your floor and looking good for decades. Alas, this isn't the case. Carpet is also short lived: 5 billion pounds of it end up in landfills every year, or enough to cover an area the size of New York City.

GOOD, GREEN FLOORS

If you do have a choice, your safest flooring options are wood, slate, marble, brick, or ceramic tile—remember, of course, to avoid toxic stains or sealants on these surfaces (go for no- or low-VOC). But do not despair if you must have something soft between your toes. There are green alternatives. Consider a washable area rug first.

TIP

GREEN SEAL OF APPROVAL FOR CARPETS

If you're shopping for carpet, look for the Green Label Plus. The Carpet and Rug Institute (www.carpet-rug.org) has established a voluntary industry-testing program for carpets and adhesives. Green Label Plus is awarded to products that meet criteria for low chemical emissions set by an independent, certified lab. You might be wary of anything industry driven, but the tests were developed in cooperation with the Environmental Protection Agency, and the label goes so far as to meet California's stringent (more so than other states) indoor quality standards. It's a good start.

When you move from your apartment, condo, or house you can take it with you. And it's easier to maintain and rid of all those trapped toxins. Shaking and airing it outside will do wonders.

ANIMAL, VEGETABLE, RECYCLABLE

For rug or wall-to-wall carpet, perhaps your best choice for material is wool, especially organic wool that hasn't been treated with moth-killing pesticides. It's spendy but extremely hardy, often lasting up to fifty years. It's also naturally flame-, stain-, mold-, and mildew resistant.

If you'd rather go vegan, there are many plant-fiber options to choose from: sisal, which is made from the stems and leaves of the agave plant; coir, or the husk of a coconut; jute, from a woody herb found in India; and seagrass, which, as the name implies, is made from seagrass. You can also try cotton, which is durable and pretty—especially if you choose organic. For the bookish among you, there's even a paper carpet, whose yarns have been spun from the pulp of coniferous softwoods.

Finally, for the latest in commercial green carpeting, check out carpet tiles, which allow you to replace worn-out carpet in pieces on an as-needed basis. Two brands stand out for their recycled and low-VOC

IT'S A JUNGLE IN HERE: CLEANING YOUR HOME WITH PLANTS

They cost less than a housekeeper. Houseplants will do more than add décor to a room or bring the lovely green of the outdoors in. Potted foliage actually cleans the air in your home.

You probably learned how plants recycle oxygen in seventh-grade biology, but did you know that they are also effective at breaking down pollutants in the air? NASA proved it by placing various plants in sealed chambers and then exposing them to high concentrations of chemicals. Some were better at ridding the air of toxins than others. The top-ten winners (listed below) were able to remove 90 percent of nasty chemicals like benzene, formaldehyde, and trichloroethylene in fewer than twenty-four hours.

Here's how it works: The chemicals are absorbed by the plants leaves, and then the bacteria hanging out with the roots help break down the toxins, which are then absorbed as nutrients. Even a measly 6-inch plant can do the job—one per 100 square feet of a home will excel at taking out toxic substances. The healthier the plant, the better it performs this purifying task. So don't forget to water.

TOP-TEN POLLUTANT-BUSTING HOUSEPLANTS

- Bamboo palm (*Chamaedorea seifrizii*)
- Chinese evergreen (*Aglaonema modestum*)
- English ivy (*Hedera helix*)
- Gerbera daisy (*Gerbera jamesonii*)
- Janet Craig (*Dracaena deremensis*)
- Marginata (*Dracaena marginata*)
- Mass cane/corn plant (*Dracaena fragrans* 'Massangeana')
- Mother-in-law's tongue (*Sansevieria trifasciata* 'Laurentii')
- Pot mum (*Chrysanthemum morifolium*)
- Peace lily (*Spathiphyllum* 'Mauna Loa')

content and the fact that they'll take back and recycle your tired tiles for you. The Flor line turns your old tiles into their new product. EcoWorx tiles are PVC-free.

UNDER THE RUG

Whatever ecocarpet you decide on, it's important to remember what lies beneath. For the backing, avoid combinations of styrene, butadiene, and rubber latex and also polyurethane—back it up with jute, hemp, cotton, or natural latex instead. Of course, stay away from adhesives that contain formaldehyde and VOCs. Use glue derived from the rubber tree or tacks to hold it all together. Plastic, foam, or synthetic rubber are commonly used as carpet pads. But you'll extend the life of your carpet and absorb shock just as well with natural materials such as jute, hemp, cotton, wool, natural rubber, horsehair, and felt.

Luckily, more and more of these natural materials are becoming readily available—if not at your local floor store, than at least from a green online retailer. When I decided to put a stair runner on my steep, angled wooden stairs, I was unable to find good green options in my rural community. I was, however, able to find what I needed—organic wool carpeting, felt padding, and low-VOC adhesive—online. I acquired samples and took them to my local floor store in the hopes that they would use them and their expertise to install the runner. The owners were reluctant, at first, to work with materials they didn't sell in the store. They finally agreed that the carpet and padding would do the job but wanted to stick with the adhesives they always used to attach the binding. I convinced them to at least test the low-VOC option. They called back, surprised and amazed, that it actually held. They were professionals, a family operation, and had been in flooring for decades. I can't help but think that seeing that green glue stick may have influenced the course of their business for decades to come.

THE USUAL SUSPECTS: LEAD, MOLD, ASBESTOS, AND OTHER COMMON POLLUTANTS

So far we've spent a lot of time talking about what, to most of us at least, are fairly new and scary toxins lurking in our homes. There are, however, a host of indoor pollutants that we've all grown up hearing about. They're more commonly recognized by government and industry as a threat, and they haven't necessarily left our homes just because they've been identified as dangerous. These unhealthy regulars include mold and mildew, radon and lead, and carbon monoxide and asbestos. Just because they're familiar doesn't mean they're more benign than their less well known chemical counterparts.

GETTING THE LEAD OUT

Lead has been banned from paint for more than three decades now. Yet how many of us live in homes that have been around for more than thirty years? A lot. That means that lead is an inevitable presence—if not in the interior paint, then maybe in our drinking water from lead pipes or lead solder on copper pipes, or perhaps in the soil around our homes (from generations of paint scraping and flaking), which gets tracked in and becomes a component of household dust.

There's a reason, after years of prevalent use, that lead was finally banned. Its neurotoxic effects on our health—for growing infants, children, and babes in utero especially—are disastrous: reduced IQ, delayed puberty, and compromised cognitive development. Blood levels as low as 10 micrograms per deciliter can impair mental and physical development; high levels (80 micrograms or above) can cause convulsions, coma, and even death.

If you have a major lead paint problem, don't try to remove the paint yourself—you'll most likely make matters worse. Scraping, sanding, or using a heat gun to remove lead paint can create concentrations of airborne lead particles and

TIP

LANDFILL-FREE

Avoid adding your old carpet to the billions of pounds piling up in our country's landfills: check out Earth911, where you can enter your zip code and find a recycler. Nonprofits like Habitat for Humanity will also sometimes accept carpet still in good repair and reuse it.

lead dust. Seek professional help. (See the Environmental Protection Agency's "Lead in Paint, Dust, and Soil" webpage to find remediation and abatement professionals.)

First, find out if you have lead paint; buy an inexpensive test kit from your local hardware store. Then, as a rule of thumb, if your lead-based paint is in good shape, leave it alone—it usually won't cause a problem. The exceptions are places where painted surfaces grind against each other and create dust. It was for this reason that we sent all of our old wood windows and doors away to have the paint professionally stripped.

Other safety precautions, according to the EPA, include the following:

I **Keep the dust down:** Areas where children play should be as dust-free and clean as possible. Mop floors and wipe window ledges and chewable surfaces with a solution of powdered automatic dishwasher detergent in warm water. (Dishwasher detergents are recommended because of their high content of phosphates.) Wash toys and stuffed animals regularly. Make sure that children wash their hands before meals, naptime, and bedtime.

I **Use a doormat:** Wiping your feet helps minimize lead dust being inadvertently tracked into your home. In our house, we also make sure that we wipe our dog's feet every time he comes in.

I **Test your water:** Most municipal and well water doesn't inherently contain lead, but water can pick up lead found in your household plumbing. Find out how to test your water by contacting your local health department or water supplier. If you do discover lead, the EPA has information on what to do about it. Call their Safe Drinking Water Hotline: 800-426-4791.

I **Seek out calcium and iron:** A diet high in these two elements will actually result in less lead absorption.

There is an abundance of information on lead. Check out these resources for a start: the Office of Healthy Homes and Lead Hazard Control (run by the U.S. Department of Housing and Urban Development); the Centers for Disease Control and Prevention (CDC) Childhood Lead Poisoning Prevention Branch; the Lead Poisoning Prevention Outreach Program of the National Safety Council; and the EPA's National Lead Information Center.

Dr. Julia Brody is executive director of the Silent Spring Institute and a leader in research on breast cancer and the environment. In collaboration with Communities for a Better Environment and researchers at Brown University and the University of California, Berkeley, her current research focuses on connecting breast cancer advocacy and environmental justice in a study of household exposures to endocrine disruptors and air pollutants. Since 1996, Brody has been the principal investigator of the Cape Cod Breast Cancer and Environment Study.

How did you become interested in household exposure to chemicals and air pollutants?

Through my work with Silent Spring Institute, which researches environmental factors in the causes of breast cancer. I started to focus on everyday exposures, places where we spend a lot of time, and pollution in the home became a strong candidate. Many everyday pollutants mimic estrogen, which is an established breast cancer risk factor.

Describe the work of your organization.

Silent Spring Institute was founded by a partnership of scientists, physicians, and activists dedicated to studying the environmental links to women's health and breast cancer. The collaboration between activists and scientists inspires us to take on questions about environmental factors and prevention that have been downplayed by the major cancer organizations. Early detection and better treatment are important, but we need to focus more resources on finding ways to prevent breast cancer. The environment is an understudied area that can lead to the discovery of preventable causes of cancer.

Tell me about the Cape Cod Household Exposure Study. What were the most significant findings?

Silent Spring Institute researchers took indoor air and dust samples from 120 homes on Cape Cod and measured the concentrations of eighty-nine chemicals identified as endocrine disrupting compounds (chemicals that mimic or interfere with human hormones). The researchers detected a total of sixty-seven endocrine disruptors in the air and dust. We found phthalates—which have been shown to have effects on sperm quality and the development of baby boys—in all of the homes, while parabens—an estrogenic class of chemicals—were found in 90 percent of the homes.

The study provided the first report of the levels in U.S. household dust of PBDE flame retardants found in carpets, draperies, furniture foam, electrical appliances, televisions, and computers. PBDEs disrupt thyroid hormones, which affect the developing brain. The researchers found PBDE levels to be ten times higher in Cape Cod homes than European homes. PBDEs are less frequently used in Europe because of their suspected toxic effects.

Many of the chemicals we found were banned many years ago, suggesting that they do not break down indoors. We found DDT in dust in two-thirds of the homes even though it's been banned in the United States since 1972.

What are the most prevalent pollutants in a typical American home? And what are the best strategies for mitigating their presence?

Indoor exposure to pollution is actually higher than outdoor. In your home you're likely to be exposed to a complex mix of endocrine disrupters that come from everyday products: phthalates, parabens, phenols, brominated fire retardants.

One way for someone to reduce exposures in the home is to avoid products with fragrance. Shoppers can also read product labels and avoid phthalates and parabens, for example, in cosmetics. Use a damp cloth or mop to remove dust. Avoid dryer sheets and air fresheners. Choose furniture, carpets, and bedding made from natural fibers such as wool, cotton, and hemp, which are naturally flame retardant. Decline stain-resistant treatment of furnishings and fabrics. Avoid furniture made from particleboard, which releases formaldehyde, and stay away from phthalates in vinyl flooring, wall coverings, and shower curtains. Buy an effective vacuum cleaner with a strong suction and multilayered bag for dust collection (*Consumer Reports* rates them).

Keep in mind, though, that while individuals can have some influence on personal exposures, it's impossible to know what's in many products, because the manufacturer is not required to disclose complete information. Better solutions will come from systematic screening of chemicals for health effects before they are put into consumer products.

If these chemicals are so dangerous, why aren't they more strictly regulated?

This might be a better question for a political scientist. The main problem is that in the United States chemicals are assumed innocent until proven guilty. We need new laws that shift the burden of proof to require manufacturers to find out if chemicals are safe before they're put in products. We need to do more substantial testing before products are put on the market. Our most important strategy is to reform chemicals policies, such as the Toxic Substances Control Act, and practices at the Consumer Product Safety Commission and the Food and Drug Administration.

One of our goals as a research institute is to inspire green chemistry solutions, so we don't just ban one chemical and then substitute another one that is hazardous too. For example, manufacturers have stopped producing PBDEs in the U.S., but we are concerned that the substitutes might be just as bad, possibly causing cancer. We need someone looking over the shoulder of industry to assure that the substitutes aren't as bad as the chemicals being removed.

MICROBIAL WARFARE

You might think something biological like mold couldn't be considered a major health hazard, but you'd be wrong. Mold releases it own special brand of VOCs, called MVOCs. Some varieties of mold are more toxic than others. Most all have the potential to cause respiratory problems, allergic reactions, and asthma.

Mold's needs are pretty simple: water and food. Unfortunately, your home is usually all too willing to serve up a meal. Items on the menu include damp wood, paper, carpet, plastic, and textiles from mattresses to upholstered couches. High relative humidity (caused by places where cold and warm air meet) will foster mold growth in places like wall cavities. So will just plain water leakage, which can often happen in your home's plumbing, joists, gutters and drains, chimney flashing, roof, and basement.

To help prevent mold, keep your home well ventilated, use air conditioning or a dehumidifier when necessary (Energy Star rates them), and find and stop leaks. If your mold problem is large, contact a professional. For smaller problems, don't resort to chemical solutions. Annie Bond, author of *Home Enlightenment*, recommends a mixture of 1 gallon water and 0.25 cup unscented detergent; then dry with clean rags and fans. Check out her "Favorite Mold Helpers" as well. I used the tea tree oil solution to attack mold growing above my shower.

ABATING ASBESTOS

Once upon a time asbestos was commonly used in buildings as insulation and as a fire retardant. After discovering that it causes a lot of problems in the lungs, most notably cancer, the EPA banned it from several products and manufacturers have voluntarily cut back on its use.

It still can be found in older homes in the form of pipe and furnace insulation, shingles, floor tiles, millboard, and even some textured paints. If left intact, which is what the EPA recommends you do if it's in good shape and not likely to be disturbed, you don't have much reason to worry. But if there's any chance it will be messed with—say through a green remodeling project—or if it's already deteriorating, your choice is simple: hire a trained and qualified professional contractor to clean it up.

RIDDING RADON

As bad as asbestos is on your lungs, radon is probably worse if only because its effects are much more prevalent. Radon is the second-leading cause of lung cancer, eclipsed only by cigarette smoke. The EPA estimates that it causes about 21,000 lung cancer deaths in the United States each year. This scary statistic is compounded by the fact that almost one out of every fifteen American homes has high radon levels.

With this colorless, odorless, tasteless, radioactive gas, your chances of discovering radon's presence without assistance are slim. It originates from the natural breakdown of uranium in soil, rocks, and water and then filters up through the ground, into the air, and seeps in through cracks in your home's foundation, other holes, and sometimes through the water supply, finally collecting and building up—unbeknownst to you—in your residence.

But you aren't defenseless against this stealth gas. You can purchase a test kit to detect its presence, either from your local hardware store or from the National Safety Council. A professional can assist as well. More help is available via EPA's website, where you can connect with your state radon contact. And radon-reduction systems are fairly inexpensive and have the potential to reduce levels in your home by 99 percent.

ANOTHER CARBON PROBLEM

Like radon, carbon monoxide (CO) is invisible, and you can't smell or taste it either. These secretive qualities are especially frightening considering the fact that this gas has, in large amounts, the potential to lay you in the grave before you're aware of its presence in your home.

In smaller doses, it'll make you feel like you've got a bad hangover, with symptoms ranging from headaches and dizziness to nausea and fatigue. CO enters your home from myriad sources, which include but aren't limited to gas stoves and water heaters; woodstoves and fireplaces; leaking chimneys and furnaces; unvented kerosene and gas space heaters; and automobile exhaust filtering in from an attached garage.

Your best defense against CO poisoning, aside from prevention, is to place battery-operated carbon monoxide detectors in rooms where you spend a lot of time. The bedroom is a good choice, since you'll be sure to hear the alarm even in the depths of slumber. Don't forget to change the batteries on a regular basis.

You can prevent or limit CO from taking up residence in the first place by properly maintaining your gas appliances and combustion devices (like boilers and furnaces); not leaving your car idling in the garage; ventilating to the outdoors by installing exhaust fans over gas stoves and opening flues when you're keeping warm by the fire; choosing a woodstove that is size-appropriate and EPA-certified to meet emission standards; and hiring a professional to check out, clean, repair, and tune up your central heating system, including furnaces, flues, and chimneys.

CHAPTER 5

CLEANLINESS IS NEXT TO GODLINESS:
GETTING HOLY WITHOUT CHEMICALS

It used to be that we kept our homes clean by using whatever was at hand. A little baking soda from the cupboard mixed with elbow grease took out caked-on crud. Soap was soap, and it served more than one purpose, whether that was to clean your hands or the dishes. Sugar ants were best prevented by putting the sugar away.

But then things were made easier for us. A swift spray of a sickly sweet-smelling substance would kill those ants in a flash. A thick squirt of whitish goo gave the table a lustrous shine in just minutes. Grainy antiseptic scouring powder cut through the scum in the tub with little effort. Thank goodness for chemicals. At least that's what folks were told and sold and eventually wholeheartedly believed. The rapid growth of the chemical industry after World War II changed housekeeping forever and not necessarily for the better. Chemists whose previous employment was manufacturing weapons realized that similar concoctions could be used to fight agricultural pests and improve consumer products.

Since the fifties, some 75,000 chemicals have been introduced into our world. Three hundred of those can now be found within our bodies, even in the bodies of newborn babies who inherit synthetic chemicals from their mothers. All those cleaning products and pesticides in the cupboard are more than evidence of a well-kept home. They are a toxic testimony of the chemicals that we willingly bring into our lives in the name of cleanliness. The average American uses about 25 gallons of hazardous chemical products in his or her home—the majority coming from cleaning products. Every day, more than 32 million pounds of household cleaning products are poured down the drain in this country. Despite the best efforts of wastewater treatment plants, many of the toxic substances within these products find their way to our rivers.

The news on household chemicals is sobering, the stats are startling, and the studies scary. Even the fairly conservative Environmental Protection Agency encourages folks to use alternatives to conventional cleaning products such as glass, oven, drain, and toilet cleaners; furniture polish; rug deodorizers; and flea and tick products. Cleaners and pesticides with toxic, ignitable, corrosive, or reactive ingredients are classified as "household hazardous waste" by the agency—alongside oils, batteries, and paints—and special caution is urged for their disposal.

In the early eighties, a study by the EPA concluded that concentrations of twenty cancer-causing chemicals were up to fifty times higher indoors than out—most appeared in an average bottle of all-purpose cleaner, toilet-bowl cleaner, or dish soap. According to the Consumer Products Safety Commission, 150 common household chemicals are linked to allergies, birth defects, cancer, and psychological abnormalities. The health effects are indeed vast, and the effects of each and every one of these chemicals too numerous to detail. For illumination's sake, here's one potent example: Isobutene, a volatile organic compound, is a propellant you'll probably find in your bottle of conventional glass cleaner. Isobutene also accumulates in breast milk. Prolonged exposure can cause headaches, nausea, and, in very extreme cases, coma.

More than 1.4 million Americans exposed to household chemicals were referred to poison control centers in 2001—824,000 were children under the age of six. In 2009, while my friend was scrubbing her bathtub, her curious and precocious toddler picked up a bottle of all-purpose cleaner and sprayed himself in the face. His mom called poison control, but after reading the ingredients over the phone,

What ubiquitous household disinfectant that cleans mold and mildew, whitens clothes, and kills germs is actually classified by the Environmental Protection Agency as a pesticide that attacks mucous membranes (like those in your lungs) and contributes to indoor air pollution? The answer is bleach, also known as chlorine bleach, household bleach, or Clorox—a classic example of a product whose purpose is to protect us (from germs and bacteria) but that actually does us (and the environment) much more harm than good.

It's the chlorine in bleach that's particularly bad. Chlorine is a highly reactive gas that the chemical industry turns into a liquid or powder form for cleaning products. It cleans and whitens so well because it reacts with the grease that causes stains. Unfortunately, it also reacts with organic compounds to create a class of chemicals known as chlorinated hydrocarbons (such as dioxins and chloroform) and organochlorines, both of which are recognized carcinogens. Virtually all studied chlorinated compounds have very bad health effects, ranging from reproductive disorders to endocrine disruption to birth defects to developmental impairment to cancer. The use of bleach may produce other chemicals that are a mouthful to pronounce: trihalomethanes, which are linked to cancer, and absorbable organic halides, which are harmful to marine organisms.

Oxygen bleach is the green solution. In fact, oxygen does a better job of loosening stains and odors from fabrics than its toxic rival, though you may need to give it longer to do the job. Oxygen bleach is available in three forms: hydrogen peroxide (a liquid) and sodium percarbonate and sodium perborate (both powders). Both of the sodium p's are good for laundry and other household cleaning projects, including cleaning carpet and upholstery and automatic dishwashing. Because it acts as a disinfectant; brightens fabrics; can be mixed safely with other household cleaners; is nontoxic to plants, animals, and humans; and, after the oxygen is released, breaks down into natural soda ash and/or borax, oxygen bleach is the clear winner in the which-bleach-is-better smackdown. There's really no reason to reach for the chlorinated contender again.

she was told she didn't need to bring him in. It was a natural citrus-based cleaner. The remedy was to flush his eyes with lots of water. And the little boy suffered little more than tears.

SPARKLING GREEN

So there is a better, safer way. We have the power to restore what's divine in the act of cleaning—just get rid of the chemicals. This is both easy to say and easy to do because there are many options for substitutes. If your preference is to pick up a bottle of this or that while out shopping, you'll find a diverse array of green cleaners stocked on the shelves of even the most conventional grocery stores. If you're into saving money or using whatever is at hand, you'd be surprised at what just a few simple ingredients can do—some of which you might already have in your pantry.

TAKING NAMES

First, spend a weekend going through all those old half-used bottles sitting under the kitchen sink. The purists among you will probably want to get rid of all them. Remember, many of these concoctions are classified as household hazardous waste. Be responsible and dispose of them properly (follow the disposal directions on the bottle and call your local environmental, health, or solid waste agency for information).

What if you want to keep some of your favorite, time-tested products? Or at least use that little bit up? By my reading almost all of the chemicals in conventional cleaners are pretty bad, though there also seem to be degrees of badness. Here are few products and/or ingredients you should try to stop using right now:

- **Ethylene-based glycol** is often used as a water-soluble solvent in many cleaning agents. It's classified as an air pollutant by the EPA.
- **Synthetic terpenes** (as opposed to the terpenes found in some essential oils) are a class of chemicals found in orange, lemon, and pine oils. They have the potential to become carcinogenic compounds when mixed with ground-level ozone.
- **Chlorine**, often appearing in a list of ingredients as sodium hypochlorite or hypochlorite, is in too many household cleaners to count. Breathing it in is

bad for your lungs and is especially risky if you already have heart or respiratory problems.

I **Crystalline silica** is an eye and lung irritant and likely carcinogen, according to the Cancer Prevention Coalition.

I **Butyl cellosolve**, also IDed by the Cancer Prevention Coalition as a possible carcinogen, has been tied to kidney, liver, and lymphatic problems; is an eye and skin irritant; and is toxic to newly forming and regenerating cells.

I **Diethylene glycol monobutyl ether** can also injure your lungs, kidneys, and nervous system.

I **Ammonia**, like many of the others in this list, is bad for the eyes, skin, and lungs. It might also burn you.

I Finally, if you want to zero in on the three most dangerous products themselves, you'd do well to avoid **drain, oven**, and **acid-based toilet bowl cleaners**, according to Philip Dickey, former staff scientist at the Washington Toxics Coalition. All are corrosive and can cause both external and internal (if swallowed) burns.

READ THE LABEL: WHAT DOES NONTOXIC REALLY MEAN?

Buyer, be aware. The claims on household products are not regulated or certified by independent organizations. While it's reassuring to see the words *natural, nontoxic*, or *biodegradable* on a cleaner, keep in mind that these words may not mean much. Even the term *organic* loses definition when found on a spray bottle; while the USDA regulates what foods can claim to be organic, there is no such standard for cleaning products (even if some ingredients may be USDA-certified organic).

Looking at the label doesn't always help. Active ingredients are usually listed, but ingredients like "fragrance" in cleaning supplies and inert ingredients in household pesticides do not have to be disclosed on the label. "Fragrance" can contain up to four thousand separate ingredients, most of which are synthetic and many of which are toxic and suspected or proven carcinogens. In fact, only 1 percent of toxins are required to be listed, since companies are allowed to classify their formulas as "trade secrets."

To learn more about the chemicals you do see on a label, look to the National Library of Medicine Household Products Database. There you'll find toxicity studies summarized in plain English, giving you a snapshot of the danger of any product you may be considering. Search by product name, a chemical name, or by manufacturer.

There are common-sense alternatives to cleaning without chemicals. You probably have most of what you need on hand and would use them if it weren't so easy to grab a bottle and spray or pour. But we've all been seduced by the quick and easy promise of chemicals. Now that we're beginning to realize that this promise isn't worth the toxic trade-off, it's time to get back to basics. It turns out those basics are green. They also cost a whole lot less than all those colorful containers lining the cleaning-product aisle.

First up, **distilled white vinegar**. It's the main ingredient in many homemade cleaning recipes, including cleaners for glass, tub and tile, toilet bowls, floors, windows, drains, and mildew. This is because of its deodorizing and sanitizing properties and acidic nature, which help it dispel bacteria, germs, and mold. Vinegar works well as a fabric softener too, dissolving detergent residue and helping to wash away smells, even those wrapped up in your partner's stinky white gym socks.

Next on the list, **baking soda**. The folks at Arm & Hammer don't lie when they boast of their product's many uses (visit their website for a lengthy list). Because it's abrasive, use it as a scouring powder to make sinks, counters, and tubs sparkle. It takes a little extra effort on your part, but since you'll be breathing easier you might not even notice the added labor. You may already know that baking soda will absorb carpet and fridge odors; thanks to the fact that it creates a good pH level in the wash, it'll deodorize your laundry, too, as well as make it brighter.

Third, **liquid castile soap**. It's the sudsy base for a lot of homemade cleaning recipes. Plus, you can use it to wash your hands. Castile soap is very mild. It used to be made exclusively from olive oil, but now you'll find it made from other vegetable oils too. Unlike in other liquid soaps, you won't find any petroleum products and their associated contaminants.

On to **essential oils**, or concentrated plant oils. These are derived from bark, flower petals, roots, or fruits. Talk about getting back to basics: essential oils have been used for centuries for cleaning. Today you can find them online or in small vials in your local health-food store. Some are antibacterial, including cinnamon, clove, eucalyptus, lavender, lemon, lemongrass, rose, rosemary, tea tree, and thyme.

Try using lemon oil (not the commercial variety made from petroleum distillate) as furniture polish, eucalyptus to cut grease, thyme as a cleaning disinfectant. Do keep in mind that essential oils are potent and some may irritate your skin. And they are the one green-cleaning item that isn't cheap (we paid $11 each for our 1-ounce bottles), but they are concentrated—one bottle will last you a year.

Last but not least, there's **water**. It's the universal solvent in many green-cleaning recipes and is much better for you than the petroleum-based solvents found in many conventional cleaners. You can't get any safer or simpler.

That's it. Distilled white vinegar, baking soda, liquid castile soap, essential oils, and water. Buy some spray bottles and other containers and mix away. Label those concoctions you can make in advance and store them for easy use. Books, websites, and magazines are good sources for a variety of these recipes. Some of my favorite go-to references include two of Annie Bond's books, *Home Enlightenment* and *Better Basics for the Home*, and Renée Loux's *Easy Green Living*, as well as the websites for Women's Voices for the Earth, Care2, and the Green Guide.

Each of these five raw ingredients has a role to play, and you might get creative and experiment with different mixing ratios for different purposes. Cleaning glass? Use more vinegar for cleanliness and essential oils for a fresh scent, less soap to prevent streaking. Cleaning tile? Use more baking soda for the scrubbing power. Cleaning your toilet bowl? Use more vinegar for its antibacterial qualities.

As you might expect, bleach is not on the list of fundamentals, nor is ammonia. Never mix the two, as this act releases chlorine gas and potentially other hazardous gases. In fact, it's a good idea to never mix commercial cleaning products. Stick with the green fundamentals for your homebrews.

The big five should get you through most cleaning situations, but some homemade green-cleaning recipes call for washing soda or borax. Both are alkaline. Washing soda can potentially scratch some surfaces, so rein in the creativity if you add it to the mix. Borax is a heavy hitter, most often brought in for tough scouring. It's not quite as benign as baking soda and carries the warning to keep out of reach of children. If you must take your cleaning to the borax level, stick to the uses recommended on the box.

Elbow grease and prevention also have their role to play. Keep the drain clog-free by using a trap or screen on your drain as prevention. If you do get a clog, pour boiling water, vinegar, or baking soda in various combinations down the drain. If the clog is immobile and you're desperate for a commercial, conventional solution, try enzyme-based cleaners. Keep your oven clean without getting chemically burned by lining the bottom with foil as good preventive medicine, or simply clean up spills as soon as they happen.

It's a tough shift from throwing the cheapest conventional cleaner in the shopping cart to reading the labels and picking an ecofriendly option. Are green products really safer? Are they effective? How do they compare? I decided to test a variety of commercial green cleaners and homemade recipes with my former neighbor, Tes Reed, who has a lot more sparkling toilets under her belt than I do.

Tes prefers not to spend her days cleaning, but she does like a clean home. When playing in the woods falls short of paying the bills, Tes makes extra income with house-cleaning jobs. She has used a wide range of products on all levels of dirt and grime and, after running these tests, is confident that healthier, Earth-friendly products can get the job done.

Here's how a handful of green cleaners measured up to Tes's standards when used in my family's home, which—thanks to the presence of our five-month-old daughter—hadn't seen a decent cleaning in about as many months. For each contender, problematic ingredients appear in italics.

■ TEST NO. 1: GLASS CLEANERS

You don't want streaks or cloudiness when you look in the mirror or out the window, but you also don't want chemicals to get between you and your view. Green glass cleaners promise to clear it up with minimal toxic filminess.

NATURAL GLASS AND SURFACE CLEANER, RUBY GRAPEFRUIT AND HERB
by Seventh Generation
Cost: $3.79 for 16 ounces or $6.49 for 32 ounces
Ingredients: Seventh Generation helpfully explains each ingredient on the label: aqua (water), lauryl glucoside (plant-derived cleaning agent), tetrasodium iminodisuccinate (water softener), essential oils and botanical extracts (citrus paradisi [ruby grapefruit], pelargonium graveolens [geranium], ocimum basilicum [basil linalool], *methylisothiazolinone and benzisothiazolinone* [preservative])

Tes says: Glass was streak-free after a few squirts from this handy spray bottle, and it worked on the stovetop too, cutting through grease. I like how Seventh Generation lists ingredients pretty clearly and describes what they do—the company also provides further explanation of ingredients on its website. The Environmental Working Group's Skin Safety Database lists methylisothiazolinone and benzisothiazolinone as causing possible immune-system toxicity and classifies them as eye, skin, or lung irritants. Seventh Gen says that, while not ideal, these synthetic preservatives are biodegradable and exist in safe amounts in their products.

CLUB SODA AND ESSENTIAL OILS
from Annie Bond's *Better Basics for the Home*
Cost: about $1 for 16 ounces
Ingredients: club soda, essential oils of lemon and lime
Tes says: This isn't the most effective recipe for a glass cleaner, but it's creative, simple, cheap,

and definitely safe. Though citrus essential oils are revitalizing, I'd use a fresh lemon and a lime so that after cleaning I could squeeze the rest into a little vodka and celebrate a job all done.

GLASS AND SURFACE CLEANER
by Ecover

Cost: $4.29 for 16 ounces

Ingredients: aqua, alcohol, capryl glucoside, *parfum*, *sodium laurylsulfate*, rhamnolipid, citric acid

Tes says: This works on both stovetop grease and leaves your mirror without streaks. The "floral" scent is a little strong. Maybe that's because this stuff is about 4 percent volatile organic compounds, most likely from the parfum (fragrance). Companies are not required to list the ingredients in fragrance, since they're considered trade secrets. The Environmental Working Group gives parfum a high-risk score of 8, listing allergies, immunotoxicity, and data gaps as cause for concern. Sodium laurylsufate is a skin irritant and possible allergen. Rhamnolipid, though it sounds scary, is not too worrisome; it's a biosurfactant, or a biological agent that loosens the surface tension of water.

CLEAR AND CLEAN GLASS SPRAY
from Renée Loux's *Easy Green Living*

Cost: about $1 for 16 ounces

Ingredients: water, distilled white vinegar, liquid castile soap, eight drops essential oils (lemon, lime)

Tes says: This was more effective than the other homebrew cleaner and just about as effective as the commercial brands. I got streak-free glass after just a few swipes. Make sure you mix in enough of the essential oils, lemon and lime in this case. Otherwise they get overpowered by the smell of vinegar. The ingredients are all known quantities—you can't do better than that when assessing the safety of the stuff in your bottle. If you're short on soap, vinegar with essential oils added for scent will clean glass pretty well. Try citrus, orange, or lavender.

The bottom line: Tes's work requires speed, ease, and practicality, so Seventh Generation was her top pick, even though the preservatives aren't too lovely. Ecover fell behind because of its parfum-y scent. Renée Loux's vinegar-based cleaner beat out Annie Bond's club soda concoction, though both homemade recipes got accolades for simple, safe ingredients and the nicest prices.

■ TEST NO. 2: TOILET BOWL CLEANERS

The truth is, you don't really need a specialized toilet bowl cleaner. A toilet is just porcelain, after all, not much different than a sink or a tub, though it might warrant a more antibacterial approach. Still, many folks like the ergonomic squeeze bottle and having a specialized cleaner for this particular job. For this reason there's a lot of competition on the cleaning-aisle shelves, green cleaners included.

TOILET BOWL CLEANER
by Ecover

Cost: $4.21 for a quart

Ingredients: aqua, citric acid, lauryl polyglucose, sodium citrate, xanthan gum, *parfum*, sodium benzoate, linalool, limonene

Tes says: For a decent price you get an effective cleaner. It's not watery. The thickness helps the cleaner go to work. I like the scent—smells like Grandpa, maybe Bengay or hair cream. And the bottle is easy to hold, not too heavy when you're a-squirtin'. I just wish I liked what's actually inside the bottle as much (there's that dreaded parfum again). Not listing the chemical constituents of the fragrance irks me. Linalool and limonene are found in citrus-peel extract and can be allergens for some folks.

BASIC SODA FIZZ TOILET SCRUB
from Renée Loux's *Easy Green Living*
Cost: about $2 for a quart
Ingredients: liquid castile soap, baking soda, distilled white vinegar, essential oil of lavender or rosemary
Tes says: This basic recipe gets the job done. The ingredients are safe. Nothing funky and difficult to pronounce, and you know exactly what you're dealing with. Use whatever essential oils you want, but lavender and rosemary combine antibacterial power with those floral scents most of us associate with cleanliness.

This is also a fun science experiment for the kids—mixing vinegar and baking soda makes a big fizz—but then see if you can get them to clean the toilet bowl! Having to mix it up right before you use it can be problematic. Cleaning the toilet bowl is usually one of those last-minute rush jobs that gets done as company is pulling in the driveway. Right? Plan ahead!

NATURAL TOILET BOWL CLEANER, EMERALD CYPRESS AND FIR
by Seventh Generation
Cost: $6.29 for a quart
Ingredients: aqua (water), *lactic acid* (plant-derived demineralizer), polyglucose, coceth-7, coceth-4 and deceth-5 (plant-derived cleaning agents), xanthan gum (natural thickener), *peg-15 cocomonium chloride* (plant-containing cleaning agent), essential oils and botanical extracts (citrus aurantifolia [lime], abies balsamea [balsam fir], calilistris columellaris [emerald cypress])

Tes says: Quick and clean, this is another effective toilet bowl cleaner. It's a heavy bottle to hold and squirt with one hand, though, and not a great smell. You can always buy an unscented version. The National Library of Medicine Household Products Database says Seventh Generation toilet bowl cleaners have moderate health effects. In this case, it may be due to the lactic acid and peg-15 cocomonium chloride, which the Environmental Working Group lists as ingredients with moderate to high health hazards.

CLEAN DAY TOILET BOWL CLEANER
by Mrs. Meyer's
Cost: $5.79 for a quart
Ingredients: water, *surfactant, natural thickener, lactic acid, certified color, fragrance,* essential oils of lemongrass, lemon, peppermint, fir needles
Tes says: This stuff is blue, and though that shows what surface you've squirted, it makes it hard to see if you've missed scrubbing any spots without an extra flush, which is wasteful. They say the blue color helps you see where the cleaner is going and that you should wait for five to ten minutes before brushing and flushing, but who has time when you're cleaning a toilet? Speaking of color, what the heck is "certified color"? These ingredients are too vague to analyze; some of them are trade secrets that don't need to be disclosed. What kind of surfactant? What kind of natural thickener? And there's the scary, unknowable fragrance again.

The bottom line: All these products did their job: they cleaned the toilet, and they did it well. The difference was in how. Mrs. Meyer's made Tes a little blue because of ambiguities and trade secrets. Ecover's scent brought back old memories, but its chemical makeup ushered in new fears. Seventh Generation beats out the conventional crew any day, but its moderate risks left it lacking against Tes's top pick: Renée Loux's Basic Soda Fizz was the clean winner—safe, cheap, fun, and an educational opportunity for the kids.

■ TEST NO. 3: TUB AND TILE CLEANERS

Tubs and tiles can be some of the most difficult places to clean, which is why they're often not cleaned—resulting in a lot of scummy buildup that requires hardcore help. When I asked Tes if she'd test green cleaners for me, she insisted that tub and tile cleaners be a part of our experiment. A green cleaner that can shine up these forgotten areas is worth its weight in gold.

NATURALLY IT'S CLEAN TUB AND TILE CLEANER
by Enzyme Fresh Home
Cost: $5.49 for 16 ounces
Ingredients: water, plant-based enzyme blend, coconut oil surfactants, essential oil lavender scent
Tes says: This is too expensive for sixteen ounces. The ingredients look good, but they don't really work well on anything too dirty. It might work if you clean every day and keep the house practically spotless—it's good for touch ups—but I clean when things have gotten bad, so I need cleaners that can work on tough jobs.

TUB AND TILE CLEANER (FRAGRANCE-FREE)
by Ecodiscoveries
Cost: $10.49 for a quart
Ingredients: water, coconut-based surfactants, organic salts
Tes says: Though the ingredients are as safe as can be, this didn't really work on soap scum. The packaging is ridiculous—an empty spray bottle taped to a two-ounce concentrate that, when diluted, fills the bottle. It's way too expensive;

I can get an empty spray bottle at the hardware store for 79 cents.

HOMEMADE TUB AND TILE CLEANER
from Annie Bond's *Better Basics for the Home*
Cost: about $2 for a quart
Ingredients: hot water, borax, liquid detergent, Citrasolv Valencia orange, distilled white vinegar
Tes says: Not worth the effort to make. This didn't work on soap scum, the primary target of tub and tile cleaner. (Ouch!)

NATURAL TUB AND TILE CLEANER, EMERALD CYPRESS AND FIR
by Seventh Generation
Cost: $3.79 for a quart
Ingredients: aqua (water), polyglucose, coceth-4 and deceth-5 (plant-derived cleaning agents), *lactic acid* (soap scum and lime scale remover), *sodium hydroxide* (pH adjuster), *peg-15 cocomonium chloride* (plant-containing cleaning agent), essential oils and botanical extracts (citrus aurantifolia [lime], abies balsamea [balsam fir], calilistris columellaris [cypress])
Tes says: This one wins hands down as the soap scum beater. It acts and looks more like conventional tub and tile cleaner. Unfortunately, it also has a few conventional drawbacks. According to the National Library of Medicine Household Products Database, lactic acid and sodium hydroxide both have moderate health concerns (respectively, respiratory irritation and an irritant to skin, eyes, and mucous membranes). The Environmental Working Group say peg-15 cocomonium chloride has moderate to high health concerns—be careful using it around broken skin. If you feel comfortable trading a little safety for a kick-ass tub and tile cleaner, this is the best of the lot.

The bottom line: When it comes to cleaning tub and tile, Tes wants a product that destroys soap scum. Seventh Generation did, albeit not perfectly safely. Naturally It's Clean couldn't clean the scum, and, despite pure ingredients, neither could Annie Bond's homemade recipe. Ecodiscoveries failed on that front, too, and got an F for excess packaging.

▪ TEST NO. 4: ALL-PURPOSE CLEANERS

Clean it all with one bottle. That's a hefty promise, and not even every conventional all-purpose cleaner can make good on it. Can nontoxic ingredients take on the dirt and grime of every substance and on any surface? Tes put these four green cleaners to the ultimate test.

FREE AND CLEAR NATURAL ALL-PURPOSE CLEANER
by Seventh Generation
Cost: $3.29 for 16 ounces
Ingredients: aqua (water), polyglucose, sodium lauriminodipropionate and coceth-7 (plant-derived cleaning agents), sodium carbonate (mineral-derived alkalinity builder), sodium citrate (pH stabilizer), essential oils and botanical extracts (citrus reticulata [green mandarin], mentha spicata [spearmint], citrus aurantium amara [petitgrain], citrus aurantium bigarade [petitigrain bigarade]), *methylisothiazolinone and benzisothiazolinone* (preservative)
Tes says: I want an all-purpose cleaner that works on glass. Period. This was too streaky. We've got some problematic ingredients again, too. The National Library of Medicine Household Products Database lists this product as an irritant to the eyes and skin, plus problems if you ingest it (I'm not planning on it, but a curious kid might be tempted). Also see comments on Seventh Gen's preservatives for glass cleaner in Test

no. 1, above. Same issues here, but I'll add that benzisothiazolinone is also classified as toxic to wildlife by the EU. Eew.

CLEAN DAY LEMON VERBENA ALL-PURPOSE CLEANER
by Mrs. Meyer's
Cost: $7.99 for 32 ounces of concentrate
Ingredients: water, anionic surfactants from plant sources, solubilizing agents, sodium citrate, chelating agent, essential oils of lemon, lemongrass, peppermint, clover, geranium, and fir needle, *fragrance, preservative*
Tes says: Good all-purpose concentrate—decent price, effective, mild, and it gets your home smelling clean. This bottle, like all Mrs. Meyer's bottles, has roadside appeal, stopping you in the shopping aisle. But I'd like to know more about the ingredients. Particularly the preservative and fragrance.

CITRASOLV
Cost: $5.59 for 22 ounces
Ingredients: water, d-limonene, orange oil, biodegradable cleaning agents derived from coconut
Tes says: Citrasolv has a nice citrus-y smell (hence the name) and is pretty effective at cleaning *most* surfaces. I can't help but streak glass when I use it though, and for me this is a deal breaker. Maybe this is because the fluid is a little thick. On the upside, the ingredients are nice, safe, and simple.

HOMEMADE ALL-PURPOSE CITRUS SPRAY
by Renée Loux, from *Easy Green Living*
Cost: about $2 for a quart
Ingredients: distilled white vinegar, liquid castile soap, Citrasolv concentrate, water, antibacterial essential oils (try eucalyptus, lavender, lemon, lemongrass, rosemary, tea tree, or thyme)

Tes says: OK, so this includes Citrasolv and adds some of our household standards. It works better than Citrasolv on its own. It's safe, it cleans pretty well, and you can change the scent with essential oils of your choosing.

The bottom line: For Tes, it's not all-purpose if it doesn't clean glass. Seventh Generation and Citrasolv left streaks. Both Renée Loux's homegrown recipe and the Mrs. Meyer's commercial concoction did well on glass and other sticky surfaces. But Mrs. Meyer's edged out Ms. Loux based on speed, ease of use, and sexy packaging. In the end, Tes was willing to live with the Mrs. Meyer's mysteries.

A Final Note on Homegrown Contenders

A visit to any of the green-cleaning companies' websites to find out more about ingredients is a reminder of why it's great to make your own

recipes at home. Even so-called eco-friendly products are manufactured in industrial settings and are subject to the vicissitudes of mass production. "Trace materials" are present and can include a wide array of chemicals. The best labels can be difficult to decipher. Lax labeling regulations allow the terms *fragrance* and *preservative* to be used in lieu of more specific information.

Though only one homemade recipe got a blue ribbon for effectiveness in Tes's tests, price and the safety of pantry ingredients may make up the difference in your own home. What's most important to you? You might experiment and come up with more effective recipes too!

BRAND-NAME COMPETITORS

If the thought of making your own cleaning products seems too time-consuming, cumbersome, or stressful (maybe you have a hard enough time following a recipe for dinner?), there are still green-cleaning options for you. Eco name-brand cleaners are available for just about every household chore. Notable brands include Seventh Generation, Biokleen, Ecover, Method, and Mrs. Meyer's, just to name a few (see "Tes's Tests," above, for some recommendations). Do make sure that you check the label before you buy, because *natural* doesn't always mean natural.

If you need to go even more DDIY (don't do it yourself), you may be in luck. Ecocleaning services are wiping down the dust in communities everywhere. Check the yellow pages or look for ecofriendly cleaning services online at the Great Green List. Be sure to ask what cleaning products a service uses and then verify that they really are safe. If you depend on a conventional cleaning service, it wouldn't hurt to give them a bottle of green cleaner and encourage them to test it out it. You all might be pleasantly surprised.

THE DIRT ON GERMS

Squeaky clean isn't all it appears to be. In our quest for spotlessness and our aversion to dirt, germs, and bacteria, we may have gone overboard. Obsession with hygiene has led to the development and marketing of innumerable antibacterial soaps and cleaning products—as well as more esoteric devices such as elbow-operated doorknobs and personal subway handstraps.

Some researchers say this craze has also prompted an increase in asthma and allergies. According to the "hygiene hypothesis," our immune system evolved two different types of biological defenses. When one lacks practice staving off bacteria and viruses, say from an oversanitary lifestyle, the other system grows more powerful and overreacts, causing allergies to harmless substances, such as pollen. This phenomenon may be behind the results of other studies, which have shown that children with many siblings or pets and who lived on farms or went to daycare within their first year of life were less likely to develop allergic diseases than children who led more sequestered urban lives or washed their hands or bathed excessively. Time to skip baths and let the housecleaning go?

No one is suggesting that. But it's certainly time to give up one common antibacterial chemical: triclosan. You'll find this ingredient in everything from toothpaste to liquid soap to mattresses and deodorant. Its stated purpose is to kill germs. That it may do, but it's also linked to liver and inhalation toxicity and thyroid functioning problems. As a phenol, which is a persistent organic pollutant, it sticks around, bioaccumulating in humans and animals, and is found in fatty tissues and breast milk. If combined with chlorine, it reacts to create carcinogenic chloroform and chlorinated dioxins. And if combined with aquatic life, the results are deadly. This happens whenever triclosan ends up in our rivers and other water bodies—which it does often, as wastewater treatment doesn't remove all of the chemical. The Environmental Protection Agency registers triclosan as a pesticide. The Danish EPA recommends avoiding it altogether. Given that soap and water will do just as good a job at getting your hands and home clean, it's certainly not bad advice.

THE WAR ON PESTS: BANNING BIOWEAPONRY

They say an ounce of prevention is worth a pound of cure. This is definitely true if you want to keep your home free of pests, especially if the cure is a common pesticide or poison, which when it comes to unwanted critters it all too often is. Say *cockroach* and even your green pacifist roommate will resort to whatever it takes to get rid of that particular creepy crawly.

It's not just the ick factor that causes us to reach for the nearest can of Raid. Rats, mice, and bugs are seriously annoying and can cause major health problems. You don't have to resort to that pound of cure if it's poison, though. There are healthier alternatives, the first and most important one being prevention. Stop those unwelcome guests at the door before they let themselves inside.

Most of this is common sense, appealing to the basic standards of cleanliness. Keep your food in tight containers and thoroughly clean up the kitchen after you've prepared food—wipe and dry surfaces, sweep away crumbs. If you're too tired to do the dishes before going to bed, leave them soaking in soapy water. If you have pets, put away their food dishes and any leftover food at night. Your garbage should have a tight lid; empty it regularly. Vacuum with a HEPA filter; sweep and mop often. Basically, don't give pests any reason to want to visit. Next, don't give them easy access. Caulk, weatherstrip, and seal around pipes—this, of course, is good for weatherizing your home as well—and block any openings.

Really, that's about it. Simple, inexpensive, and safe.

Safe is key here, because the conventional method—calling the bug guy—is a terribly unsafe option. In 2005, the Centers for Disease Control found that 90 percent of people in the United States had a mix of up to forty-three pesticides in their blood. A study published in the journal *Environmental Health Perspectives* revealed that more than 75 percent of 230 women in New York City had common household insecticides in their blood, including in their umbilical cord blood. Over 95 percent of the infants in the same study had insecticide residues in their first bowel movement.

The consequences to human health are innumerable. One particularly scary example is the correlation between household pesticide use with childhood acute leukemia and non-Hodgkin's lymphoma (NHL). One study showed that in homes where mothers reported pesticide use between one and two days a week, children were three times more likely to develop NHL than in homes where pesticides were used less. In homes where pesticides were used "on most days," children's risk of NHL was seven times greater than in homes where they were used less than once a week. How about not using them at all?

It's entirely doable. Here are a few tips, in addition to the clean standards outlined above, for your typical pest varieties.

SOLDIER ANTS

Keep wood and surfaces dry, since insects are attracted to all things wet. Mint, pine, and citrus oils are reported to repel ants. Try washing your floors with a citrus cleaner. Make your own ant trap by mixing equal parts borax, sugar, and water in a jar and punch holes in the lid. Another version is sugar mixed with boric acid on a cardboard square.

If you want a little immediate gratification, soapy water or citrus oil and water will kill ants on contact—this includes carpenter ants, and you can also spray this mixture in areas where they're active to destroy their chemical trails.

Since carpenter ants like wet, decaying wood, it only makes sense to fix leaks and replace any wood if it's rotten. Another preventive measure is to trim shrubs, bushes, or trees that touch the house, since they provide ladders that ants climb in order to crawl inside your house. Big carpenter ant problems can be remedied by borax spray, or Boracare. Since these pests can do a great deal of damage to your home, hiring an exterminator, though one who uses ecofriendly methods, is warranted.

FOUR-LEGGED FOES

In terms of prevention, in addition to not tempting rodents with snacks and sealing up holes and cracks, stack woodpiles away from your house or building. If you're unable to keep cats, which have excelled at keeping rodents at bay in our home, there are a few good options for ridding your home of mice and rats.

You'll certainly want to do so, since their droppings and dander are a significant source of allergies in children. But avoid using poison, since this is obviously even worse for children (and for pets too).

Traps are a better option. We've used the Havahart type, which allowed us to transport the unharmed, furry critters to more suitable living quarters in the woods down the road.

Healthy-home maven Annie Bond found two mice-ridding solutions worked especially well for her. One is called Fresh Cab, which is a potent-smelling mixture of corncob chips mixed with essential oils. It's designed for camper cabs and cabins, and Bond says it will put off flies, moths, and mosquitoes as well. Her other recommendation is Pest-A-Cator, which sends a pulse through the building's wiring that drives out the mice—in her case initially right into her living space, but then away completely. This solution requires a little patience. Give it a couple weeks.

FALLOUT SURVIVORS

Cockroaches may be able to survive atomic fallout, but they don't like boric acid. If you know where they're entering your apartment building or home, try drawing a line with it. Apply with caution—although it's natural, it's also moderately toxic, though unlike some other toxic substances it doesn't evaporate into the air. To play it safe, try to put it, or products that contain it, in places like cracks and crevices where there's less of a chance of human or pet exposure, and use eye protection and a mask while doing so.

Catnip is the least toxic roach repellent. Roaches appear to be repelled by nepetalactone, the thing that drives cats crazy. What roaches love: dirty, damp mops and clutter (as it makes for good hiding places), so clean up.

WOOD WARRIORS

Termites are not to be taken lightly as they're a danger to the structural integrity of your home. There are three different types: dampwood, subterranean, and drywood. Determine what kind you have, since treatments differ (the University of California integrated pest management (IPM) website has extensive information on how to identify your wood-eating bug).

There are a few green control options. Parasitic nematodes attack termite larvae: they're effective against subterranean and some dampwood termites but not their drywood relatives. Dampwood termites can also be expelled by turning up the heat in your home for an extended period of time (drying up their food source and home), and another option for fighting the subterraneans includes excavating the colony.

There aren't many good green options for drywood termites. Experts recommend a high-voltage electric gun, which will require a professional, who will also be able to accurately pinpoint the location of the colony.

THE BITERS

It's probably unnecessary to say that those flea bombs, foggers, and broadcast sprayers are a bad idea—but even targeted application can be dangerous. If you need a specific reason to stay away from these pesticides, consider a study of Los

Angeles County children with brain tumors. They were twice as likely as kids without the disease to have mothers who treated their dogs for ticks or fleas during pregnancy—those diagnosed before the age of five had a fivefold increase.

A better route is to multiply the pest cleanliness rule by three: wash your pets and their bedding regularly; wash area rugs and vacuum carpeting as much as possible; steam-clean rugs and upholstery if the problem persists.

Annie Bond recommends treating your floors with citrus-peel extract because its components, d-limonene and linalool, kill all stages of the flea life cycle—though she does urge caution for folks with asthma and cats, who are sensitive to d-limonene.

There are a host of natural topical treatments on the market. I can't personally attest to their efficacy, but the folks at the former web magazine *Ideal Bite* recommend both Sentry Natural Defense Flea and Tick Squeeze-On (a plant-based solution you rub on Spot) and Only Natural Pet All-in-One Flea Remedy (a powder you sprinkle on Fido and around the house and yard). Test these treatments out and see if they work for you and your furry friends, but be sure to review the ingredients carefully before doing so.

CLOTHING MONGERS

Prevention is your best line of defense against attire-eating moths. Clean your shelves and vacuum regularly. Any retro or vintage thrift shop purchases should be closely inspected and washed as soon as you get them home.

Avoid these two moth-killing chemicals especially: naphthalene, which can damage the liver and red blood cells, and paradichlorobenzene, which is an allergen and suspected carcinogen.

Cedar chests and closets have historically been used to keep moths at bay, but it turns out that tight construction using any type of wood is more important than the wood itself. While aromatic eastern red cedar does contain an oil that can kill small larvae, it has no effect on the big guys. Worse yet, after several years the cedar loses this quality altogether.

NIGHT RANGERS

After fading away for decades, bedbugs are making a comeback. They're certainly annoying, but they're not known to spread disease. Apartment dwellers are especially vulnerable because of the large number and high turnover of beds. When bed-bugs are entrenched, deny them sleeping rights by moving your bed away from the walls and keeping your blankets from touching the floor. Wash all your linens in hot water and dry on high too. If you must call a pro, ask him to try to avoid using pyrethrins, which potentially cause skin and respiratory irritation. Derived from a flowering plant, pyrethrins are strong pesticides and are generally considered safer than organophosphates, but be aware that they're toxic to fish and amphibians. Recent animal studies have also linked pyrethrins to neurological, immune, and reproductive system damage.

It's worth repeating: prevention is your strongest ally in keeping pests at bay. This may be more of a challenge in apartment buildings and other multi-unit or shared settings. How do you convince your co-tenants to up their cleanliness standards or your landlord to seal around gaps or pipes or insist on regular garbage pickup? And what should you do if you receive a notice that the building is going to be sprayed next week (other than plan a last-minute vacation)?

Cheesy as it may sound, education is probably the only way to prevent chemical warfare or to urge the guys in 4C to mop their floors. Good resource groups include Beyond Pesticides, Northwest Coalition for Alternatives to Pesticides, Pesticide Action Network North America, Environmental Research Foundation, University of California integrated pest management (IPM) program, Safer Pest Control Project, and Washington Toxics Coalition. Talk to both tenants and landlords alike about the dangers of pesticides and the simplicity of deterrence. If you've managed to generate strong building-wide support, you can work to keep common spaces and the recycling and garbage areas clean. Like most noble efforts, it won't work unless you're all in it together.

If you do face a situation where you must hire a professional bug guy—and let's face it, sometimes you really have to hire a bug guy—see if you can't find one who practices integrated pest management. Practitioners follow a step-by-step approach that integrates preventing, monitoring, and controlling pests so that pesticide application might be both minimized and used as a last resort. Some even use natural or organic methods. Green Shield Certified makes sure that IPM companies are what they say they are and that they meet tough prevention-based standards.

CHAPTER 6

YOUR YARD:
OVERCOMING AN
AMERICAN OBSESSION

"I believe a leaf of grass is no less than the journey work of the stars," wrote Walt Whitman in *Leaves of Grass*, arguably one of the greatest works of American poetry. When Whitman first published his magnum opus in 1855, the American landscape had not yet been transformed. True, where once stood vast forests, stretched native prairies, and flowed wild rivers there were cities and railroads, farms and ranches, fences and roads. But there wasn't so much lawn. If as many manicured leaves of grass covered as much territory then as it does today, would Whitman have picked them to symbolize the beauty of nature, the vastness of the universe, the mystery of the self?

Today there are a little less than 32 million acres of turf in this country. That's about 50,000 square miles, larger than the state of Ohio, and it takes in more acreage (three times as much) than is devoted to corn—making it the largest single irrigated "crop" in America. This crop is grown for schoolyards, parks, football fields, golf courses, business lots, and, yes, the front and backyards of our homes. About 80 percent of us have a lawn of some sort. Kentucky bluegrass is so ubiquitous most of us wouldn't think about landscaping without it. And if that grass is found sporting dandelions or a shaggy cut, we might find ourselves judged by the neighbors such that we feel morally bankrupt. What kind of person doesn't take care of her lawn?

Whoever she is, she might ask the 54 million of us who mow our lawn each week the very same question. By performing this quintessential American chore, we use 800 million gallons of gas a year. Our mowers and weed whackers and other motorized devices contribute to 5 percent of urban air pollution. We dump 100 million pounds of synthetic pesticides on our perfect grass—more per acre than farmers apply to their crops—and scatter 70 million tons of fertilizer annually. We use 30 percent of all water on the East Coast, 60 percent on the West, and throughout the country contribute to 18 percent of all municipal solid waste. For that uniformly green, precisely cut grass we risk poisoned ground and drinking water; sick fish, birds, and bees; cancerous dogs; and, for our own species, cancer as well as birth defects, reproductive problems, liver and kidney damage, and neurotoxicity. We're not bad people. But we've been blinded by an obsession.

And who can blame us? Lawns are nice places to lounge in the sun, throw the Frisbee for the dog, and play tag with the kids. Lawns are permeable, so they filter rain. Lawns satisfy an almost primordial need for grassy open space. Plus, many of us have no choice but to live with them.

Are there ways to make our current lawns greener? Yes. Can a lawn be replaced with something else? Most emphatically yes! Our ecofriendly options are not as limitless as the stars in the sky, but there are many, and for that Whitman might still draw on his muse for inspiration.

PUTTING THE GREEN BACK IN THE GREEN

Today's typical turf is made up of a mixture dominated by Kentucky bluegrass. This grass isn't actually from Kentucky (it's thought to be from Europe), but it does thrive in the South as well as the Northeast, where it's preferred for its ability to survive the winter. One thing it can't survive is a lack of water, and the many gallons used on lawns are a direct result of catering to this most common grass. Fortunately, we can look to nature for better landscaping ideas. Native grasses in each region are adapted to the local environment and need minimal, if any, irrigation, chemical fertilizers, or other care. If given the chance, they'll flourish in our yards.

EVERY BLADE OF GRASS

One good option for rain-starved Westerners (or other dry parts of the country) is buffalo grass (*Buchloe dactyloides*). It requires little water and is naturally resistant to insects and diseases. Turf companies sell all-female buffalo grass, which has lower flowers and seed stalks, giving it a uniform, lawnlike appearance without the frequent mowing. It's soft enough to walk on with your bare feet but tough enough for a soccer game.

Another excellent choice is blue grama (*Bouteloua gracilis*), a cold-hardy grass of the Great Plains. It flourishes during the warm months and goes dormant during the cold winters.

Native fescue is ideal for both the North and upper South due to its fine soft leaves and the fact that it greens up early in the spring and stays green into the fall. This low-maintenance, cool-season, low-growing, bunch-forming grass requires mowing only a couple times a year.

Some nonnative commercial blends of grass seed are designed to stay short as well. These are called no-mow or low-mow grasses. Be warned, however, that there isn't really a grass out there that simply grows to the perfect suburban height and stops. Despite the no-mow moniker, never mowing means accepting a bushier lawn than you or your neighbors might be used to.

If you're ready to shift your lawn paradigm in this way, versatile commercial blends are available, such as Eco-Lawn, sold by Wildflower Farm. Its mix of fescue grasses forms a dense turf in conditions ranging from full sun to deep shade. You need only mow it once a month or, if you're willing to go all out, let it flourish as a pretty meadow. Prairie Nursery sells a no-mow seed mix that's recommended for northern states, though not for wet areas or clay soils that are poorly drained. Fleur de Lawn sold by Hobbs & Hopkins includes ryegrass, clover, yarrow, and daisies, providing a fun combination of blades and blooms.

TIP

BETTER THAN AN HOUR AT THE GYM: THE PUSH MOWER

The whirl of sharp blades over grass need not be accompanied by a loud, polluting engine. A push mower, also called a reel mower, might seem old-fashioned to some, but it gets the job done simply and well, without doing damage to the planet or your lungs. In fact, your lungs and heart will get stronger through a great cardio workout, because, yes, a push mower is more difficult to use than a gas-mower—I personally can promise you that—but if you add up all the benefits, that extra pushing is more than worth it.

According to Paul Tukey, author of *The Organic Lawn Care Manual*, reel mowers actually will give your grass the cleanest, healthiest cut it's ever had. They're relatively inexpensive (you'll probably be able to find one used) and are usually well built. They require no electricity or fossil fuels to operate and produce no emissions. They're not obnoxiously loud, thereby adding to, instead of interrupting, the peace of a summer afternoon. And they do double duty as a fertilizer, by leaving the grass clippings where they lie.

Buy a reel mower with the best engineering and ergonomics that you can find, not some antique. Mow your lawn a little more frequently than you would with a gasoline mower and keep the blades sharp.

See, too, what your agricultural extension service has to offer in the way of advice on lawns. You might pick up some great insight from the local office on grass species (not necessarily native) that won't require much water or fertilizers. Or stop by your local native nursery—more and more of these are popping up across the country as people learn to appreciate the utility and beauty of native flora. Native plants, by virtue of their nativeness, don't need extra water or chemicals in the form of pesticides, fertilizers, or herbicides. Besides native grasses, you'll discover diverse species of groundcover that are great for high traffic areas—take a lesson from nature and mix and match for diversity. Or you could buddy up with some sedges.

SEDGES HAVE EDGES

Sedges aren't a true grass (unlike grass, sedges have triangular instead of round stems), but they look like grass and can serve the same purpose in your backyard. There are some two thousand varieties native to the United States, many of which will work great as a lawn. While quite a few love moisture, many others thrive in droughty conditions. They grow from plugs and need only be mowed occasionally.

Gardening guru Barbara Damrosch, author of most serious gardeners' go-to, *The Garden Primer*, recommends Pennsylvania sedge (*Carex pensylvanica*), which easily spreads and tolerates drought and some shade; Texas sedge or catlin sedge (*Carex texensis*), which is adaptable to a variety of conditions, including foot traffic; and California meadow sedge (*Carex pansa*), which is a great performer in the West.

Speaking of performers, there's even a low mop-head sedge cultivar called 'The Beatles.' Tune in or see if there are any locally grown sedge bands just right for a lawn performance in your region.

LOVING YOUR LAWN NATURALLY

Let's say you must love the lawn you're with. Maybe your landlord isn't willing to rip up his sod, or the turf is necessary to preserve marital accord, or your neighborhood covenants bind you to Kentucky bluegrass. Your tactic should then be to convince said landlord, spouse, or neighborhood association board that the grass can be kept green without synthetic chemicals.

Whether you've got a conventional or native-grass lawn, natural supplements and organic fertilizers are actually easier on both it and the environment. Concentrations of nitrogen, potassium, and phosphorus are far lower in organic fertilizers, which means the grass won't get "burned." If you're feeling the pressure to produce lush, emerald grass, try plant by-products such as alfalfa or cottonseed meal, corn gluten, seaweed, or wood ash instead of chemical fertilizers; or, in the animal realm, try blood, bone, or feather meal, bat guano, and fish products. These are sold either individually or in commercial mixtures. Those who recycle their food scraps, otherwise known as composters, can also use their black gold as a lawn supplement.

There's also no need to poison weeds with the scary wand and pump. Those implements of destruction are overkill in more ways than one. For those who might miss the excitement of the total eradication promised by the weed wand, there are portable propane torches, or flamers, which you can pick up at the hardware store and which give you the option of zapping the weed with heat rather than poison.

Some folks swear by spot-treating weeds with vinegar, garlic, soap, or boiling water. I personally take great satisfaction in hand-pulling weeds. There's something very meditative about taking them out taproot and all. Renters may want to volunteer their time in exchange for an herbicide-free lawn and/or a reduction in rent. Get to know your upstairs neighbors better by organizing a weed-pulling party.

MOSS OR NOT?

Moss takes over turf where conditions are right: compacted or shallow soil, too much moisture, low fertility, acidity, and shade. There are organic applications that kill moss, many of which are soap products high in phosphorus. But killing off your moss is likely a temporary solution—it will return unless you fix the underlying

---

FOR THE BIRDS

Think about it. If peregrine falcons nest on skyscrapers or bridge abutments, and coyotes roam the streets of Los Angeles, you can take a step toward making your habitat, however urban or suburban, wildlife friendly. Or maybe five steps.

Whether you have an apartment balcony or 40 acres, the National Wildlife Federation (NWF) lists five criteria for making your space a functioning habitat:

- Wildlife need food. Give them something to eat. Plenty of forbs, shrubs, and trees provide the necessary foodstuffs: berries, foliage, nectar, pollen, or nuts.
- Wildlife need water. Provide a birdbath or pond for drinking and bathing.
- Wildlife need cover. To feel safe, wildlife need to be able to hide from predators and people. Shrubs and trees provide cover, but so can brush piles and dead snags.
- Wildlife need nurseries. Create places to raise young. Plant butterfly-friendly bushes or a wildflower meadow.
- Wildlife need you to clean up your act. Use mulch and compost and other sustainable gardening practices and reduce space devoted to turf grass and the chemicals that come with it.

Once you have taken these steps, apply to NWF for certification. To date, more than 150,000 backyards have been certified wildlife friendly in the United States. Want more habitat? Reach out to your neighbors or local schools to bring more wildlife to your neighborhood and schoolyards—create an urban sanctuary.

problems. Loosening the soil, letting in more sun, and improving drainage all help. Or leave it alone and live and let live. Moss is about as green as grass after all.

PREYING ON PESTS

As a first step in evicting pests from the yard, the National Wildlife Federation recommends putting a couple tablespoons of detergent in a gallon of water and pouring it over a suspicious spot of dead grass. This won't kill the invaders, but it will drive subterranean bugs to the surface where you can collect them and find out exactly what you're dealing with.

Once you've done that, botanical pesticides are available for a less toxic routing. Neem oil, made from an evergreen tree that grows in India, is a popular botanical pest killer. It's an effective pesticide against moths, mites, and worms and can be used to spot-treat your lawn if diluted. Insect parasitic nematodes are also an option. These worms prey on pests like mole crickets and white grubs.

Remember that our lawns are extensions of our homes. The chemicals we use on the lawn are tracked back inside by our pets or on the soles of shoes and then ground into the carpeting or set free to drift about on the floor. Ever more reason to go organic.

LET IT GROW

Grass is also healthier without a military cut. Allowing it to grow a few inches helps protect surface roots and topsoil. Leaving grass clippings in place returns nutrients to the ground. And, of course, avoiding gas-guzzling, air-polluting mowers for your trims will help reduce air pollution. The Environmental Protection Agency estimates that running a mower for an hour is the same as getting in your car and driving twenty miles.

There are many electric- and battery-powered mowers on the market today. Each have their drawbacks: for electric, you're limited by the length of the cord, and electricity isn't without its cost; for battery, price can be prohibitive, and necessary recharging can be irritating if you have a large lawn.

Push mowers have been around for quite a while longer and, if properly maintained, will cut grass just fine. We owned a scythe when we lived in Massachusetts—it was useful for grass that had grown too long for our push mower to

FRITZ HAEG'S EDIBLE ESTATES

Is a lawn a manicured microcosm of the American dream, or is it an artless act of conformity that separates you from your community? Artist and architect Fritz Haeg has a vision to convert unproductive lawns to productive gardens. Part horticulture, part multimedia art project, part grassroots movement, the Edible Estates project hopes to inspire lawnowners across the country to become landowners.

"The Edible Estates project proposes the replacement of the domestic front lawn with a highly productive edible landscape," writes Haeg in a book profiling his project, *Edible Estates: Attack on the Front Lawn*. Beginning with pilot gardens created in 2005 together with homeowners, including one in the dead center of the country in Salina, Kansas, and others in Maplewood, New Jersey, and Lakewood, California, Haeg's goal is to convince others that they can grow food in place of a front lawn. Though credit can't be directly attributed to Haeg, even the White House lawn was partially transformed into a vegetable garden in 2008, where carrots were last seen when the Roosevelts were in residence.

Converting lawn to garden has benefits: it's better for the soil to recycle nutrients; better for the community to build a space that's useful and welcoming; better for the atmosphere to eliminate the pollution of chemical fertilizers and exhaust from lawn mowers; and better for our health to eat fresh, local produce and reconnect with the ecology of the place we live in through gardening.

It might be better for our artistic sensibilities as well. "The banal lifeless space of uniform grass in front of the house will be replaced with the chaotic abundance of biodiversity," writes Haeg in his book. Compared to pushing a lawn mower back and forth across a flat expanse of green, gardening is a work of art.

handle. I felt a little medieval every time I used it, but it was always effective. If I were a golfer it might have helped me improve my swing.

A LAWNLESS LANDSCAPE

Finally, it's worthwhile rethinking the necessity of a lawn altogether. Aesthetically pleasing home landscaping is achievable otherwise. Consider paths winding around wildflower islands and wildlife habitat, interspersed with native shrubs and trees, accented by mulched areas, complemented by a rock or water garden, and perhaps centered on a vegetable garden.

Sound more interesting than a flat expanse of grass? This sort of approach is greener than grass too. And if a garden is possible in your backyard or the common outdoor area of your apartment building, your carbon homeprint is about to get smaller. The ability to grow what you eat where you live not only rids your life of the carbon calories of well-traveled vegetables, it's a whole lot of fun.

HARVEST YOUR YARD

Many herbivores like vegetables better than grass, which is why gardens have fences. And though a deer might not appreciate the subtle difference between a vegetable shipped from another state and one grown in your backyard, your palate will. Garden-grown vegetables taste much better. The commercial varieties found in most supermarkets are bred for things besides taste: ease of transport, uniformity of size and color, and the plants' ability to bear its crop all at once. In contrast, homegrown veggies can be selected for taste and quality or even natural resistance to local pests. Which of these vegetables would you want on your dinner plate?

Whether or not you're sure, your planet has a clear preference. Today most food travels between 1,500 and 2,500 miles before it reaches your table. A head of lettuce grown in California's Salinas Valley and shipped 3,000 miles to Washington DC requires approximately thirty-six times as much fossil fuel energy in transport as it provides in food energy when it's eaten. A typical meal using local ingredients requires four to seventeen times less petroleum consumption than the same meal with conventional ingredients. Yet most typical American meals contain ingredients with an average of five different countries of origin! That's a lot of miles and a lot of fossil fuel that end up parked at your dinner table, which, of course, getting back to our focus, sits in the dining room or kitchen of your home. You are what you eat. Goats will happily graze your lawn, but wouldn't you rather have a salad made up of baby carrots, spring greens, and spicy radishes?

PLOTTING YOUR GARDEN

Are you ready to get your hands dirty? Do you, or rather does your outdoor space, have what it takes? Gardens have three basic necessities: good soil, good light, and water. Make a plan that includes these three elements; don't just go crazy digging up the earth on a warm spring day.

For **light**, it might seem obvious to pick the sunniest spot. If you live in the Northern Hemisphere, you should also orient your garden slightly to the south. Most vegetables require at minimum six hours of sun each day, but some—such as salad greens like arugula and other greens you can't find in many supermarkets—will get by on less.

To see if you have good **soil**, get it tested. Many public universities have soil-testing labs, as do local extension services, and private labs abound. A soil test will tell you both the nutrient content and the pH of your soil. It's far easier to successfully grow organic vegetables if you know your soil's shortcomings and can target soil amendments to your specific problem.

Most plants will tolerate a wide range of pH, and it's only when you have highly acidic or alkaline soil that you need to do something about it. Poor soil can be remedied with organic matter like dried manure, peat moss, or compost. All three are available at nurseries. The third option can also be found in your compost bin (see "Compost: The Gold Standard of Fertilizers" a bit later in this chapter).

If the land is too sloped, consider terracing. If you don't have adequate drainage, consider building raised beds—which will also solve the problem of having troubled soil in general (the bad stuff gets buried under the good stuff you truck in).

Finally, make sure your **water** supply is within easy reach—via a hose or, better yet, a rain barrel.

PUT YOUR GARDEN WHERE YOUR GRASS IS

If that perfect sunny spot is covered in lawn, you'll have to address that problem first. There are two methods for getting rid of the sod.

The first is to work through some aggression by using a spade to cut it up (and then dump it in the compost pile). Then mix in your homemade compost or trucked-in yummy, rich soil. This involves more backbreaking work than you might imagine, but you'll establish a nice plot rather quickly.

Option number two is for the lazy. Cover the grass with something that blocks the light. Cardboard is a good option; a blanket will do the trick too. Many folks recommend newspaper; but while some newspaper inks are soy-based, others contain heavy metals, which seems like a good reason to not use your local daily for this job unless you can determine the source of its ink. Deprived of light, the grass will die in about two months. Leave the soy-inked newspaper or cardboard in place and add a thick layer of soil or compost on top. Plant your seeds. This stacking of mulch and newspaper is also often called the lasagna method. Food-related metaphors work well in gardening, of course.

SOWING THE SEEDS

There are a lot of great books on gardening, books devoted entirely to the subject, which you should consult and reference for detailed advice. Of the many, Barbara Damrosch's *Garden Primer* is used often and you'll come across dirt-stained copies that prove it. *Sunset National Garden Book*, by *Sunset* magazine, is another go-to guide. Started in the West, *Sunset*'s garden guide has gained a national reputation. Growing up in the Pacific Northwest, I relied heavily on *Growing Vegetables West of the Cascades*, by Steve Solomon. Gardeners in your region likely have a favorite resource book as well.

You'll find information on seed saving, companion planting, schedules, and styles of gardening. I'd recommend sitting down with a few of these books on the darkest winter day and finding what works for you and your region. To get you started on your garden reveries, some basic tips follow.

Start simple: Novices should start with crops that are both delicious and easy to grow, such as lettuce, radishes, beets, summer squash, cucumbers, and swiss chard.

Go local: Buy your plants or seeds from your local garden center or farm, not a mega store. You'll find healthier plants and advice from knowledgeable employees.

Know the light: Fruiting vegetables like squash, cucumbers, peppers, and tomatoes are adamant about getting a minimal four or five hours of direct sunlight, plus some residual heat and reflected light. (To increase reflective light, use foil, marble chips or white painted walls.)

If you're unlucky in the light department but dying for homegrown tomatoes, plant cherry tomatoes, which need less sun to get juicy. Or bury seeds of banana or chili peppers, which fruit with less solar energy than their plumper cousin, the bell pepper. And remember that leafy veggies such as spinach, kale, chard, rhubarb, broccoli, and cabbage are fantastic in shadier spots.

An ounce of prevention: The best way to fight weeds and pests is to prevent them from taking root. Work hard to keep your plants healthy. Don't give weeds opportunities, like bare soil. Keep your soil fully planted. Mulch! A fluffy layer of organic material—such as leaves, straw, peat, or bark—spread generously about is a deterrent to weeds. Secondly, weed often. Don't let weeds get a foothold.

…is worth a pound of chemicals: Fight pests with natural approaches. Allow predators like ladybugs, lizards, frogs, and toads to coexist in your garden. Attract predatory insects by planting natives that produce small blossoms. When pests do show up, try blending chili, garlic, liquid detergent, and water in a spray bottle and then spraying the leaves of the affected plant.

Believe it or not, picking insects off by hand is one of the most effective ways to eliminate pests. For cabbageworms or caterpillar problems, consider using *Bacillus thuringiensis*, commonly referred to as Bt. This microbial insecticide consists of spores produced by a bacterium that lives in soil. Use it as a last resort, however, since beneficial insects may fall prey to it alongside the wormy invaders.

If nothing works, be generous and plant extra for the pests. In the balance of nature (if nature is allowed to balance in your garden), something is likely to come along and eliminate your pest population.

Respect your soil: Don't use chemical fertilizers. Instead, use organic fertilizers or natural soil amendments (like "rock powders"), both of which are a natural source of minerals that help plants. They tend to be slow release, helping over time and leading to sturdier plants and sweeter fruits and vegetables.

Determine your motives: Are you in it for the bounty or the fun? Experimentation, fresh air, or exercise? Or all of the above? If the former, you may want to consider a schedule for your garden plot. Sowing particular crops too early or too late can lead to failed crops. Master gardeners plant their crops in smooth succession, often following a meticulous schedule, ensuring fresh veggies for many months of the year: for example, an early crop of leafy greens planted in spring, followed by a second crop of heat-loving tomatoes and squashes planted as seedlings in midsummer.

But don't feel overwhelmed or compelled to get your plants in step, perhaps especially if you're a beginner. You many not harvest as big a crop, but experiment, have fun, and learn as you go…or hoe.

SHARE THE WEALTH: GROW COMMUNITY AND A GARDEN

Though many gardeners claim to get their best thinking done while spending hours alone tending their vegetables, gardening need not be a solitary experience. In fact, it's a fantastic way to make friends, meet like-minded individuals, and learn from and teach others. In other words, community gardens, well, build community.

That may be why there were an estimated 150,000 community gardens in the United States in 2004. A community garden is any piece of land gardened by a group of people. Perhaps the best part about a community garden is that it allows those without suitable land to get their hands dirty and grow their own fresh, local food. A garden might exist on an empty lot or your neighbor's large lot; it might be shared outdoor apartment space or donated land on a suburban/rural farm.

Gardening groups are usually bound together by a common thread: a neighborhood, perhaps, or church or other organization. Students at the regional high school where we used to live in Massachusetts started a community garden to help supply food for their cafeteria.

Each garden works differently. Some gardeners or families have their individual plots within the larger garden space. Some gardens are shared: all members work in the garden and all receive a share of the harvest. Some gardens are food-bank gardens, donating their harvest for distribution to those in need. Some gardens are market gardens, where all the produce is grown for a farmers market.

Maybe you know of the perfect sunny spot to set up a garden in your condo complex? Does that weedy patch behind the apartment building look appealing for sun-loving tomatoes and peppers? Even if your landlord or neighborhood association isn't convinced by the beautiful utility of a garden, he, she, or they might be swayed by the social benefits shared vegetables can bring. Studies have shown that community gardens have a positive effect on urbanites' quality of life and also stabilize neighborhoods. The American Community Garden Association's list of benefits is near utopian: community gardens provide a catalyst for neighborhood and community development; beautify neighborhoods; reduce family food budgets; reduce crime; preserve green space; create income opportunities and economic development; reduce city heat from streets and parking lots; and provide opportunities for intergenerational and cross-cultural connections.

People have been gardening and farming land communally forever, but the modern community garden movement can be traced to a dawning ecological

Raina Weber is the founder of Project Native (www.projectnative.org), a nonprofit in the Berkshire-Taconic region of western Massachusetts with a mission to inspire the stewardship of natural resources by cultivating native plants and restoring the local landscape. Project Native cultivates over 170 varieties of organically grown perennials, including wildflowers, ferns, grasses, wetland species, and flowering shrubs.

Why go native?

Aesthetically, native plants give the appearance of belonging. Because they evolved in a specific place over time, along with natural weather patterns and native fauna, if planted in the right locations they generally require less human intervention and maintenance to thrive. The long process of evolution developed interdependent relationships between species. Some native insects and birds cannot survive without the presence of certain native plants and vice versa.

How can native plants help eliminate chemical use and water abuse in our yards?

Native plants can solve a wide range of home landscape issues. Rain gardens designed using native plants will absorb excess water from your roof and gutters or from your sinks, commonly called gray water. Properly placed native plants can keep chemical runoff from roads and homes from entering waterways and other natural areas.

And as I mentioned earlier, because native plants are adapted to the environment you're planting them in, they generally require less water and don't need chemical fertilizers. Not using chemical fertilizers and fungicides and insecticides is also often about aesthetics. Powdery mildew is a part of the growth of beebalm as aphids are a part of butterflyweed. Most insects and fungus will not harm a plant and in some cases are beneficial, particularly native insects and fungus. Sustainable gardening requires a new perspective, one that enjoys leaves that have been munched. Eventually, like me, you'll look at an ox-eye sunflower whose stem is covered in neon red aphids and say, "how beautiful!"

Are natives always the better choice?

Not all nonnative plants are invasive. In fact most are not. In a more formal garden, favorite exotic plants incorporated with a native plant design produces stunning results. Project Native's landscaping services tend to mix gardens with 75 percent native and 25 percent exotic.

It is very important that you understand the growth patterns of the plant you are purchasing and planting. Old favorites like English roses and lilacs have been around New England gardens a long time and have shown no signs of "jumping ship" and taking over natural habitats. Others such as barberry and burning bush have devastated whole ecosystems by competing for light, nutrients, and water and crowding out all the native understory plants in the forest. Others are newly developed and should only be purchased with extreme caution. Watch out for "aggressive grower," "drought-tolerant" or "flood-tolerant," and evergreens.

How can I get started?

Many landscapers and nursery centers are now making an effort to incorporate native plants. If you cannot find them, ask for them to be sourced. Otherwise, several fantastic books to use as reference are Douglas Tallamy's *Bringing Nature Home*; *Noah's Garden*, by Sara Stein; and *Guide to Growing and Propagating Wildflowers of the United States and Canada*, by William Cullina. To find a rough—and not entirely accurate—listing of what is native to your area, see the USDA plants database. Or better yet, contact a local environmental group to find out if any local botanist or ecologist has completed a vegetation classification in your area.

What are some common pitfalls to be avoided?

Like all functioning home landscapes, natives must be incorporated appropriately. A shade-loving spring ephemeral that goes dormant in the summer, such as bloodroot, will not work in the full sun and as a cornerstone plant. Likewise the ever-blooming summer perennials such as blue-eyed grass need afternoon sun and moist soil to thrive. Even though certain plants are native to a region doesn't mean they will thrive any place planted. It is important to note the conditions the desired plant is found in its natural habitat and emulate that setting as much as possible.

To truly "go native" one must change the entire way one thinks about gardening. Bugs aren't all bad. A healthy functioning garden has some leaf damage from the native caterpillars, native aphids of various colors and sizes lining the stems, powdery mildew dusting the surface of flowers in August, and berries that feed the migrating birds in late fall and winter. A native garden is not meant to be sanitary but instead rich in the diversity of life.

Tell me about the founding of Project Native and your current projects. How did you get interested in native plants?

No one is a better landscaper than Mother Nature. I started out as a garden designer. After I bought my first field guide, I discovered that the plants and design combinations that were so inspiring in natural settings were not available at any local nursery centers.

The conception of Project Native was at first just about aesthetics. I quickly learned about the wildlife connection and ecological value thereafter. I have gardened at pristine and visually stunning gardens where if I stop working and observe I notice the complete and utter lack of life. No bees, no butterflies, no birds, no nature. It is a painting and no better food or shelter for native fauna than your driveway.

Project Native now has a 54-acre native plant farm on which we grow over 180 varieties of regional native plants, have a small roots-style garden shop, offer walks through habitat trails and demonstration gardens, have cultivated seed banks that preserve and protect regionally native flora—and we sell the seed harvested from the seed banks. We offer a wide variety of education programs to schools, camps, clubs, landscape professionals, and the general community. We also provide landscape consultations, designs and installations for private and public venues and sites deemed for restoration, particularly wetlands.

What are your favorite native plants?

I have many favorite native plants! One I will mention because I think it is highly underutilized and sadly ostracized from the human landscape design. *Rhus typhina*, commonly known as staghorn sumac. It has fantastic fall foliage color, the seed cones are visually stunning and provide a much needed food source for birds throughout the entire winter, and sumac grows very quickly and in average or poor soils. I'll admit that Dr Seuss's book *The Lorax* was a childhood favorite, and the sumac reminds me of the Truffula trees.

awareness in the 1970s. Seattle, New York City, Boston, and Chicago all established community gardens in those heady days, and many continue to produce. If you're ready for your own contemporary movement and have a critical mass of interested neighbors or co-tenants but not a lot of know-how, the aforementioned American Community Gardening Association has great website resources. You'll find detailed information about how to start a community garden, including everything from site selection to considering insurance.

Do you need some inspiration to plant those first seeds with your neighbors? Consider these community gardens and projects as just a few examples of the many creative ways people share the bounty:

- **Community Roots** (Boulder; www.communityrootsboulder.com): This group began in 2005 in the yards of churches and suburban ranch houses. Thirteen front and backyards, ranging in size from 600 to 3,500 square feet and totaling less than an acre altogether, feed fifty families. The gardens are so productive that this group sells CSA (community supported agriculture) shares to the public.
- **P-Patch Community Gardens** (Seattle; www.seattle.gov/neighborhoods /ppatch): Seattle hosts the most community gardens per capita of U.S. cities, in part because of more than three decades of the P-Patch program. This effort alone includes sixty-eight gardens (and counting) and provides 1,900 plots of land for 3,800 urban gardeners. Cooperatively run by a city agency and a nonprofit, the program has converted 23 acres of the Emerald City to garden.
- **Green Thumb** (New York City; www.greenthumbnyc.org): The largest urban gardening program in the country, with 600 gardens founded on vacant lots, converting crime-ridden eyesores into community resources.
- **Village Harvest** (San Francisco Bay Area; www.villageharvest.org), **Portland Fruit Tree Project** (Portland, OR; www.portlandfruit.org), and **Fallen Fruit**

(Los Angeles; www.fallenfruit.org): These nonprofit volunteer organizations harvest fruit from backyards, small orchards, and public spaces and then pass the bounty along to local food agencies and to volunteers. The Portland Fruit Tree Project also registers fruit and nut trees throughout the city and teaches tree care and food preservation in hands-on workshops. Fallen Fruit takes advantage of the fact that fruit hanging above sidewalks is public property; the group keeps an archive of fruit-tree locations in Los Angeles.

COMPOST: THE GOLD STANDARD OF FERTILIZERS

Compost is miraculous. Take a mix of organic materials like food waste, grass clippings, leaves, and dirt, mix it all together, and you end up with a sweet-smelling, crumbly fertilizer. The biological process goes like this: organic material is digested by soil microorganisms, things like bacteria and fungi, as well as their larger dirt buddies like earthworms and mites. The bacteria drive up the temperature of the pile, which produces an even more favorable environment for themselves. Eventually, all the big stuff is broken down, and the temperature drops, but the worms keep chomping and pooping. In the end you are left with a nutrient-rich mix.

Though there are means and methods of achieving this perfection and of speeding up the process, a somewhat sloppy, haphazard composter will still, eventually, get compost. Things rot. It's only a matter of time. Why let your food and yard waste decompose? According to the U.S. Composting Council, approximately 70 percent of the municipal waste stream destined for landfills is organic. Of that, 12 percent is food scraps and 13 percent is yard debris. That equals about 63.5 million tons of trash. Buried food in landfills is not a good thing. Cut off from air, it releases methane—twice as much as the same amount of buried paper—and methane is a greenhouse gas. There's really no sense in giving up something so useful in exchange for climate change. Compost is good for the yard and garden, around trees and shrubs, or even for a window box or potted plants. Putting it in places like these instead of your trash can will eliminate about a third of your household waste.

Not much is necessary to make compost. You eat food, you've got food scraps. Do yard work, and you've got yard waste. The key is where to put the leftovers. I've known folks to toss their waste in a pile, turn it on occasion, and let nature take care of the rest. Be aware, though, that this low-maintenance method could very well annoy human neighbors and attract animal ones. It will also take longer to achieve the desired composted results. Binning your compost is in most cases the best idea.

CONTAINING YOUR COMPOST

In general, a bin should be big enough, or hold enough material, to allow heat to build up in the center, but it should also be small enough so that oxygen easily enters and moves about and works its magic. Many experts suggest that 3 feet wide by 3 feet long by 3 feet deep is a good size. If the bin is in direct sunlight, and the base touches the soil you'll have better results too.

There are different types of bins and bin systems for different tastes. You've probably seen the square black plastic types. They're sold at local hardware stores and by upscale vendors. Staking out a circle of wire mesh, about three feet high, is another type of compost holder. If you elect to buy or build a bin of this variety, keep in mind it's nice to have access to the bottom of the pile. If you are continuously adding new scraps, the stuff at the bottom will become compost first. At some point, you'll need to stop adding stuff so the top of the pile can break down too. You can get a little more complex and build a system with multiple cells for holding compost as it moves through the decomposition process, keeping it in the first cell as it heats up, moving it to a second cell as it cools down but continues to decompose, and moving it to a final cell once it's all done. When the first cell is emptied, you begin again with new waste.

LET IT BREATHE

Turning your compost helps bring in oxygen, and you can buy a tool designed specifically for the job, called a compost aerator or compost turner, or use a shovel or pitchfork just as well. Or make turning a little easier by purchasing a tumbler unit, which looks like a barrel on a spit. Turning the spit turns the compost inside, exposing it to air and making the mixture uniform.

Gardening guru Barbara Damrosch calls compost a "casserole of organic matter" that you have to let cook for a while. Depending on your climate, this can be a few weeks or a few months. Compost is ready for your garden and plants to eat when it's crumbly and brown like coffee grounds. You'll achieve this texture, what some folks call black gold, with enough warmth, moisture, and air. If you want to be precise, your bin should be about 160º F (measure the temperature with a soil thermometer). Or take the more intuitive approach; if it feels warm to the touch, if it steams on cool mornings, it's hot enough. A too-cold compost casserole will reheat with more frequent turning and adjusting of ingredients.

Most people turn the pile weekly, but some don't turn it at all. Turning, as noted above, adds oxygen, mixes ingredients more uniformly throughout the pile, and is thought to speed the composting process by keeping those microorganisms centered in the pile, eating and generating heat. The process will go on even without turning, though, and if you are willing to wait between six months and two years, some people argue that the end result holds more nutrients than if you regularly turn the pile.

THE COMPOST RECIPE

While you don't *have* to follow a specific recipe, the right ingredients, or rather the right ratio of ingredients, will cook faster. Technically this is **thirty parts carbon to one part nitrogen**. Or, for the more visually inclined, **two parts brown to one part green**. By brown I mean stuff like dried leaves, straw, wood, or wood chips—even cardboard or egg cartons. By green I mean fresh food scraps, grass clippings, plant trimmings, and manure.

At our Massachusetts home, my family had a small flock of chickens, and their poop worked wonders, in small amounts though. We dumped in a much bigger pile of dead leaves whenever we added it.

Top your casserole with a little soil to help introduce beneficial microorganisms. Add water when it feels dry, though you're aiming for moist, not soaking. If the pile gets too wet, add more "brown" to help absorb excess moisture.

With the right amount of attention and balance of ingredients, the pile will cook down to about a third of its original size.

Any good cook knows what will spoil a perfect dish. In their zest to recycle organic matter, composters should be careful to avoid certain materials. These include dog or cat waste (potential parasites), vegetation or wood that's been treated with chemicals and weed killers (defeats the purpose of organic), and weeds or diseased plants (the temperature might not be hot enough to kill them and you'll end up with more weeds).

So-called putrescent wastes, things like meat scraps and dairy, can be difficult for many microorganisms to digest, and including too much can slow down the composting of your pile. If you really want to keep your putrescents from going to the landfill, consider the newest fad in composting: black soldier-fly larvae. Black soldier flies (*Hermetia illucens*) aren't like houseflies—they don't transmit disease. Their larvae, little grubs, plow through putrescent waste, getting fatter and producing good compost. They are known for their speed and efficiency, and after they've eaten their fill the protein-rich grubs can be fed to chickens or fish, or you might just enjoy watching the wild birds they attract.

FIGHT THE FREEZE

Perhaps a composter's biggest challenge is not meat, not dairy, but cold. Residents of warmer climes have an easier row to hoe when it comes to compost. Those who live in an area that imports its weather from Canada face the challenge of keeping their compost alive and hot.

A frozen compost pile isn't composting and turning it is as easy as lifting a small boulder. That's OK. It will return to work in the spring after a dormant winter.

If you're serious about composting in the winter, you can take steps to fight the freeze. Most of the heat in a compost pile comes from the metabolism of the critters, and it's hottest in the middle. Keeping the mix ratio right keeps the bacteria munching at their greatest efficiency and producing the most heat. Try protecting that heat by insulating your bin. Dig a hole 6 inches deep and put your bin over the hole. Surround it with straw bales as a form of insulation, and let the snow fall on it (which also provides good insulation). If this fails, or if you can't take it outside, consider bringing the composting indoors. Like urbanites can and should do.

VERMICOMPOSTING

Don't have a backyard? Residing on the ninth floor of an apartment building? Short on space? City dwellers, dorm residents, and renters have no excuse not to compost. Just pick up some worms and a small bin and get ready for the fun-filled practice of vermicomposting. Worms will eat about half their body weight in a day. Their poop, or castings, is the finished product, and it's rich in nitrogen, phosphorous, and potassium. These castings are ready to use in about four and a half months.

Spread them around your plants or windowsill herbs or make new friends by gifting them to your neighbors. Worms are about the most useful and low-maintenance pets around. Sustain them with your food waste (though avoid dairy, meat, and

TIP

BACK TO THE (KITCHEN) GARDEN!

Americans tend to hide the garden in the back corner of the lawn, treating it as a messy jumble of plants. But there are other traditions that approach gardening differently. The French use the term *potager* to describe a kitchen garden that grows food and is aesthetically pleasing, a designed space that serves both purposes. It becomes a fundamental element of the landscape. Kitchen gardens date back to at least medieval times. Monasteries, country estates, and castles each had their own. A twenty-first century renaissance might change the way we think about our own urban fiefdoms.

bread), but leave on a three-week river trip and they'll be just fine while you're gone. All they ask for is modest living quarters.

In general, small worm bins are about 16.5 inches wide and 12 inches tall, and 24 inches long, lined with moist newspaper, and drilled with air holes. Build one yourself or buy one online, worms and all. The City Farmer News blog has tips like how to combat fruit flies, how much food your worms can take, and how to keep your working worms from escaping the bin. Worm composting has taken off in cities like New York, Chicago, and Vancouver, B.C. where there's even a worm composting hotline.

Urbanites, in fact, are leading the way on the composting front. New York boasts several groups that collect food scraps. The Lower East Side Ecology Center has it own composting facility and picks up food waste at two Manhattan locations. Seattle and San Francisco have both codified composting into law. San Franciscans are especially forward thinking in terms of reusing, reducing, recycling, and rotting. The city's goal is to send nothing to landfills by 2020. Green carts are provided for compost material. In June 2009, 27 percent of the city's 9,000 large apartment buildings composted, but as of October that number had rapidly risen to 37 percent. The end result? About 500 tons of compost per year for farmers and the region's famed vintners.

CONTAINMENT: BRINGING YOUR GARDEN INDOORS

Those peering down from the tenth floor of an apartment building in the downtown of a major city might consider gardens something out of a paperback fantasy novel. This isn't necessarily a bad thing. As R. J. Ruppenthal writes in *Fresh Food from Small Places*, "we may be limited by the amount of free space we have, but not by our imaginations." Ruppenthal insists that you don't need ground to grow your own food. Landless dwellers of apartments, condos, townhouses, or homes can use one or two strategies outlined in his extremely practical and fun book, and, he says, grow 10 to 20 percent of their own food. Every square inch, even vertical square inches, are potentially productive, and just about anything grown outdoors can do well inside.

Ruppenthal takes container, indoor, and limited-space gardening to its maximum potential. He uses trellises, gutters, walls, and doors and grows everything from sprouts to berries, chickens to yeast, garden-variety vegetables to mushrooms. You can too, or at the very least dabble by putting some pots on your doorstep, windowsill, patio, porch, or even a fire escape.

In fact, container gardening has its advantages over gardening on a plot of land. Soils can be manipulated—sand, loam, clay, and different pHs—on a container-by-container basis to suit the needs of different plants. Garden pests are also more easily addressed, one container at a time; and some, such as snails, slugs and soil-based pests, are much less of a concern than they are in a regular garden. Many plants will take maximum advantage of containers: herbs, carrots, radishes, and lettuce, to name a few.

But containing your vegetables also presents unique challenges. You must water more frequently, as the thinner, lighter soils have the potential to dry out quickly. You also need to consider where that water is going—since the containers need to be perforated at the bottom.

Light is perhaps the biggest constraining factor in apartments and condos. Ruppenthal's advice is the same as for any gardener who faces a low-light or shady situation, whether indoors or out, with a lot of space or a little. Plant whatever accepts or even thrives with little sun: smaller fruiting veggies like cherry tomatoes, banana peppers, roots and tubers, and mushrooms. You can even use indirect, reflective light to grow veggies like bush peas and beans. Light and heat bounce off of south-facing walls, even more so if they're painted white. Any white or light-colored surface will make a great backdrop for containers.

Peas indoors? What are you waiting for?

PART 3

REDUCE, REUSE, RECYCLE, REMODEL

We ask a lot of the planet, and it delivers: food, water, shelter, life. Unfortunately, we take more than we need; more, in fact, than Earth has to give. We're not great in terms of reciprocity either. What we do give back—clear-cut forests, dewatered rivers, overflowing landfills—isn't by anyone's measure an equal exchange. We're like a bunch of very bad houseguests. Yet improving our manners isn't tough at all. It just takes a little thoughtfulness. By understanding the full impact of our resource use, and cutting back on what we consume and throw away, there'll be room enough for us and other species to continue living under this planet's big-domed roof.

CHAPTER 7

WATER RIGHTS:

WHERE YOUR WATER FLOWS AND HOW TO USE LESS

Though scientists have discovered water on the moon, we can't transport it back to Earth like filling up a bucket at the well. For this reason, as well as many others, we should treat our planet's water like the precious and finite resource it is.

Unfortunately, our history of water use is one of loss. Every day in the United States, an estimated 7 billion gallons of clean drinking water leak out of pipes. We aren't much better when we're being more purposeful about water consumption. According to the Environmental Protection Agency, the average American uses 100 gallons a day, while the rest of the world's inhabitants eke by on about 2.5 gallons.

With at least thirty-six states facing anticipated local, regional, or statewide water shortages by 2013, more and more of us will need to change our water ways, and fast. Conserving water, like conserving energy, should become a mantra in your household. Doing so will have the added bonus of damming up the flow of money from your bank account, since the average American spends $474 per year on water bills.

The four biggest water users and losers in a typical home are toilets (26 percent), clothes washers (22 percent), showers (17 percent), and faucets (16 percent). Let's look at these one by one, or drip by drip.

DOWN THE TOILET

An average 22 gallons of water per toilet per day is flushed away. That's a lot of water devoted to waste. Besides not flushing after every pee (if it's yellow, let it mellow) or installing a composting toilet (an option for serious water conservers, though not as radical as you might think), there are a few good ways to conserve.

The old-fashioned way is to place a brick or a full half-gallon bottle in the tank. Doing this will displace an equal amount of water, keeping it from being flushed away and refilled with each flush. It's a great option for renters and those who don't want to spend money on a new low-flow or dual-flush toilet.

Keep in mind that if your toilet was made after 1994, it's already outperforming its predecessors: 1.6 gallons per flush versus an average of 3.5 gallons per flush. Installing a super-efficient low-flow or dual-flush toilet is a great move. Dual-flush toilets save water by giving you the choice of tailoring the flush to what's in the toilet: small flush for number one, big flush for number two. These modern units use less than a gallon for a short flush and about 1.6 gallons for a long flush, and they claim to save 67 percent of the water you would have used with a conventional toilet.

Low-flow toilets, also called high-efficiency, use about 1.3 gallons per flush, though some designs use even less. Toilets that have met the EPA's water-efficient WaterSense standards will save more than 16,500 gallons a year over other toilets.

No matter what type of toilet you have, and whether you rent or own it, keep your ears tuned for leaks, which happen when too much water runs from the tank to the bowl and then to the sewer or septic system. A toilet that proclaims its leak by "running" can waste up to 2 gallons of water a minute. Stealth toilets with silent leaks will cost you up to 7,000 extra gallons of water per month.

To confirm that you have a leak, put a few drops of food coloring in the tank, don't flush, and then check the bowl about ten minutes later. A brightly colored bowl means you've got a leak. Leaks are generally either caused by a bad flapper or faulty fill valve that doesn't shut off when the tank is full. The flapper is the little flappy gizmo at the bottom of the tank that lifts up when you push the flush handle, allowing water to pass through. If it's broken, simply replace it—it'll run you anywhere from $2 to $4. That's a good deal considering you're potentially saving gallons and gallons of water.

GREENWASHING

Washing machines use as much as 55 gallons of water for a normal load. Please see chapter 2 for tips on how to save energy when washing clothes as well as the virtues of newer energy-efficient models. Saving water and energy go hand in hand when it comes to clothes washers. That's because a lot (90 percent of a machine's energy) goes into heating water to wash your clothes. So wash in cold whenever possible, run only full loads, and if you need to upgrade consider a front-loader over a top-loader. It'll use about 40 percent less water than a top-loading machine.

SHOWERHEADS AND FAUCETS: STEMMING THE FLOW

I lump these together since a shower is essentially a big faucet. If a faucet leaks in a slow and steady way—say 100 drops a minute—you'll be wasting about 350 gallons a month. A small stream will consume 2,000 to 2,700 gallons in the same amount of time. Replacing a worn washer or gasket will usually fix the problem, and it's pretty easy to do, especially for do-it-yourselfers. Most leaky showerheads can be fixed by tightening their connection to the pipe sticking out of the shower wall using pipe tape and a wrench.

On the conservation front, upgrading is key. If your showerhead was forged before 1992, it's gushing out about 5 gallons of water each minute you're in the shower. After that year, all showerheads and faucets had to cut that number in half, due to the Energy Policy Act. So convert existing fixtures if you can.

A step beyond is to install an aerating and/or a low-flow showerhead. Aerating showerheads mix air in with the water and are the most common type of low-flow showerhead. Nonaerating low-flow showerheads are available too, and they rely on

WATER CONSERVATION IS ENERGY CONSERVATION

Turn the handle and water comes out of the faucet, but a whole lot goes into getting it to do so. If you live in a rural area, it might be a well and a pump; in urban areas it can be as complex as a network of dams, pumps, massive pipelines, and treatment plants. Either way, getting water to your home and out of the faucet requires energy. Which means that saving water saves energy.

Energy is used to extract and convey water, to treat water so that it's potable, to distribute water, to use water, and to collect and treat wastewater. Even if you're on a simpler well system, energy is used to pump drinkable water into your home and also to pump wastewater into a septic system.

Temperature makes a difference. From an energy perspective, saving cold outdoor water is good. Saving cold indoor water is better. Saving hot indoor water is better still. Why? Expelled indoor water ends up using energy as it's treated in the wastewater system, and hot water requires the additional energy to heat it up in the first place.

Faced with complex energy and water problems, the State of California took a look at the relationship between the two and discovered that supplying municipal water took 19 percent of the electricity used in the state. Seventy-five percent of the cost of water comes from the cost of the electricity used to provide it.

"The nation's water and energy resources are inextricably entwined," noted the California Energy Commission. And so are your home's. Which means it's smart to conserve water no matter where you live, whether it's an arid place like the California desert or a soggy place like the Pacific Northwest coast. Wet or dry, save water and you'll be saving energy.

sending out pulses of water to reduce usage. These cheap fixes can cost in the range of $5 to $30. You'll reduce water usage by 30 percent, and as a bonus you won't sacrifice water pressure either. Or choose one with the WaterSense label, which according to the EPA will save 20,000 gallons of water annually.

LOCATING LEAKS

Household leaks are serious. The yearly amount of water lost in U.S. homes equals the annual water use of Los Angeles, Chicago, and Miami combined—about 1 trillion gallons a year. According to the EPA, an average home will waste about 11,000

Too much of landscaping these days is hard work. Pray for rain. Curse the sun. Haul out the hose. Remember to turn on the sprinkler. Pick up bags of soil amendments at the garden store. Dig up that once flowering shrub because it wilted and died. It doesn't have to be this way.

Instead of fighting the weather, a pretty much useless task when you think about it, why not work with it? Or as Olivier Filippi says in *The Dry Gardening Handbook*, "Rather than changing the growing conditions, what you need to change is the range of plants you grow." This means choosing plants that are adapted to your local environment and acknowledging water conservation and natural ecological processes while you landscape. It's called xeriscaping, and it brings functionality, beauty, and freedom to yard work.

Xeric describes something adapted to a dry habitat, or that which is drought tolerant. The term *xeriscaping* was first coined in the dry state of Arizona, and its practice there allowed landscapers to cut their water use by half. Why worry about water conservation if you're not a desert dweller? Climatologically speaking, all of our gardens are slowly heading south. Xeriscaping is just good practice in a world undergoing climate change.

According to Gayle Weinstein, author of *Xeriscape Handbook*, this progressive practice involves seven principles: (1) integrate irrigation and maintenance into your landscape plan; (2) cut back on the turf and other high-water-use areas; (3) use smart and natural approaches to soil amendments and aeration; (4) pick the right plants for the site; (5) mulch your soil to prevent erosion and reduce evaporative water loss; (6) be efficient when irrigating; and (7) make sure your maintenance routine uses resources efficiently.

The fun part, of course, is picking the plants. Lots of herbs, flowers, shrubs, and trees are xeric. Natives are an excellent option, of course, as they are hardy and by definition suited to your growing conditions. Don't despair if you're in love with vibrant, showy flower gardens. Plenty of aesthetically pleasing species are drought tolerant. Some of my favorites include delicate lavender, hardy stonecrops, and the amazing agaves. Remember to stay away from invasive species—lots of these are xeric too.

To find out more about what not to plant, what to plant, and how best to do it, consult *Dryland Gardening*, by Jennifer Bennett, and the aforementioned *Dry Gardening Handbook*, by Olivier Filippi, and *Xeriscape Handbook* by Gayle Weinstein. You'll discover that you can do more with dry conditions besides curse them.

gallons annually, which would fill a backyard swimming pool. Sleuth out that *drip drop drip*.

As discussed above, you'll find its source in leaking toilet flappers, dripping faucets, and faulty valves. All are easily and cheaply stopped, which means both renters and owners ought to try—especially since doing so can save up to 10 percent on water bills.

Don't forget where the hose meets your outdoor spigot either. You don't have to buy a whole new hose if you've got a leak at this connection; simply replace the nylon or rubber hose washer and ensure a tight connection to the spigot using pipe tape and a wrench.

Finally, to find out if your home is leaking in copious amounts, the EPA recommends two methods. One involves monitoring your winter water usage. A family of four has a definite leak problem if it's using more than 12,000 gallons a month. For quicker results, check out your water meter before and after a two-hour period when you're sure no water is being used. Does it read exactly the same? If not, you've probably got a leak on your hands.

BREAKING THE SPRINKLER HABIT

Our homes, condos, and apartment buildings are situated on a piece of ground, sometimes filled with grass, sometimes shrubs, trees, and other landscaping features, maybe just concrete dotted with potted plants. This isn't breaking news, of course. What might be surprising to learn, however, is that outdoor watering accounts for about a third of all domestic water use—or about 30 gallons a day.

We can get that number down without having to live with dead grass and plants. Aside from planting with native and drought-hardy species, reusing gray water, and practicing the arts of xeriscaping or rainwater harvesting (which we'll get to next), there are simple strategies that any of us can pursue to green up our yards and common areas.

But before we get to those, it's time to admit that we humans have a tendency to overwater. It's an understandable flaw, since intuitively it makes sense that to keep something alive you feed and water it. But drinking and eating in excess isn't healthy—not for you and not for your lawn or plants. The ironic fact is that overwatered

lawns are a much more prevalent problem than thirsty ones. Too much water harms plants by flooding their root systems, which deprives them of oxygen. This is compounded by the reality that most of us live in regions dominated by clay soils that hold onto water, rather than sandy soils that whisk it away into the ground, and so more plants end up dying of overwatering than underwatering. Check your impulse and remember this when you reach for the hose.

When it is appropriate to turn on the spigot, follow these simple practices to reduce your water use.

TIP

HARVESTING WATER FROM THE SKY

Way back when, farmhouses often had cisterns in their basements, which were filled by rain runoff from the roof. Farmers then pumped out the water for use in irrigation. You don't need a farm to use a cistern, which these days can be above or below ground and made from plastic, metal, wood, or concrete. In fact, cisterns are just one of many ways you can catch, store, and use water from the sky. Other options include rain barrels, landscaping ponds, and swales. You can even install a rooftop catchment system that reduces runoff by channeling rainwater through gutters and downspouts to a storage area, where it's available for landscape irrigation.

Simple rain barrels, however, are one of the more popular options and are available from your local garden store or online retailers—sometimes even for free from municipalities (New York City and Philadelphia are just two cities that have giveaway programs), state and county agencies, and green groups. Elevating the barrel (uphill or on a stand) and using a short hose will help improve water pressure.

Pour rainwater in your toilet to flush it. Use it to wash your hair, hands, or clothes. Water your garden. It's possible to drink it yourself if you treat it (the collected water will have run over your roof tiles, through your gutters, and into a stagnant barrel; you never know what it might have picked up along the way).

Or consider making a rain garden. In a low-lying area of your yard, dig out the soil 2 to 4 feet down, mix the soil with mulch, and refill the hole. Build a berm so the water is detained. Then fill the area with water-loving shrubs and plants—if they're native, all the better. Sit back and enjoy. You've just reduced runoff, created a new habitat, and added beauty to a landscape that might otherwise just be a yard.

Take aim: Instead of broadcasting water wildly, target your watering exactly where it's needed. More than 50 percent of water used in landscaping is wasted due to runoff or evaporation. But you can save 50 percent or more water if you use a soaker hose instead of a sprinkler. You'll get similar results with trickle or drip irrigation. The point is to put water where it's needed, not where it's not.

Time it right: Water at the right time of day, when it's cool. As much as 30 percent of water is lost to evaporation during the hot hours. In a desert-type climate, if your sprinkler is running at high noon that number can be as high as 50 percent. Watering during the cool hours (some experts recommend from midnight to 9:00 AM) both prevents evaporation and gives the water a better chance of getting down to the roots.

Go deep: Water thoroughly but less often. You'll use less water and your grass and plants, both garden and ornamental, will like it more. Frequent, brief watering promotes shallow root systems because water is left near the surface. You want root systems at a depth of 3 to 6 inches. To get them, water for ten minutes until the soil is saturated, wait for about thirty minutes, and then water a few minutes more. With this method the water percolates into the soil, quenches the roots, and promotes healthier growth.

Be precise: Your average lawn needs about an inch of water a week to remain green, including rain. Native and drought-tolerant grasses need less. Joe Lamp'l, author of the *Green Gardener's Guide*, wisely explains that "knowing just how much is enough when it comes to watering your lawn and landscape will allow you to use less while achieving the same great results as before." Buy a rain gauge, or make one yourself with a can or jar, to measure how much rain you've received and to figure out how much more you need to water.

Get creative: Use swales, berms, depressions, contours, and ponds to keep water working for you and cycling in areas where you want it. Detaining water stops it from running off and eroding your soil, and it gives it time to infiltrate deeper. It's not difficult to design landscaping to conserve both water and soil. In some case you'll just need a shovel (dig out a swale and create a berm). Or use microclimates. Bunch plants that require more water in the wettest spot of your property. Plant dry-tolerant plants in drier or sandier areas of your lot.

Mulch: Defined as a protective covering of organic matter, usually leaves, straw, or bark, mulch is one of the most versatile additions to your landscape and garden. It saves water by reducing evaporation from the soil. It prevents erosion by keeping rain from hitting bare soil. Deep mulch troughs can provide underground reservoirs that water deeper roots directly. Mulch is good. Spread it around.

Choose wisely: Plant with drought tolerance in mind. Think native and xeric. And make a plan before getting out the shovel. The EPA has a free water-friendly landscape-planning program available for download at their website.

WORKING WITH WATER

Nobody should face a challenge empty handed. Like any chore or responsibility, keeping a small suite of tools readily available will help you in your quest to quench your landscape's thirst accurately and responsibly.

Consider the aforementioned **rain gauge**. As noted above, buy one at a gardening store or use a can or jar. Place whatever container you've chosen in a spot with an unobstructed opening to the sky and simply keep track of how much water accumulates. Chart this progress daily, as the water will evaporate, messing with your results.

If the gauge shows the heavens have let down an inch on the lawn, you have no work to do that week. If the gauge is empty, start up the sprinkler and measure how much you yourself water by using a recycled can—set out your can and monitor it until it holds an inch of water. Then your job is done.

Consider the handy **moisture tester**. For less than $10 you can purchase this little device that resembles a meat thermometer. Push it into the soil at different depths to see if your plant roots are getting the moisture they need.

The familiar **spray nozzle** functions like an off/on switch and in this way prevents water waste.

You probably already own a **hose**. We've talked about the importance of checking for and fixing leaks. Getting off the track of water conservation for a moment, recall the evils of PVC discussed in chapter 4. Most hoses are made out of it, but you can find vinyl-free polyurethane or rubber hoses that are safer for you and your plants to drink from.

A **soaker hose** is an essential piece in your hose repertoire. It facilitates both deep and targeted watering. If you don't want to purchase a special one, you'll achieve the same effect by taking a nail and puncturing a regular hose with holes.

Water is recyclable. Of course, most environmentally aware folks understand that water flows through a cycle of use and re-use on a planetary level. But how many of us have thought about reusing water in our very own homes? If caught and diverted for another purpose, gray water—or leftover water from cooking and washing—both conserves and uses water to its fullest potential. And since dish, shower, sink, and laundry water make up about 50 to 80 percent of residential "waste" water, recycling gray water makes a big splash when it comes to mitigating our homes' draw on this most precious of resources.

The benefits of gray water recycling are many. Besides the obvious plus of lowering your freshwater use, you'll put less strain on septic tanks or sewage treatment plants, you'll conserve energy and use fewer chemicals because less water is treated, and you'll help with groundwater recharge, promote plant growth, and reclaim the otherwise wasted nutrients found in gray water.

While complex gray water systems (like disconnecting the drain on your washing machine and running it outside your house into a filtration system) that are subject to municipal plumbing codes and regulations are embraced by the hardcore, and innovative products abound (such as the Take-Away Sink, which detaches from the pedestal allowing you to directly reuse your leftover tooth-brushing and face-washing water), catching gray water in your house or apartment can be as simple as pouring cooking water in the garden or using shower water collected in a bucket to quench the houseplants' thirst.

Seeing as how an average household wastes 150 gallons of gray water a day, you've got a lot of opportunities to be creative with water reuse. Heather Flores, author of *Food Not Lawns*, recommends wrenching open your sink drain (and covering the outlet pipe to the sewer to prevent gases from entering the house), putting a five gallon bucket beneath the pipe, and gathering the water for later use, including dumping it in the toilet after you've gone pee to trigger a flush.

Gray water with a lot of soap residue can be used if treated by running it thorough an old tub or catchment filled with gravel and planted with water-loving plants like cattails or reeds. The plants and gravel will pull solids and contaminants from the water, which you can then use for your garden.

Attaching a **timer** where your hose and sprinkler connect will allow you to water during the midnight hours without getting out of bed. Programmable, sophisticated timers facilitate complex watering schedules and weekly watering.

For those with deeper pockets, or if you or your landlord are planning a bigger landscaping overhaul, **drip irrigation** is the key to using between 20 to 50 percent less water over conventional in-ground sprinkler systems. Drip irrigation also outperforms regular sprinklers because it eliminates loss to wind, runoff, and evaporation. Instead, the bulk of the water directly reaches the roots because water is allowed to drip slowly in place over the soil or onto the root zone through a network of hoses, pumps, plastic tubing, valves, and pipes.

There is a downside. Aside from the cost, which is likely to run into the thousands of dollars, said system can be a little ugly and overbearing, and the plastic tubing is potentially toxic. Weigh the trade-offs, your landscaping options, and water needs carefully.

GREENING THE COMMONS: WATER CONSERVATION IN SHARED SPACES

Like community gardens (discussed in chapter 6), conserving water benefits from a team effort. You could be just the person to inspire others, including your landlord, to green up the greenspace around your building.

Arm yourself with statistics on the benefits of water conservation. Better yet, live by example. Show your neighbors how easily it's done. Convince your condo association of the merits of watering the lawns at night by doing so with your own—perhaps you'll get a water-saving regulation in place. Invite others to join you in a deep-watering session—a good opportunity to share gossip or catch up on the neighborhood news. Drop some literature off for your landlord on the ease of connecting the building's downspouts to rain barrels (see "Disconnect…and Protect Your Watershed"). Conspicuously dump gray water on the plants of your shared rooftop terrace, and hope someone will ask some questions.

Your roof's ability to shed water is one trait you probably really like about it. Without it your home would be uninhabitable. This impermeability becomes a problem, however, in urban areas, which abound in watertight surfaces: roads, parking lots, sidewalks. It all makes for a mess when it rains. Streets flood, and many cities and towns struggle with combined sewer overflows (CSOs), which happen when all that stormwater gets dumped into the sewage treatment system, and then the sewage treatment plant overflows into the local river.

Retrofit and disconnect your downspouts for about $9 each, and you'll take your roof out of this wet equation. It's simple. Connected gutters run into downspouts that run into a standpipe that in turn is hooked up to your city's sewer system. Disconnect by cutting the gutters off 6 inches above the ground, attaching an elbow to the downspout, and directing the water onto your lawn, garden, or into a rain barrel. If you don't have a rain barrel, make sure you direct the water more than 2 feet away from your house and that the area meant to absorb the water is at least 10 percent of the surface area of your roof. Whatever you do, don't direct your water onto another impermeable surface.

Many municipalities have changed their zoning ordinances to allow for the disconnection of downspouts. (A few still do not allow you to disconnect, fearing stormwater problems on streets and erosion on tightly packed urban lots.) Toronto has taken things a step further by requiring disconnection. The city estimates that 20 percent of the urban area is made up of rooftops and that CSOs could be eliminated if two-thirds of the houses in the city disconnected. Not only that, disconnected downspouts save the city $25 per house in wastewater treatment costs. What's more, only one hundred disconnected houses prevent 2.6 million gallons of stormwater from running into the street and causing erosion annually.

Cities across the country have downspout disconnect deals—Portland, Philadelphia, Milwaukee, Chicago, and Seattle, to name a few, all have programs. Find out if your community has resources that will help you take rainwater off the sewage grid.

CHAPTER 8

TREE HUGGER:
MAKING YOUR HOME FOREST-FRIENDLY

Much of the wood that went into home construction during the past century came from the old-growth forests that used to blanket the continent. Over 97 percent of those forests no longer exist in North America, and, today, protecting this elderly flora as well as letting younger trees age gracefully is one of the priorities of almost every nonprofit dedicated to conservation. Yet old-growth cutting still persists, and one-third of the wood devoted to building products comes from ancient trees. Given the choice between a standing old-growth Douglas fir, hung with ferns and mosses, or a piece of particle board, which would you choose?

All of which makes wood a green remodeling conundrum. In some situations, it may be one of the best choices you can make. Choosing remilled boards from a local barn that was demolished over vinyl flooring is a pretty green choice. But if you decide to buy a teak dining table from an unknown source, you've probably just cost an orangutan his home.

Choice matters. Despite the fact that the size of the average American family is much smaller these days, their average newly built home is twice as large as one built in the sixties. The vast majority of these supersized homes are made of wood— so much wood that it takes about an acre of forest to build just one house. Much of the most destructive logging around the country, and even around the world, feeds this construction, or overconstruction, habit. Despite the fact that the United States is home to only 5 percent of the world's population, Americans consume 15 percent of the world's wood.

When you choose to remodel, you enter this equation. Roughly one-third of the softwood lumber used in the United States goes toward remodeling and refurbishing our buildings and homes. Replacing floors, countertops, and cabinets, or framing up an addition can all lead you to consider wood. A few general principles will help minimize your impact on native forests.

Make plans that create less waste: Choose remodeling dimensions that match lumber dimensions, or choose structural materials that might also look nice as a finished material (a concrete floor is one example, so is an exposed wooden beam).

Consider the entire life cycle of a product: Look at the source of each raw material, transport to your home, manufacturing required, primary use, and whether it can be recycled or reused at the end of its days. Certification of a product as environmentally friendly is helpful—this research has been done for you (see "Certifiably Green" in this chapter).

Avoid volatile organic compounds: These come in the form of wood sealers and finishes as well as the glues in pressboard, particleboard, and plywood (see chapter 4 for more on VOCs).

Reuse materials from building deconstructions: Check out the Building Materials Reuse Association (BMRA), a nonprofit dedicated to the deconstruction and reuse of building materials. BMRA maintains a state-by-state directory that allows you to search for reusable building supplies near your home.

Look for remodeling supplies that are recycled: Glass and concrete are both materials that can incorporate recycled content.

Repair or rehabilitate first: Does your remodeling project require demolition and new materials? Or can any part be spiffed up and made almost good as new?

Third-party certification, or certification by someone other than the buyer or the producer of a product, has become a growing trend in our conscientious consumer culture. Informed consumers want to know the history behind the products they buy. Like any recognizable brand with cachet, certified products satisfy this need by bearing a logo that identifies them as having met stringent standards. Certified wood often sells for a premium because people value the guarantee that a two-by-four came from a sustainably managed forest.

With certification, you get what you pay for. Among certification systems for wood, these are some of the most widely recognized programs:

- **The Forest Stewardship Council (FSC) (www .fsc.org):** The Forest Stewardship Council is an international, independent, nongovernmental organization established to promote the responsible management of the world's forests. FSC-certified operations follow ten principles that protect environmental values, indigenous rights, and a variety of health, safety, occupational, and community standards. Importantly, the organization also backs up these principles with extensive monitoring. FSC has certified forests in eighty-two countries. More than 261 million acres have been FSC-certified around the world, and over 96 million of those acres are in North America.

- **Smartwood (www.smartwood.org):** Initiated in 1989 by the Rainforest Alliance, Smartwood was the very first forest certification program. Smartwood certifies a host of different factors, such as whether or not a forest meets FSC standards, if wood was harvested legally, or if a company's claim that a forest is sequestering carbon is true. The Rainforest Alliance is distinguished by its global reach, with 1,600 partners in sixty countries worldwide, and by experience, with twenty years in the certification business.

- **Cradle to Cradle (C2C) (www.c2ccertified .com):** Cradle to Cradle certification looks at the whole life cycle of a product. C2C evaluates whether a product is made from healthy and environmentally friendly materials, whether the materials are reusable after a product's lifetime, whether energy and water are used efficiently, and whether the manufacturing process is socially responsible. Depending on how well a product measures up, it can earn silver, gold, or platinum ratings. Everything from flooring to furniture can be certified.

- **Sustainable Forestry Initiative (SFI) (www .sfiprogram.org):** This nonprofit certifies wood from forests that meet thirteen performance standards; over 135 million acres in North America are certified. SFI requires that loggers follow best-management practices, that standards for endangered species habitat are met, and that reforestation occurs. SFI only certifies lands in Canada and the United States. A warning: SFI has been criticized for being overly influenced by the timber industry and for being lax in monitoring its certified forests. The U.S. Green Building Council's LEED standards give recognition and credit to construction projects that use wood from forests certified by FSC but not SFI.

Look for a certified green remodeler: If you're not a do-it-yourselfer, there's help. Several nonprofits offer green certification programs for contractors, including the U.S. Green Building Council and the National Association of the Remodeling Industry. The programs are different, but all involve coursework and testing in green principles and practices.

REMODELING WITH RESOURCES IN MIND

Wood is warm, elemental, and beautiful, and there are many good reasons to use it for a remodeling project. Untreated wood requires less industrial processing than some other materials, like glass, tile or concrete. Perhaps it's obvious that using wood is not necessarily environmentally friendly, however. Using wood contributes to deforestation, for every plank or two-by-four was once a living tree.

WOOD WITH STANDARDS

Nonetheless, trees can be harvested and forests can be managed in a responsible and sustainable manner, and you can encourage this through your purchasing power. When you buy wood, buy wood that is certified, preferably by the Forest Steward-ship Council (FSC), which is by far the most ecostringent certification around (see "Certifiably Green" in this chapter for a deeper explanation of certification). FSC-certified oak and maple, two of the most common types of hardwood floors, are widely available, as are FSC Douglas fir floor planks and other domestic and exotic tree species.

If you're framing up an addition or interior wall, FSC-certified softwoods, like Douglas fir and southern yellow pine, are the best choices. Consider low-VOC FSC plywood to green up your remodel as well. Are you installing new cabinets for that long-dreamed of kitchen remodel? FSC products such as finish-grade hardwoods, like maple and poplar, are also on the market. Are you ripping out those dingy Formica plastic laminate countertops for something more natural? FSC-wood is also milled into counters. Your dream kitchen will be even greener if the FSC wood used is from a local forest, eliminating the energy used to ship it to your doorstep.

SALVAGED MATERIAL

Continuing on the topic of reuse, wood is built for it. Why fell a standing tree when gently used boards or even finished products like countertops and cabinets are available for a second or third life? Consider reusing a floor. Perfectly functional and beautiful hardwood floors can often be scavenged from a demolition project or another homeowner's remodeling "waste" (Habitat for Humanity runs a number of ReStores with reusable building supplies).

"Reclaimed" wood is a prettier name for this waste, and these days it's not too hard to find highly marketable reclaimed wood, much of it with romantic pasts—everything from old-character boards from a demolished tobacco barn in North Carolina to wood milled from recovered trees that sank to the bottom of rivers and lakes during the logging booms of the last century.

Columbia Riverwood is one company that salvages sunken logs. The outer several inches are saturated with grit that requires special milling, but the core wood is well preserved by submersion in the water. The Rainforest Alliance has a program to monitor reclaimed wood providers to make sure their claims aren't bogus. The organization's Rediscovered Wood and Underwater Salvage certification verifies the sourcing of reclaimed wood and ensures that it's harvested without harm to the environment, workers, or the surrounding community.

LIKE WOOD, BUT NOT

Of course, another way to save trees is to choose a different material altogether. There is a tree that keeps on giving, because its yield doesn't require a chainsaw or axe.

The **cork oak** grows in the dry, sunny Mediterranean countries of Spain and Portugal, where a centuries-old tradition of harvesting its bark has kept forests of this tree intact. The bark is stripped and then grows back—up to twenty times during a tree's life cycle, or about every ten years. Harvests are made from both plantations and wild cork forests, and conservation organizations like the World Wildlife Fund believe that encouraging the purchase of sustainably harvested cork products (FSC certifies them!) helps keep the wild forests, and the species they support, intact.

Oenophiles have long been aware of the virtue of cork in stopping up a good bottle of wine. It also makes for great stomping grounds for your family's feet. As flooring, cork is extremely resilient. Cork floors in the New York Public Library have held up for over fifty years.

Indeed, the virtues of cork flooring are voluminous: it absorbs vibration and noise; it's a good shock absorber and is thus easy on your feet; it has natural antiallergenic and insect-resistant properties as well as being moisture, mold, and flame resistant (all of which reduces the need for chemical additives); and it's easy to both clean (a bucket and mop will do the job) and install (you have your choice of slabs, tiles, rolls, and floating tongue-and-groove planks; we found this last option great for our laundry room).

As always, beware of added chemicals. Avoid cork flooring that uses fiberboard panels as backing and VOC-containing glues. According to the U.S. Green Building Council, you can do this by purchasing solid cork tiles, products with no added formaldehyde content, and by using tile adhesives with no- or low-VOC glues.

Bamboo is another green substitute for "traditional" wood that measures up in terms of performance, beauty, and longevity. You'll find a wide variety of forms, including flooring, butcher-block style countertops, and cabinets for your remodeling needs. Bamboo boards look like wood—they are flexible, dense, and durable, even harder than red oak—but, in fact, bamboo is a grass. It grows quickly, with typical harvests in four or five years. When done right, it's grown without pesticides, and this is usually the case.

Nonetheless, overharvesting is a problem, especially in some areas of China, where much of this grass grows and where its harvesting is unregulated. Luckily, FSC certifies both boards and plywood, so look for the label, which ensures more sustainable management.

Bamboo's sustainability can be called into question, however, when you consider that it's shipped from China or other faraway places, making for a big carbon footprint on your new bamboo floors. Also, unrolling all that round bamboo grass into flat boards requires a labor- and energy-intensive process.

So in this case, as with many others, weigh your options. If this grass is greener or more economical in your home, be sure to find it in a formaldehyde-free form. Bamboo requires laminate and glue to hold it together, and many producers use urea-formaldehyde glue, which is of course bad for indoor air quality. A few suppliers claim to sell low- or no-VOC bamboo floors (e.g., Bamboo Mountain and

Green Floors). One stellar brand is EcoTop which manufactures a 50 percent bamboo fiber, 50 percent postconsumer recycled paper countertop, with a water-based binding system in lieu of conventional glues.

GREEN MOSAIC: STONE, CONCRETE, AND TILE

Wood or woody substances aren't the only natural materials available for green remodels. **Locally sourced stone** is an attractive and durable option for countertops and is far cheaper than marble or granite, which are usually imported anyway and thus colored with an abundance of carbon. In contrast, most areas of the country have local quarries, stonecutters, and masons. Find these and other experts in your community to make sure your stone is responsibly quarried from an environmentally appropriate location. *Local* doesn't necessarily mean *green*, but chances are your hometown quarry has more stringent environmental regulations than those overseas.

If modern and/or man-made materials better suit your remodeling tastes, you don't have to feel left out. *Natural* doesn't have the corner on green materials. **Concrete** is a good example. What could be more unnatural? And yet concrete can be an environmentally friendly material for floors and countertops.

Yes, the raw materials are resource intensive, the production process takes a good deal of energy, and it's not exactly biodegradable, but it can be greened. It's obviously durable and also easy to clean; and, if purchased locally, it has a somewhat lower carbon footprint. Plus, if concrete is your "finished" floor, you've saved resources in the form of materials that you might have placed on top of it, like carpeting or wood. Since it conducts and retains heat well, concrete is a great match for in-floor radiant heating, which can be a highly efficient way to heat your home.

The basic ingredients of concrete are usually a mix of gravel, sand, water, and Portland cement. About 1 ton of carbon dioxide is produced for each ton of concrete made with Portland cement. But a slightly more environmentally friendly concrete utilizes fly ash instead. I say *slightly* because fly ash is a byproduct of dreaded coal-fired power plants. We'd live in a better (and cooler world) without coal energy, but as long as it exists you can help mitigate its impacts by diverting fly-ash that would otherwise end up in landfills. In comparison to Portland cement, fly-ash concrete actually produces fewer global warming gases and uses less water.

There are plenty of other materials that can be salvaged from the waste stream and mixed into concrete, adding aesthetically pleasing accents to that modern gray: mix in recycled or reclaimed glass or ceramic for a bit of color. Two companies are among a handful that provide solid examples of this ecomixing. Brooklyn-based IceStone mixes concrete with 100 percent postconsumer recycled glass. The company takes its recycling a step further by accepting its older concrete products and grinding them into reusable material for future countertops destined for another kitchen. On the other coast, Squak Mountain Stone is manufactured in Washington State. It's made with over 50 percent recycled content, including waste paper, crushed glass, fly ash, and cement, and illustrates that giving waste a second life transforms it into something functional, beautiful, and planet-friendly.

Recycling is also key to transforming **tile** into a green remodeling material for your countertops or floors. There are many sources of tile, both ceramic and glass, that are made from postindustrial waste and postconsumer waste. Not only does using recycled materials keep glass and ceramics out of the waste stream, it also saves energy, as making tiles from recycled products uses less energy than making them from raw materials.

Choose recycled glass tile made from window glass, windshields, and bottles. One company, Fireclay Tile, has a line of tile called Bottlestone that's 80 percent postconsumer waste—that's empty bottles to you and me—generated near the manufacturing site in Northern California. The company's Debris series incorporates waste glass, granite dust, and used sandblasting abrasives to make ceramic tiles. No matter what company or tile you choose, be sure to seek out low-VOC mastics and glues to hold the tiles in place. Unlike vinyl, tile in and of itself won't off-gas dangerous chemicals, but most conventional glues associated with it will.

Another material that is unlike vinyl, but is often mistaken for vinyl, is **natural linoleum**. Made from renewable materials like linseed oil, pine rosin, limestone dust, cork and jute, natural linoleum is a virtually chemical-free alternative to vinyl for floors and countertops. Natural linoleum was a much more common product fifty years ago but was usurped by vinyl. Now, with increased attention to health and environmental concerns, and recognition of vinyl's toxicity, natural linoleum can reclaim its place on your countertop.

THE NATURE OF FURNITURE

Even the most austere Thoreauvian disciple's home is usually furnished: a table or desk, a simple chair, perhaps a bed frame. Quite a few of us claim a much longer list of furniture items—end tables, side tables, coffee tables, nightstands and plant stands, desks and dressers, book shelves and clothing shelves, cribs and cradles. When we move out, these once essential items are often discarded. When we move in, we replace what we previously threw away with other things that more often than not are destined for the dump too. In fact, discarded furniture is the fourth-greatest contributor to landfills. It accounted for more than 18 million pounds of waste in 2006, the most of any durable good. Worse yet, a recent report by the Environmental Investigation Agency estimated that 10 percent of furniture used in the United States probably comes from illegal sources—like an officially protected rainforest.

And yet, the impulse to furnish your home, to make it feel habited and habitable, shouldn't be shunned, nor does it have to be wasteful. There are plenty of creative, inexpensive, and stylish ways to keep outdated couches from being tossed on the street or mahogany trees from ending up as five-piece dinette sets.

STEP 1: REPAIR RATHER THAN REPLACE

If the wood is scratched, worn, or water stained, try stripping, sanding, and restaining it with a low- or no-VOC stain. And here's a plug for old, well-made furniture: Traditionally, furniture was made to last a lifetime, and if it became broken or worn it was easily repaired. One reason this is so is that older furniture is often made with all wood joinery—instead of adhesives—making fixes a simpler affair. Even furniture held together with nails is relatively easy to repair compared to furniture held together with glues. (The lack of adhesives means you'll get fewer VOCs with that rocker as well.)

Such a hand-crafted approach to making furniture also encourages a more sustainable relationship between you and your chair. If you see it as an heirloom rather than a disposable commodity you're more likely to take better care of it, take it with you, and buy less new furniture overall (saving money in the long run, even if that chair costs more up front, and saving planetary resources too).

This philosophy is applicable to upholstered items as well. If you're tired of that old print, or if the couch is looking a little grungy because you can't keep the dog from sleeping on it, you don't need to start looking for department-store sales. Give that couch a facelift by reupholstering it with a stylish new fabric. You could go vintage, retro, modern, or organic—just try to make sure your choice bypasses chemicals (plant-based fibers rarely have them) and is easy on the earth. The Association for Contract Textiles has an online life-cycle evaluation tool for its members that sheds light on a particular textiles' environmental impact—for example, resources used, toxic emissions involved, and biodegradability. In a similar effort, the Institute for Market Transformation to Sustainability has approved a voluntary sustainable textile standard, with a precise rating system (sustainable, silver, gold, and platinum).

STEP 2: WHEN IT'S TIME TO BUY, BUY USED

Call it antique or secondhand or previously loved. It's furniture that had a life before you but is quite willing to be of service in your house or apartment today. Not only does such furniture tend to be cheaper (there are of course expensive antiques), it's not difficult to find. Peruse your local paper's classified ads or get online and search Craigslist for more FSBO items in your city or region. Many schools or universities discard furniture, appliances, and fixtures at the end of the term—see if there are educational opportunities for you. Join Freecycle, a network of over 4,800 groups and 6 million members, where you can find used stuff for free and get rid of your own used stuff for the same price. Even eBay has a "green team" that promotes the idea that the most ecofriendly product is one that already exists.

Step 2 has a part B, and that is to make sure that your own unwanted furniture makes it to the secondhand market instead of being tossed in the waste stream. Classified ads don't cost much (they're free on Craigslist), and you'd be surprised how much truth there is to that saying about one person's trash being another person's treasure. Freecycle in particular exemplifies this—I haven't had a single item I've offered up go unwanted. Or perhaps your local municipality can help facilitate an exchange. New York City government is so concerned about waste in general and furniture waste in particular that the city created a "Wastele$$" program, which enables Gothamites to sell, donate, or find used stuff.

Do keep in mind that used furniture often contains particleboard, especially if it's of the mass-produced variety. In general, particleboard should be avoided because of its propensity to offgas VOCs (though it may have gassed out by the time it reaches your home) and because it's just not as long lasting as something made of solid wood. But if you're extending a garage-sale bookcase's life by trucking it back to your apartment, you've made an undoubtedly solid green choice.

STEP 3: IF YOU MUST BUY NEW, BUY GREEN

Take this step only if steps 1 and 2 aren't an option, because any new piece of wood furniture means felled trees. Look for certification to ensure credentials (see "Certifiably Green" in this chapter). The Forest Stewardship Council certifies wood included in furniture as well as particular furniture manufacturers (it hosts a database of furniture manufacturers who use FSC-certified wood).

There are actually quite a few environmentally sensitive furniture manufacturers, in part because the demand for sustainable furniture is growing—their market share was 8 percent in 2009, which may not seem like much, but that's twice the level of 2008. As the furniture business is an $8.3 billion industry, there's a lot of opportunity to make a big impact. One nonprofit organization is making it easier for consumers to do just that. The Sustainable Furnishings Council (SFC) promotes green practices in the furniture industry, including among manufacturers, distributors, and retailers. Both the Rainforest Alliance and World Wildlife Fund have begun working with SFC, lending green credibility. The group's website is most useful for its searchable database of green manufacturers and retailers.

When you've hit the streets, real or virtual, in search of ecofurniture, be prepared with a list of questions for your friendly and hopefully helpful retailer. He or she should be able to tell you who made your furniture, what products went in to it, what's in the finish, and where the wood came from. These are a few furniture companies that an ecohip salesperson might recommend: Team 7 is an Austrian company that makes modern furniture lines with sustainable wood and low-VOC finishes and glues; EcoBalanza designs and manufactures ecofriendly upholstered furniture with FSC-certified wood, natural latex foam, and organic hemp, cotton, and wool fabric; Furnature makes furniture with certified wood and organic textiles, with a special focus on providing safe furniture for folks with chemical sensitivities; and the Q Collection and Q Collection Junior (the company's line of furniture for kids) take ecomaterials to the limit, using everything from certified solid wood to water-based adhesives to recycled metals to organic cotton batting to vegetable fabric dyes. Sound comfy?

CHAPTER 9

THE PITFALLS OF LANDFILLS:
STEPPING OUT OF THE WASTE STREAM

Out of sight, out of mind is either wishful thinking or willful ignorance. When you throw something away, it ends up landing somewhere. That "somewhere" might be the roadside or a parking lot or a more sanctioned place like a landfill. Yet even the sanctity of a landfill is an illusion. They all eventually leak into the environment, and since many landfills have been repositories for hazardous waste, that leaching is often toxic, leading to contaminated groundwater and drinking water. Many chemicals, from mercury to arsenic, have been found in wells contaminated by leaking landfills. Landfill space is limited too. Many are full to overflowing, causing waste to be shipped great distances to other available space. But nobody wants a dump in their backyard.

What's more, landfills are the largest human-related source of methane in the United States—accounting for a whopping 34 percent. Methane is produced as open dumps and waste decompose under low-oxygen, or anaerobic conditions. The gas is particularly problematic because it's twenty times more effective at trapping heat in the atmosphere than carbon dioxide. All this gives the act of taking the trash out to the curb a whole new meaning.

In fact, every garbage can left out for pickup is actually the equivalent of seventy-one cans of waste created in logging, mining, agriculture, oil and gas exploration, and the processes used to convert raw materials into finished products and their packaging. Because Americans waste or cause to be wasted nearly 1 million pounds of materials per person per year, that's a lot of cans in toto. Take into consideration that about 55 to 65 percent of municipal solid waste comes from our houses and apartments, and home sweet home starts to smell a little stinky.

LESS GARBAGE IN, LESS GARBAGE OUT

Every holiday season, economic pundits ponder how much we spend and, from these numbers, draw conclusions about the health of our economy. Buying lots of stuff is good; if there's measly spending in December, our society is on an ambulance ride to the ER. Yet if we considered all the effects of our hyper spending—overwhelming debt, depleted natural resources, buying as a substitute for true happiness—we might not see purchasing power as an indicator of health and vitality.

Buy less: The truth is, we should buy less stuff. Less stuff means less trash (and less energy and resource consumption). If you're not bringing bags of goodies home, you're not throwing bags of goody leftovers and goody packaging away. It's that simple. Less stuff also means less clutter, which frees up your mind for better focusing and your body for better functioning, or so the spiritual home-organization consultants advise. Prioritize what you *actually* need, lessen the amount you buy, and you've taken the simplest step in reducing your home's garbage.

Buy local and buy in bulk: When you do buy, buying from the shop on Main Street often reduces the need for packaging that's used for shipping. Buying in bulk also cuts back on the amount of packaging that ends up being tossed. Why is packaging such a big deal? One out of every ten dollars you spend buying stuff goes to disposable packaging. Packaging makes up about 65 percent of your home's trash. And about one-third of a typical dump is made up of packaging material.

Buy products made from recycled materials: Any given item's environmental impact generally occurs in the extracting of raw materials and the manufacturing process. Once it's on the shelf, it has already stamped out its footprint. Buying recycled goods makes that footprint a little smaller.

Borrow rather than buy: Your neighbor is probably good for more than a cup of sugar. Or see what lending organizations exist in your town. When I was a graduate student in Missoula, Montana, my household had a membership to our neighborhood's tool-lending library. Similar opportunities may be available in your neighborhood. If not, go to LendList.org, which helps you organize a group made up of members who list what they're willing to lend. LendList.org keeps track of who's borrowed what.

Reuse: Before you throw away, before you even recycle, reuse. Reuse cans, bottles, and plastic containers for garden or art projects or storage. Wrap presents in newspaper or previously used wrapping paper. And don't forget to compost organic material (see chapter 6).

Finally, a word on junk mail. In delivering an average of 560 pieces of junk mail to each American, junk mail purveyors use 100 million trees, waste eight hours of your time, and use as much energy as 2.8 million cars use in a year. There are ways to put a stop to this. Sign up with Directmail.com's National Do Not Mail List, a free service that removes you from most commercial mailing lists. Or pay for a service called Mailstopper from Tonic, which promises to get rid of 90 percent of your junk mail in ninety days. Catalog Choice prevents unwanted catalogs from piling up in your mailbox. The organization claims to have helped remove more than 85 million unwanted catalogs a year from the mail, saving more than 192,000 trees and preventing 82 million pounds of greenhouse gas emissions, the equivalent of removing about 7,500 cars from the road. Stop receiving those unwise credit-card offers in the mail by signing up at OptOutPrescreen.com. Last but not least, these days with a little useful invention called the Internet, you probably don't need a phone book. At YellowPagesGoesGreen.org, you can drop your name from the phone book distribution list, allowing you to opt out of receiving one of the 540 million unsolicited phone books that are sent to Americans every year.

ONE'S PERSON'S JUNK IS ANOTHER'S TREASURE

Salvage is a sexy word for reuse, and it's a great way to remodel green. According to the *Waste Business Journal*, in 2008 the United States generated about 143.5 million tons of building-related construction and demolition debris. Only 28 percent was reused, recycled, or sent to waste-to-energy facilities. From all this "waste," remodelers might have found lumber, millwork, windows, cabinets, plumbing fixtures, lighting fixtures, countertops, appliances, tile, piping, and hardware—full of character, in styles retro, modern, and antique, and in most case at lower prices than brand-new materials. Incorporating salvaged goods into your remodel not only diverts these dusty jewels from the waste stream, it saves resources and the energy required to manufacture new stuff. The benefits are so huge, that Leadership in Energy and Environmental Design (LEED), the most popular and respected certification for green building, will give certification points for incorporating reclaimed materials into a building.

Finding salvaged stuff isn't tough. Talk to the friendly folks at your local dump and ask if they ever receive building materials you could lay claim to. Look for houses under construction and get permission to dumpster-dive. Call up a few local remodeling contractors and find out what they do with older fixtures, lights, doors, windows, or sinks that they've replaced with newer items. You might be able to strike a deal. Habitat for Humanity sells salvaged material from demolished buildings at ReStores throughout the country.

If you can't find what you need through on-the-ground sleuthing, the Internet is a treasure trove of salvaged goods. The Building Materials Reuse Association's directory of members contains many retailers who stock reclaimed building materials. You'll also find them at Freecycle and Craigslist; the latter even has a separate section for your salvage-remodeling needs.

Finally, in many towns and cities across the country, you'll find architectural salvage stores and warehouses dedicated to the resale of goods from demolitions and remodeling projects. I was able to uncover quite a few just by searching the web. Here's a taste: Dixie Salvage, Fort Payne, Alabama; Recycling the Past, Barnegat, New Jersey; the Salvage Barn, Iowa City, Iowa; ReNew Building Materials and Salvage, Brattleboro, Vermont; Urban Ore, Berkeley, California; ReSource, Boulder and

Fort Collins, Colorado; and Second Use, Seattle, Washington. Your community might have one of these fantastic salvage centers, places for you to lose yourself for a few hours and, perhaps, to imagine a creative use for that funky chandelier.

THE BIG SORT: HOW AND WHAT TO RECYCLE

Once you've taken a vow to create less waste in the first place, your next assignment is to recycle whatever and whenever you can. Recycling has many cheerleaders. The Natural Resources Defense Council sums it up this way on its website: "Recycling is one of the most feel-good and useful environmental practices around. The benefits go way beyond reducing piles of garbage—recycling protects habitat and biodiversity, and saves energy, water, and resources such as trees and metal ores. Recycling also cuts global warming pollution from manufacturing, landfilling and incinerating."

And one commenter to *Grist* magazine gently reminds us, "Recycling isn't a hassle, it's a privilege."

Odds are your city or town has a local curbside recycling program (if not, visit Earth911 online to find one near you). These things have sprouted up like mushrooms recycling nutrients on the forest floor. Before 1973, no curbside recycling programs existed in the United States. By 2006, about 8,660 programs were collecting cans and bottles across the nation. The programs have played a part in upping our numbers: from 5 percent of waste recycled in 1970 to 32.5 percent in 2010.

You can turn that number even higher in your home, apartment, and apartment building. Make recycling convenient. Put bins in multiple places around the house or in common spaces—kitchen, laundry room, home office, garage—and use different bins that follow your city's recycling policies so you don't have to sort it out later. Good news, though. Advances in sorting technology have allowed many communities to shift to commingled or single-stream recycling. In this system built for the laissez-faire crowd, you don't have to sort recyclables at all—just throw them all in a single bin. In some areas where commingled recycling programs have been initiated, recycling rates have increased by 30 percent.

Recycling has expanded beyond the world of bottles, cans, plastic, and paper, although it's still critically important to give these items an opportunity for rebirth.

For a little inspiration in the art of deconstruction and reuse, visit the ReBuilding Center in Portland, Oregon (or check out their website, www.rebuildingcenter.org). Started by a volunteer group, in 1998, the center has grown into the Northwest's largest provider of reusable building materials recovered from demolitions. A stroll through the warehouse uncovers doors, windows, molding, tiles, sinks, tubs, pipes, and every other construction material imaginable, all saved from the dark fate of being landfilled.

The center gets its merchandise from donations (it offers a free pick-up service) and from demolitions managed by its own DeConstruction Services program. DeConstruction Services dismantles buildings or rooms that might otherwise face conventional demolition. For about the same price, the center takes apart buildings by hand and salvages materials for reuse. The ReBuilding Center estimates that its deconstruction of an average house results in these benefits as well: 2,400 gallons of water and thirty-three mature trees saved; over 900 hours of living-wage employment provided; and greenhouse gases—equivalent to those produced by almost three cars used for over a year—kept from being released.

The fruits of the center's demolition labor are recycled and sold at the warehouse. Some pieces are used to build new ReFind furniture. Everything from tables to picture frames is reconstructed out of old construction waste, including reclaimed old-growth Douglas fir from the Portland area. Each piece has a story to tell.

Building community is also a core part of the center's work, and there are numerous volunteer opportunities as well as workshops and classes on how to safely and creatively work with used building materials. But maybe the most impressive aspect of the ReBuilding Center is that it is ReTurning a profit. Aside from some initial start-up grants from nonprofits and local government, the center stays in the black through its sales and services, keeping the cycle of reuse spinning.

Here are a few creative ways to expand the recycling paradigm in your home.

Media: Keep your unwanted media products from piling up in your closet or getting mixed in the trash. If you've seen it, read it, or heard it too many times, SwapTree and BarterBee are just two sites that allow you to swap books, CDs, DVDs, and other media with people around the country. BookMooch and PaperBackSwap focus exclusively on trading books for books. And don't forget that you can help keep used-book stores (the best kind) thriving by selling or trading back books. Charities are another fine way to share the love of reading with others.

Electronics: About 70 percent of the toxic waste in landfills is attributable to e-waste—all those unwanted computers, cords, motherboards, MP3 players, and cell phones. Since these electronics contain heavy metals like lead and mercury, it's important to recycle them and keep them out of the environment, water supplies in particular. The EPA estimates that as much as 40 percent of the lead in landfills comes from electronics.

Some manufacturers have trade-in or buy-back programs for their electronics that provide cash, store credit, or tax incentives. Other companies will accept electronics for recycling. Still other manufacturers will refurbish old machines for use in schools or nonprofits. Recyclers recoup more than 100 million pounds of materials from e-waste every year, and some of those metals and plastics can be made into new machines. Even old CDs can be recycled.

Sign up with one of the many places that will help you start your e-cycling quest: Gazelle offers cash for recyclable e-waste and has partnered with Costco to put drop boxes at retail stores. Earth911 has a searchable database of drop-off spots for recyclables. CollectiveGood accepts donations of cell phones and will either fix them for someone else's use or recycle them. GreenDisk will also recycle old electronics, even the small stuff like cables. Some 1,500 post offices accept electronics for recycling; call and find out if yours is one of them. Newer computer products can find a home at TechSoup, a nonprofit that helps provide technology to schools and nonprofits. The National Cristina Foundation looks for new homes for old computers and software. Finally, the EPA lists its "Plug-In to eCycling Partners"—companies with their own trade-in programs, such as Dell and HP.

A word of caution: Some recyclers melt electronic components, a practice that has health risks if not done properly, and some send collected electronics overseas to countries with lax environmental laws. Your goal is to have your recycled technology used as technology or handled in a responsible way. Scrapping it for raw materials should be a recycler's last resort. Ask any company or recycler you're working with what they do with the electronic device and where it ultimately goes. To keep tabs on the proper recycling of e-waste, check out the Basel Action Network, a nonprofit fighting to make sure the lead, cadmium, and mercury in technology waste is handled responsibly.

Furniture: The EPA reported that 8.8 million tons of furniture was thrown away in 2005. There's no reason not to recycle grandma's old chair. The same places you might look for scoring used furniture (see chapter 8) are good places to unload items you're no longer into. Freecycle and Craigslist will both help you offload that couch you no longer want in your living room. Throwplace.com, which bills itself as the Internet's landfill alternative, will help you match your used furniture (and just about any other item) with a new home—charities, businesses, and individuals. Don't forget the old standbys: Goodwill and the Salvation Army pick up used furniture in good condition and sell it to fund their charitable work.

Clothing: On average an American throws away 68 pounds of clothing or textiles per year. Cleaning out your closet? Those sweaters and slacks deserve another home. Dress for Success takes donated business wear and redistributes it to those who can't afford the finery. The Glass Slipper Project will take unwanted dresses for promgoers who can't afford new ones. Even if it is beyond rewearing, your local Goodwill will take your used clothing and ship it to recycling centers that will recycle the fibers.

Swapstyle is a online location for fashion exchanges. Or organize your own clothing swap (a.k.a. Naked Lady Party) with your girlfriends. (Over the years, I have acquired some of my favorite shirts at these swaps.) Guys, there's no holding you back if you want to trade t-shirts. Or if your creative juices are flowing and you're into modifying clothing, consider finding or hosting a Swap-O-Rama-Rama event where like-minded folks bring clothes, learn how to retailor clothing, and do the work at on-site sewing stations.

Toys and kids' stuff: You know the story. The must-have-best-thing-in-the-whole-wide-world eventually gets shoved in the back of the closet because your child has moved on. Zwaggle takes donations of kids' stuff and finds a new home for it. Each donation you make earns you points toward zwaggling your way into a new traded toy. Or avoid this problem altogether. Become a member of Baby-Plays—essentially the Netflix for toys. You get a boxful each month and then send toys back when your kid is bored.

Building and remodeling waste: As noted earlier in the chapter, building waste is a ton of waste. In fact, each year more than 100 million tons get junked. Much of it could be repurposed: used drywall scraps, for example, can be made into new drywall. If you aren't doing the work yourself, make sure the contractor you hire hauls the waste to a recycling facility. The most likely recyclables are concrete, drywall, wood, metal, and shingles. Habitat for Humanity has many recycled materials outlets across the country. The Construction Materials Recycling Association has a directory of recyclers as well.

THE DEAL WITH PLASTICS

Seven is a lucky number in most cultures. It's the average number of digits easily recalled in a row—hence seven-digit phone numbers. Though recycling plastics can be tricky, fortunately they come in numbered varieties from 1 through 7. These numbers correspond to the kinds of resins in the plastic and are also helpful in identifying which plastics can be recycled, which contain estrogen emulators, and which come with (mostly) no strings attached.

I say *mostly* because all plastic has its environmental costs. Most plastic manufacturing requires petroleum—so much that just the plastic bags we throw away account for 12 million barrels of oil per year. And for all practical purposes, the plastics you use today will be kicking around the environment forever. Too, who knows what health effects will be "discovered" in the future? Also, most plastic recycling is actually downcycling; the plastic is made into another product that can't then be recycled. This is a long way of saying that before you recycle, reduce your use of plastics.

The first and most important consideration to make with any plastic is its safety. Numbers 1, 2, 4, and 5 are considered safe. They are not *known* to leach any chemicals that threaten human health. No. 3 (vinyl or polyvinyl chloride) contains phthalates, which are hormone-disrupting chemicals (see more on the evils of vinyl in chapter 4). Avoid it if you can. No. 6 is thought to contain toxins that leach when heated, and no. 7 is a catchall that includes many types of plastic materials, including potentially those with bisphenol A (BPA). You've probably heard of BPA and watched as retailers recently phased it out of many of their products. It's a chemical thought to cause problems with every organ from the heart to the brain; it's particularly bad for babies and young children because their bodies are still developing, and disruption or imbalances in the body's chemistry can have lasting effects. Some plastics are advertised as "microwave safe," but that label doesn't necessarily have your health in mind. It means the plastic can survive microwaving, but it's no guarantee the plastic won't leach carcinogens.

Which plastics are recyclable? The better question is which plastics are more easily recyclable. And this may depend on your local curbside recycling program or municipality. Some recyclers will take a specific plastic—even, for example, the difficult-to-pin-down no. 7. Some will accept that no. 7 with different plastics all mixed together, because they sort them at the end. Other programs will only accept plastic that is sorted by you. And some might not accept no. 7 plastic at all. You'll need to educate yourself on how it works in your community. Here are some general guidelines:

- **Plastic no. 1,** or polyethylene terephthalate (PETE), is the most commonly recycled and recyclable plastic. PETE can be recycled into other food and beverage bottles. It can also be downcycled into things like deli trays, carpets, clothing, and car parts. Most curbside recyclers and municipalities accept PETE.
- **Plastic no. 2,** or high-density polyethylene (HDPE), is a heavier plastic found in detergent bottles and milk jugs. It can be recycled back into detergent bottles, construction-grade imitation lumber, and, ironically enough, recycling bins, among other things.
- **Plastic no. 3,** vinyl or polyvinyl chloride (PVC), is not readily recyclable—and it's hazardous to boot. If you have vinyl or PVC, some specialty companies will accept it, though it's most likely downcycled into some other product like playground equipment or flooring tiles. Avoid bringing this plastic into your home.
- **Plastic no. 4** is low-density polyethylene. It's used in sandwich bags, grocery bags, and wrapping films, among other things. It's not recycled in most municipal programs. Many large grocery store chains are developing programs to take back the plastic no. 4 bags, however.
- **Plastic no. 5** is polypropylene. It can be recycled into car parts and packaging. Municipal programs are not likely to accept no. 5, but Whole Foods has recently partnered with Preserve Inc. on a campaign called Gimme 5. Preserve collects no. 5 plastics for recycling into new products like toothbrushes and tableware.
- **Plastic no. 6** is more widely accepted for recycling. It's polystyrene, often found in cups and packing peanuts, and can be reprocessed and downcycled into packaging and other products.
- **Plastic no. 7** is a mixed bag, made up of rare blends or combinations of resins. No. 7 is the least recyclable plastic and, coupled with the fact that many no. 7s contain BPA, this means you should reduce your use.

Recycling caps and lids isn't easy. Lids tend to be a different plastic than their bottles, and since mixed plastics can't be recycled by many programs, think twice before throwing them in the same bin. Lids and caps don't bear the numerical symbol that helps you determine how and whether you can recycle them. Some companies, like Aveda, will take back their own lids (they know they're no. 5). And some recycling centers do take lids. They sell them to companies that crush them, sort them, and run them through a pool (different density plastics will float at different levels). Recyclers can then separate out each kind of plastic. Otherwise, find a creative, artistic reuse for caps and lids.

ALL TOGETHER NOW: HOW EVERYONE CAN EMBRACE THE BINS

Not owning the home you live in may make some green renovations more difficult, but recycling shouldn't be one of them. A 2001 survey by the EPA found renters no less likely to recycle than homeowners. Homeowners barely held the lead, with 16 percent wanting to recycle and renters closing the gap at 14.6 percent. So even though homeowners may recycle more, renters still want to recycle, and with about the same fervor. There are 35 million renters in the United States; 5 million are primed to recycle. Thirty million more could be convinced. It could be the makings of a movement.

Start out green if you can. Look for rentals where recycling is obviously going on. Ask your prospective landlord if his or her building is a part of a program. And pick an apartment where you've got space for your own bins—a porch or patio makes for a good spot. Lacking that, there are great interior recycling bins that are both attractive and designed for small spaces.

If the apartment is just perfect in all other respects, but the landlord isn't, it's time to sharpen up your tools of persuasion. If he argues that space is a problem, take a walk through the building together and point out easy-to-use locations such as the mail room, laundry room, utility room, garage, space next to the dumpster, or stairwell. If that fails, try the economic angle: by reducing the amount of trash, he might reduce the rate he pays for garbage. If he counters that recycling rates are too expensive, point out that some tenants would be more likely to stay in a building with sustainable practices, thus saving him the cost of high turnover rates. In fact, with the large number of vacant rental properties in this buyer's market, you could work solo, or even better together with other tenants, to negotiate green requirements like recycling into your lease.

Still no go? Know the law before you give up. Many states and cities require that recycling be available. Wisconsin does, and county offices are outfitted to help landlords comply, with everything from site visits by an expert to labels for sorting containers. Portland, Chicago, New York, and Seattle, among other far-sighted cities, all require landlords to provide tenants with opportunities to recycle.

Make recycling easy too. Put bins next to common garbage cans so that residents have a choice about where to put that junk mail. Make signs listing what's accepted and what's not, and post educational material touting the saintly virtues of recycling. Or hold who-has-the-smallest-garbage-bag-this-week contests—the winner gets his or her beverage of choice, in a recyclable bottle of course.

CHAPTER 10

THE BLUEPRINT

Physically, your home, no matter how big or small, is a built structure divided into rooms and filled with stuff. We all know there's a whole lot more that goes on beneath your roof, but sometimes it's nice to strip all that emotional and spiritual energy away and consider the bare bones of your living structure. Thus we arrive at a room-by-room checklist—a Quick-and-Easy Green Reference Guide for Your Home—meant to inspire more research and thought and that, of course, should be supplemented with the details in the rest of this book.

Use the following checklists when you're about to begin a new project. At the end of the chapter, you'll find tips on hiring green contractors and strategies for overcoming obstacles to greening faced by renters, condo owners, and those bound by covenants. Enjoy!

WHOLE HOME

ENERGY USE

- ☐ Get a home energy audit through your local utility, or do your own energy audit so you can take a targeted approach to making your home more energy efficient.
- ☐ Buy green energy. Find out if your utility has a renewable energy option, or consider purchasing renewable energy certificates to support green energy development.
- ☐ Whether or not you're contemplating going off the grid, consider solar or wind power, and heating sources such as wood, pellets, and corn.
- ☐ Research energy-efficiency tax incentives.
- ☐ Practice conservation methods: turn off and turn down.

INSULATION

- ☐ Insulate, insulate, insulate wherever you can.
- ☐ Look for insulation certified by Energy Star, Green Seal, or Green Guard.
- ☐ Use nontoxic insulation made with recycled formaldehyde-free fiberglass, newspaper, cotton, or mineral/rock wool.
- ☐ Seek greener alternatives to chlorofluorocarbon-based foam insulation.
- ☐ Caulk and weather-strip around windows and doors, and seal up drafty air leaks inside and outside of your home with low-VOC caulk.

WINDOWS AND DAYLIGHTING

- ☐ Install storm windows.
- ☐ Caulk and weather-strip.
- ☐ Restore and weatherize old, well-made windows.
- ☐ Make sure window shades are installed close to the glass and close to the wall on the sides. Lower shades in the summer and raise on south-facing windows in winter. Try high-efficiency dual shades.

- [ ] Invest in insulating window panels, also known as pop-in shutters, or insulated drapes.
- [ ] Use sun shields, blinds, and insulating curtains to regulate temperature.
- [ ] Put an insulating layer of plastic over your windows in the winter.
- [ ] If you need a complete window upgrade, replace old or leaky, steel- or aluminum-framed, and single-pane windows with newer double- or triple-pane windows. Consider investing in coatings that increase their efficiency.
- [ ] Install new windows and skylights and arrange your furniture to take advantage of natural light.

INDOOR AIR QUALITY

- [ ] Use low-VOC, water-based paints and finishes on walls, floors, and furniture
- [ ] Avoid vinyl-based wallpaper.
- [ ] Use green cleaning products.
- [ ] Avoid phthalates, PBDEs, formaldehyde, and other chemicals in the products you choose.
- [ ] Address mold, mildew, radon, lead, and carbon monoxide problems.
- [ ] Make sure your home is ventilated. Consider whole-house ventilation for tight, energy-efficient homes. Open windows regularly.
- [ ] Choose flooring that's durable and made from FSC-certified wood, other natural materials, or from reclaimed or recycled materials.
- [ ] Institute a no-shoes policy to avoid tracking pesticides and other hazardous materials inside your home.
- [ ] Vacuum, mop, and dust with a damp cloth frequently to limit exposure to toxic chemicals in dust.

CONSERVATION PRACTICES

- [ ] Replace incandescent light bulbs with CFL bulbs or LED bulbs.
- [ ] Turn off the lights when you leave a room.
- [ ] Turn off and unplug whatever doesn't need to be on. Use power strips to make turning things off easier.

- ☐ Install a programmable thermostat. Turn down the heat when no one is home and at night.
- ☐ Put on a sweater and load the bed with blankets before raising the thermostat.

KITCHEN

ENERGY- AND WATER-SAVING APPLIANCES

- ☐ If you're shopping, replace your old refrigerator with a new energy-efficient model. Choose a model that's appropriately sized (not too big!) and that has the freezer on top. Skip extras like the ice maker and automatic water dispenser.
- ☐ Or make your old refrigerator more energy efficient. Clean the condenser coils regularly and replace cracked or broken seals around the door.
- ☐ If you like cooking with a gas stove, use one with an electric ignition. Make sure it has a ventilation fan that removes combustion products. If you prefer electric, your best bet is an induction stove.
- ☐ For energy-efficient baking, use a convection oven.
- ☐ Use metallic cookware, like stainless steel or cast iron, rather than nonstick.
- ☐ If you have the option, replace your pre-1994 dishwasher model with a newer, energy-efficient model.

ENERGY-SAVING AND WATER-SAVING PRACTICES

- ☐ Set your refrigerator's temperature at 35° F–38° F. Keep the fridge in a cool place and leave a couple of inches separating it from the wall. Keep the door closed as much as possible.
- ☐ Scrape your dishes, rather than rinsing them, before stacking them in the dishwasher.
- ☐ Don't run the machine until you've loaded it up. And when you do, set the water heater to no higher than 120° F and choose energy-saver, light wash, or shorter cycles. Air dry.

☐ If you don't have a dishwasher, put a stopper in the drain and fill the sink rather than letting the water run. Try filling one basin with soapy water for washing and another with water for rinsing.

☐ Install a low-flow faucet aerator on your sink faucet.

REDUCING WASTE

☐ Keep a recycling bin in the kitchen or in an adjacent closet or storage room.

☐ Put a compost bin on your counter to collect organic waste like food scraps, coffee grounds, and tea leaves.

GREEN CLEANING

☐ Identify and eliminate household cleaners that have toxic, ignitable, corrosive, or reactive ingredients—those classified as household hazardous waste.

☐ Dispose of hazardous products properly by following directions on the bottle. Call your local environmental, health, or solid-waste agency if you have questions about proper disposal.

☐ As an alternative to chemical cleaners, use distilled white vinegar with other pantry ingredients to clean the floor, sink, countertops, and glass surfaces.

☐ Use baking soda as a scouring powder for your floor, sink, and countertops.

☐ Or look for the best commercial green-cleaning brands.

☐ Buy dish detergents that are nontoxic, biodegradable, and vegetable- rather than petroleum-based.

BATHROOM

ENERGY- AND WATER-SAVING APPLIANCES AND PRACTICES

- ☐ For new-toilet installations, buy a low-flow or dual-flush toilet.
- ☐ To make the toilet you've got more efficient, place a brick or half-gallon jug of water or sand in the tank to displace some of the tank water.
- ☐ Upgrade to a low-flow showerhead and faucet aerator.
- ☐ Take shorter showers.
- ☐ Check your faucets for leaks and have them repaired.
- ☐ Ditto on toilet leaks. Put a few drops of food coloring in the tank, and if in about ten minutes the water in your toilet bowl is also colored, you've got a leak.

GREEN CLEANING AND AIR QUALITY

- ☐ Use distilled white vinegar to clean your toilet bowl, as a mildew cleaner, and to clean glass surfaces.
- ☐ Use baking soda as a scouring powder on the tile, tub, sink, and floor.
- ☐ Or look for commercial cleaners that are biodegradable and don't contain petroleum-based chemicals, chlorine bleach, or other toxic chemicals.
- ☐ Pour boiling water or vinegar into drains to get rid of clogs.
- ☐ Avoid commercial air fresheners.
- ☐ Avoid vinyl shower curtains and other PVC products. Consider hemp, cotton, and linen as natural water barriers.
- ☐ Install a ventilation fan.

LIVING ROOM/DINING ROOM

- ☐ Finish your floor and furniture with a water-based polyurethane finish or with drying, hardwax, or soybean-based oils.
- ☐ Avoid wall-to-wall carpeting. If you must have carpeting, choose materials made from recycled or natural fibers or that are Green Seal certified.

- [ ] Look for all-wood furniture that is FSC-certified and upholstery made with a low-VOC finish. If locally made furniture is an option, even better.
- [ ] Choose upholstery made from natural fibers—without stain treatments or fire retardants—such as cotton, hemp, linen, or wool. If you can, go organic. Add pillows stuffed with recycled-fiber filling to accessorize green.
- [ ] Find natural-fiber curtains and shades to complement your upholstery.
- [ ] Check out furniture made from reclaimed or postconsumer-waste recycled materials.
- [ ] Buy used! Visit a secondhand shop near you or check out Craigslist or Freecycle online.

LAUNDRY ROOM

- [ ] If you're in the market for a new washing machine, buy an energy-efficient front-loader.
- [ ] Whenever possible, wash your laundry on the cold/cold cycle.
- [ ] Only wash a full load of laundry.
- [ ] If weather and/or space allow, skip the dryer and take advantage of outdoor sunlight or indoor heat. Dry your laundry on a clothesline or drying rack.
- [ ] If you live in a humid climate or a tiny apartment where line drying is sometimes impractical, use your dryer's moisture-sensing option and keep the lint filter clean. Try drying clothes partially *en plein air* and finishing in the machine.
- [ ] Use biodegradable detergents made without petroleum-based chemicals, toxic dyes, or fragrances.
- [ ] Keep your whites white with oxygen bleach.

NURSERY

- [ ] Use FSC-certified wood flooring with a low-VOC finish. Avoid wall-to-wall carpeting.

- [ ] As an alternative to wall-to-wall carpeting, buy an area rug made from natural fibers to cover hard-surface flooring.
- [ ] Choose carpet padding made of new or recycled natural fibers such as felt, hemp, or jute.
- [ ] Buy a crib, changing table, rocking chair, and bureau made from FSC-certified wood treated without chemical finishes. Secondhand or locally made wood furniture is even better. Buy upholstered furniture made from natural fiber materials and without flame retardants or stain treatments.
- [ ] Choose a crib mattress made of organic wool or cotton or natural latex that meets federal flammability standards without the chemicals.
- [ ] Buy bed linens made from organic cotton.
- [ ] Avoid commercial air fresheners.
- [ ] Use toys made from FSC-certified, unfinished wood and natural fibers. If you do buy toys made from plastic, do some research before shopping, and find out whether the company has removed PVC and BPA from its products.

BEDROOM

- [ ] Avoid wall-to-wall carpeting. It's not as durable as hard-surface floors and it's likely you'll need to replace it. Carpeting also collects dust, mold, bacteria, and other unwanted substances.
- [ ] Consider area rugs and wool carpeting—wool is durable and repels bacteria and dust mites.
- [ ] Choose an organic wool or cotton or natural latex mattress that meets federal flammability standards without chemicals.
- [ ] Buy bed linens made from organic cotton or wool.
- [ ] Buy a bed frame, bureau, nightstand, and other furniture made from reused or FSC-certified wood, or purchase secondhand pieces.

HOME OFFICE

- [ ] Turn off your computer and printer when you're not using them.

- ☐ Unplug your appliances when you go away for a few days or longer.
- ☐ Use smart power strips. The smart strip will stop energy flow to computer appliances when your computer is off.
- ☐ Buy paper that contains *at least* 30 percent postconsumer recycled fiber.
- ☐ Avoid paper bleached with elemental chlorine.
- ☐ Find a computer recycler near you to recycle your old electronics, or recycle them through GreenDisk or other electronics recycling organizations. When purchasing a new computer, printer, or fax machine, find out if the retailer recycles its products in-house and has phased out PBDEs.
- ☐ Refill your ink cartridges, and find an electronics or office-supply store to recycle old cartridges.
- ☐ Keep a basket in your office to collect used batteries. Locate a battery-recycling center in your area and drop off your batteries when the basket is full.

ENTERTAINMENT CENTER

- ☐ Use smart power strips to plug in your TV, DVD player, and other home electronics. The smart strip will stop energy flow to your electronics when they are off.
- ☐ Unplug appliances if you're going away for a few days or longer.
- ☐ Reduce purchases of DVDs by subscribing to Netflix, an on-demand service, or visiting your local library.
- ☐ Recycle your old DVD and VHS videos through GreenDisk or other electronics recycling organizations.
- ☐ Replace energy-intensive electronics with Energy Star–certified alternatives.
- ☐ Reduce the number of electronics you purchase. Ask yourself if you really need something, and consider how quickly that something might become obsolete or outdated.
- ☐ Furnish your entertainment center with secondhand furniture or furniture made from reclaimed or recycled materials.

ATTIC

- ☐ Insulate! A well-insulated attic is essential to heating and cooling your home efficiently, which means saving energy and saving on utility bills.
- ☐ Paint the exterior of your home a light color to reflect light that would otherwise heat up your attic.
- ☐ Make sure the attic is properly ventilated with ridge and soffit vents or other ventilating system.

BASEMENT

- ☐ Add insulation to your basement's interior walls, first checking for leaks or cracks that need repair.
- ☐ Caulk, seal, and weather-strip around windows and doors.
- ☐ Insulate the water heater and exposed pipes connected to it.
- ☐ Set your water heater's temperature no higher than 120° F.
- ☐ Replace your old water heater with a high-efficiency gas storage water heater, a gas condensing, electric heat pump, or tankless water heater.
- ☐ If you have a sunny roof that faces south or west, consider heating your water with the sun.
- ☐ Perform regular maintenance checks on your furnace. If upgrading, consider energy-efficient and Energy Star furnaces.
- ☐ Replace your furnace's air filter regularly, preferably with a HEPA air filter.
- ☐ Consider using biodiesel if you have an oil-burning furnace.

GARAGE

- ☐ Live life without a car as much as possible. If you must own one, buy the most fuel-efficient car that fits your needs.
- ☐ Don't idle your car in your garage, since pollutants can easily enter your home.
- ☐ Keep a bike in the garage—and use it often!

- ☐ Keep your garage clean and organized to avoid pests. Sort through its contents and properly dispose of hazardous chemicals, paints, and oils according to the disposal directions. Call your local environmental, health, or solid-waste agency if you have questions about proper disposal.
- ☐ Keep recycling bins handy in the garage.

ROOF

- ☐ If you want roofing that is long-lasting, durable, attractive, and eco-friendly, check out natural roofing materials like slate, clay, cedar, and roofing made from recycled plastic and industrial rubber—an inexpensive alternative to natural slate. Or grow a green roof.
- ☐ Metal roofing is a great option for reducing heat buildup in the attic, especially if you live in a warm climate.
- ☐ Install skylights on your roof to bring in direct sunlight.
- ☐ Whether you want to establish your energy independence or stay on the grid, consider installing solar panels or shingles on a south-facing part of your roof.

GREEN REMODELING

- ☐ Paint your walls with a water-based, low- or no-VOC paint.
- ☐ Use low-VOC adhesives and finishes.
- ☐ Consider salvaged and reclaimed material. Search for reusable building supplies near your home on the Building Materials Reuse Association website.
- ☐ Avoid vinyl and laminated floors.
- ☐ Choose flooring, countertops, tables, and cabinets made of durable, long-lasting, and natural materials such as FSC-certified wood, bamboo, cork, or natural linoleum; recycled materials such as glass or concrete; or other green alternatives.
- ☐ For wood floors, use a water-based polyurethane finish or drying, hard-wax, or soybean-based oils.

- [ ] Choose ceramic or glass tile made from postconsumer or postindustrial waste.
- [ ] Install ventilation fans.
- [ ] Planning a pregnancy? Remodel beforehand so that you don't have to worry about exposure to paint fumes, dust, and debris.
- [ ] If you're hiring a remodeler, make sure he or she is certified green.

YARD

LANDSCAPING AND LAWN CARE

- [ ] Collect rainwater from the gutter in a 50-gallon barrel. Connect the barrel to a garden hose or fill a watering can to water plants and gardens.
- [ ] Plant trees and shrubs to provide shade for your yard and home, and nourishment for local wildlife.
- [ ] Choose native grasses or low-mow varieties for your lawn.
- [ ] Mow the grass to a couple inches in length, no shorter.
- [ ] Let grass clippings lie where they fall.
- [ ] Trade your gas mower for a push (reel) mower or an electric or battery-powered one.
- [ ] Apply organic fertilizers and natural supplements to your lawn, trees, and shrubs rather than using their chemical counterparts.
- [ ] Purchase long-lasting steel and metal tools for yard work.

GARDENING AND COMPOSTING

- [ ] Plant a kitchen garden or join or start a community garden. Find a gardening book you like, start small, experiment, and have fun!
- [ ] Have your soil tested so that you can take a targeted approach to keeping your soil healthy and nutrient-rich.
- [ ] Apply organic fertilizers and natural supplements to your garden.
- [ ] Pull—don't poison—weeds. Keep your garden mulched to deter weeds from sprouting.

- [ ] Keep a compost bin or pile in your yard. Your kitchen scraps and lawn clippings will provide a sustainable—not to mention free—fertilizer.

INDOOR GARDENING AND COMPOSTING

- [ ] If you live in an apartment or don't have a backyard, try vermi-composting.
- [ ] Grow potted herbs and vegetables in a sunny window indoors. Or choose varieties that can thrive without long periods of direct sunlight.
- [ ] Even if you're not ready to commit to indoor gardening, add potted plants to help keep the air in your home clean.

SIGNING ON THE DOTTED LINE: FINDING GREEN CONTRACTORS

Doing it yourself is all the rage in home remodeling these days. Thus the proliferation of big-box stores like Lowe's and Home Depot. But let's face it. Not all of us have the talent or the time. There's nothing wrong with asking for help, especially if that help wields a hammer with the earth in mind. By 2013, 20 to 30 percent of the renovation market will be green, which should mean your odds are good for finding a green contractor.

Yet what makes a contractor green? Some say the best contractor is one who will listen to you and who understands your values—it doesn't matter if she puts the correct color adjective in front of the business name. Someone who respects your choices and does good-quality work—like building lasting living spaces—is probably the best choice around. Book that person. If your market is flooded with contractors pledging green, you may need to make an evaluation. In general, a good green contractor incorporates sustainability throughout all aspects of the business (even advertising); recycles waste; uses green materials (both in terms of indoor air quality and resource use) and uses them efficiently; is versed in the latest technologies (since most new technologies are green technologies) that save you energy or water or space; and recycles or reuses the leftovers.

How does one find such a dreamy combination? Generally, word of mouth is the best way. Ask friends or neighbors. Inquire at the local hardware store. Most good contractors don't even need to advertise—their work comes through word of mouth. The web can also be very useful in helping you narrow your search. Low Impact Living has an online database of green contractors, searchable by zip code or state. Write-ups of various companies provide a little information about why they're considered green. The ReDirect Guide, an online reference (and published book) for environmental living in several western cities, has lists of ecofriendly contractors. And the U.S. Green Building Council's Green Home Guide is an online directory that features contractors and reviews from past clients.

Like good green products, many good contractors, green or not, are certified. There are an abundance of certification programs, so many it may be difficult to decide which are legitimate and which are just window dressing. One that carries some credibility is the Evergreen Institute, which has centers in Colorado, Missouri, and western New York where coursework is taught and certification is available to building professionals. Certificates in Residential Renewable Energy and Residential Green Building are available after coursework is completed. Another is the U.S. Green Building Council's LEED Accredited Professionals program. Practitioners take coursework and must pass an exam on LEED practices (LEED stands for Leadership in Energy and Environmental Design). Finally, there are several regional certifications—for example, in California, Build It Green. These programs should make you feel confident in the strong green foundation of your contractor's practices, especially if the word *remodel* seems daunting in every way.

THE SACRED COVENANTS: INFLUENCING RULES AND REGULATIONS

Living in a condominium, apartment building, and even some neighborhoods may mean that you're bound by the covenants of a homeowners' association or the decisions of a landlord. Rather than enjoying the freedom to make environmentally friendly choices for your living space, you might find yourself trying to influence people. And while leveraging opinion and plotting political tactics may sound exciting, anyone who's spent time in these trenches will attest that it can be downright discouraging. We live in changing times, though. Greening up a building or a yard is neither extravagant nor fringe. It makes economic sense and is becoming more mainstream every day. The tide is turning in your favor.

No one will argue against saving money. This is your strongest suit. Just about every green upgrade you might suggest—from replacing common-area light bulbs with CFLs to setting up a laundry line in the backyard to weatherizing or upgrading windows—can be translated into dollars saved for the renter, land-lord, or condo owner.

Take windows as an example. There are so many design options for new green windows and so many restoration choices for historic windows that even if you're facing restrictions on the style of windows allowed, you can easily meet them. And since energy costs are constantly rising, those upgraded windows will bring greater and greater financial savings. The same type of thinking is applicable to installing low-flow showerheads or an energy-efficient water heater, which will reduce water usage, water bills, sewage fees, and electricity bills. Or consider building materials. The cost is high, salvaged materials are cheaper, and they come in every style, shape, color, and vintage under the sun—any number of which could be acceptable to even the finickiest of condo associations. Even ecofriendly landscaping is less expensive. Your landlord won't have to spend money on chemicals or on companies to manage elaborate, water-intensive systems; he won't have to buy a lot of fuel to power lawn mowers, weed whackers, and other carbon-intensive gizmos.

Aside from the economics, no one will argue against happy long-term tenants and condo- or homeowners. Reducing turnover is a great incentive, and stability is a much sought after quality in tenants. People are more likely to stick around if they feel good about where they live, and nothing delivers on this front like green. Landlords and homeowners and condo associations will find the green features of their buildings and developments highly marketable. Present it this way: Who wouldn't want to live somewhere that had a community recycling program? Or chemical-free, LEED-certified landscaping? Or a community garden or rain barrels and native plants? Or a tool-lending library or solar hot water or energy-efficient appliances or no-VOC paint in all the rooms?

Finally, don't let someone's sense of aesthetics be a stumbling block. Here's where your practiced powers of persuasion will come in handy. If your homeown-ers' association's covenants prohibit laundry lines simply because they're considered too down-home, it's time for a major paradigm shift. Sure, you can bombard the naysayers with statistics and facts about how clothes dryers waste a colossal amount of energy, and how in a decade we won't need dryers in many parts of the country because clothes will practically dry of their own accord due to increasing temperature shifts upward…but c'mon, that's tacky. Even the most curmudgeonly home-owners' association president has to admit there's something simply beautiful about vibrant sheets blowing in the breeze. And there's nothing like the smell once you bring them inside.

THE REST OF THE STORY

The point is, it's time to change the rules to match the times. It's not hard to see the value of a drought-tolerant, native bunch grass or an energy audit for your entire complex, especially when you consider what's at stake. And right here in your home begins the rest of the story.

I've outlined some issues, pointed you toward resources, given you a few tools for the task. The rest is up to you. How do you want to make a difference? What motivates you each morning as you sit at the kitchen table, after coffee has cleared away the fog? Is it clean energy or clean air, vast forests or a backyard garden, the well-made beauty of that which is old or the exciting promise of the techy and new? Your home can embody all of these things. Draft your blueprint accordingly.

RECOMMENDED RESOURCES

GREEN ENERGY: EFFICIENCY AND RENEWABLES

The Carbon-Free Home: 36 Remodeling Projects to Help Kick the Fossil-Fuel Habit, by Stephen and Rebekah Hren (Chelsea Green, 2008)

The Homeowner's Guide to Renewable Energy: Achieving Energy Independence through Solar, Wind, Biomass, and Hydropower, by Dan Chiras (New Society, 2006)

The Human-Powered Home, by Tamara Dean (New Society, 2008)

Natural Home Heating: The Complete Guide to Renewable Energy Options, by Greg Pahl (Chelsea Green, 2003)

ClimateWorks Foundation, www.climateworks.org ("philanthropic network dedicated to achieving low-carbon prosperity")

Green-e.org (certification and verification program for renewable energy and emissions)

Home Power Magazine, http://homepower.com

National Renewable Energy Laboratory, www.nrel.gov

Native Energy, www.nativeenergy.com (sells carbon offsets)

Network for New Energy Choices, www.newenergychoices.org

Rocky Mountain Institute, www.rmi.org (researches efficient and sustainable resource use)

Union of Concerned Scientists, "Clean Energy," www.ucsusa.org

EFFICIENCY

Consumer Guide to Home Energy Savings, 9th ed., by Jennifer Thorne Amann, Alex Wilson, and Katie Ackerly (New Society, 2007)

Air Conditioning Contractors of America, www.acca.org

Database of State Incentives for Renewables and Energy (DSIRE), www.dsireusa.org

Energy Star, www.energystar.gov

Environmental Defense Fund, "Make the Switch to Energy-Saving Bulbs," www.edf.org/page.cfm?tagid=608

Home Energy Saver, http://hes.lbl.gov

Low-Income Home Energy Assistance Program, http://liheap.ncat.org/wwa.htm

North American Board of Certified Energy Practitioners, www.nabcep.org

RESNET (Residential Energy Services Network), www.natresnet.org

U.S. Department of Energy Weatherization Assistance Program, http://apps1.eere.energy.gov/weatherization

BIOFUELS AND WOOD

Alternative Fuels Furnace Yahoo Group, www.groups.yahoo.com/group/altfuelfurnace

Biodiesel Now www.biodieselnow.com

Biodiesel Magazine www.biodieselmagazine.com

Journey to Forever online biofuels library, www.journeytoforever.org/biofuel_library.html

National Biodiesel Board, www.biodiesel.org

Natural Resources Defense Council, "Homegrown Energy from Biofuels," www.nrdc.org/energy/biofuels.asp

U.S. Environmental Protection Agency, Burn Wise website, www.epa.gov/burnwise

WIND AND SOLAR

American Wind Energy Association, www.awea.org

Build It Solar, www.builditsolar.com (DIY solar projects)

Community Energy, www.communityenergyinc.com (promotes wind and solar energy)

Find Solar directory, www.findsolar.com

One Block Off the Grid, http://1bog.org ("solar power meets consumer power")

U.S. Department of Energy, "Estimating a Solar Water Heater System's Cost," www.energysavers.gov/your_home/water_heating/index.cfm/

AVOIDING TOXICS INSIDE AND OUT

The Body Toxic: How the Hazardous Chemistry of Everyday Things Threatens Our Health and Well-Being, by Nena Baker (North Point, 2008)

Raising Baby Green: The Earth-Friendly Guide to Pregnancy, Childbirth, and Baby Care, by Alan Greene, with Jeanette Pavini and Theresa Foy DiGeronimo (John Wiley & Sons, 2007)

Slow Death by Rubber Duck: The Secret Danger of Everyday Things, by Rick Smith and Bruce Lourie (Counterpoint, 2010)

The Toxic Consumer: Living Healthy in a Hazardous World, by Karen Ashton and Elizabeth Salter Green (Sterling, 2008)

What's In This Stuff? The Hidden Toxins in Everyday Products—and What You Can Do about Them, by Patricia Thomas (Perigee, 2008)

Cancer Prevention Coalition, "Avoidable Exposures: Consumers," www.preventcancer.com/consumers (household products information)

Coming Clean, www.chemicalbodyburden.org

Consumer Products Safety Commission, www.cpsc.gov

Environmental Health Perspectives, http://ehp.niehs.nih.gov

Environmental Working Group, "Health/Toxics," www.ewg.org/health

Greenguard Environmental Institute, www.greenguard.org (certifies products for green indoor air quality)

Washington Toxics Coalition, "Chemicals of Concern," at http://watoxics.org

LEAD AND RADON

Centers for Disease Control and Prevention, Childhood Lead Poisoning Prevention Branch, www.cdc.gov/nceh/lead/about/program.htm

National Safety Council, Lead Poisoning Prevention Outreach Program, www.nsc.org/ehc/lead.htm; and the "Environmental Health and Safety" webpage for radon, www.nsc.org/safety_home/Resources/Pages/EnvironmentalHealthandSafety.aspx

U.S. Department of Housing and Urban Development, Office of Healthy Homes and Lead Hazard Control, www.hud.gov/offices/lead/index.cfm

U.S. Environmental Protection Agency, National Lead Information Center, www.epa.gov/lead/pubs/nlic.htm; and the agency's "Radon" webpage, www.epa.gov/radon

PAINT

Natural Paint Book: A Complete Guide to Natural Paints, Recipes, and Finishes, by Lynn Edwards and Julia Lawless (Rodale, 2003)

PESTICIDES

Beyond Pesticides, www.beyondpesticides.org

Environmental Research Foundation, www.rachel.org

Green Shield Certified, www.greenshieldcertified.org (nontoxic pest control)

National Coalition for Pesticide-Free Lawns, www.beyondpesticides.org /pesticidefreelawns

Northwest Coalition for Alternatives to Pesticides, www.pesticide.org

Pesticide Action Network North America, www.panna.org

Safer Pest Control Project, www.spcpweb.org

University of California, integrated pest management (IPM) website, www.ipm
.ucdavis.edu

Washington Toxics Coalition, "Healthy Homes and Gardens," http://watoxics.org

PVC

Greenpeace, "PVC Products," www.greenpeace.org/international
/campaigns/toxics/polyvinyl-chloride/pvc-products#

Center for Health, Environment and Justice, "PVC: The Poison Plastic," www.chej
.org/BESAFE/pvc

GREEN CLEANING

Better Basics for the Home: Simple Solutions for Less Toxic Living,
Annie B. Bond (Three Rivers Press, 1999)

*Easy Green Living: The Ultimate Guide to Simple, Eco-Friendly
Choices for You and Your Home*, by Renée Loux (Rodale, 2008)

Green Housekeeping, by Ellen Sandbeck (Scribner, 2008)

*Home Enlightenment: Creating a Nurturing, Healthy and Toxin-Free
Home*, by Annie B. Bond (Rodale, 2005)

Nontoxic Housecleaners Zine, by Raleigh Briggs (Microcosm Publishing, 2008)

Care2, www.care2.com/greenliving/healthy-home/nontoxic-cleaning

Great Green List, www.greatgreenlist.com (search "eco-friendly cleaning services")

Green Guide, www.thegreenguide.com/home-garden/cleaning

National Library of Medicine Household Products Database, http://household
products.nlm.nih.gov

Women's Voices for the Earth, www.womenandenvironment.org/greencleaning

GREEN YARD CARE AND GARDENING

GARDENING, GENERAL

Eat Where You Live: How to Find and Enjoy Local and Sustainable Food No Matter Where You Live, by Lou Bendrick (Skipstone, 2008)

Ecology for Gardeners, Steven B. Carroll and Steven D. Salt (Timber Press, 2004)

Edible Estates: Attack on the Front Lawn, by Fritz Haeg (Metropolis Books, 2008)

Food Not Lawns: How to Turn Your Yard into a Garden and Your Neighborhood into a Community, by Heather Coburn Flores (Chelsea Green, 2006)

The Garden Primer, 2nd ed., by Barbara Damrosch (Workman, 2008)

The Green Gardener's Guide: Simple, Significant Actions to Protect and Preserve Our Planet, by Joe Lamp'l (Cool Springs Press, 2008)

Sunset National Garden Book (Sunset Publishing Corp., 1997)

U.S. Composting Council, www.compostingcouncil.org (about the composting industry)

You Grow Girl, "Lawns to Gardens," by Beate Schwirtlich, www.yougrowgirl.com /lawns_gardens_convert.php

URBAN, CONTAINER, AND INDOOR GARDENING

All New Square Foot Gardening: Grow More in Less Space!, by Mel Bartholomew (Cool Springs Press, 2006)

Fresh Food from Small Spaces: The Square-Inch Gardener's Guide to Year-Round Growing, Fermenting, and Sprouting, by R. J. Ruppenthal (Chelsea Green, 2008)

The Urban Homestead: Your Guide to Self-Sufficient Living in the Heart of the City, by Kelly Coyne and Erik Knutzen (Process, 2008)

City Farmer News blog, www.cityfarmer.info

Container Gardening Guide blog, http://containergardeningtips.com

Urban Gardening Help blog, www.urbangardeninghelp.com

GARDENING WITH NATIVES, WILDLIFE, AND THE CLIMATE

Bringing Nature Home: How Native Plants Sustain Wildlife in Our Gardens, by Douglas Tallamy (Timber Press, 2007)

The Dry Gardening Handbook: Plants and Practices for a Changing Climate, by Olivier Filippi (Thames & Hudson, 2008)

Dryland Gardening: Plants that Survive and Thrive in Tough Conditions, by Jennifer Bennett (Firefly Books, 2005)

Guide to Growing and Propagating Wildflowers of the United States and Canada, by William Cullina (Houghton Mifflin Harcourt, 2000)

Noah's Garden: Restoring the Ecology of Our Own Backyards, by Sara Stein (Houghton Mifflin Harcourt, 1995)

Xeriscape Handbook: A How-to Guide to Natural Resource-Wise Gardening, by Gayle Weinstein (Fulcrum, 1999)

National Wildlife Federation, "Garden for Wildlife: Making Wildlife Habitat at Home," www.nwf.org/Get-Outside/Outdoor-Activities/Garden-for-Wildlife.aspx

U.S. Department of Agriculture, plants database, http://plants.usda.gov

Wild Ones: Native Plants, Natural Landscapes, www.for-wild.org

COMMUNITY GARDENING

Sharing the Harvest: A Citizens Guide to Community Supported Agriculture, rev. ed., by Elizabeth Henderson and Robyn Van En (Chelsea Green, 2007)

American Community Garden Association, www.communitygarden.org

LAWNS

The Organic Lawn Care Manual: A Natural, Low-Maintenance System for a Beautiful, Safe Lawn, by Paul Tukey (Storey, 2007)

Safelawns.org (promotes natural lawn care)

GREEN WATER USE

Water Stewardship: A 30-Day Program On How to Protect and Conserve Our Water Resources One Drop at a Time, by David Gershon (Empowerment Institute, 2007)

U.S. Environmental Protection Agency, "Ground Water and Drinking Water," www.epa.gov/safewater/index.html; or call the agency's Safe Drinking Water Hotline, 800-426-4791

U.S. Environmental Protection Agency, "Water Efficient Landscape Planner" software, www.epa.gov/greenacres/water.html

U.S. Environmental Protection Agency, WaterSense program, www.epa.gov /watersense

CONSUMPTION BUSTING: REDUCE, REUSE, RECYCLE

REDUCE

Catalog Choice, www.catalogchoice.org

41pounds.org, "Junk Mail Impact," www.41pounds.org/impact

Life without Plastic, www.lifewithoutplastic.com

Mailstopper service from Tonic, http://precycle.tonic.com

National Do Not Mail List, www.directmail.com/directory/mail_preference

OptOutPrescreen.com (to opt in or out of credit and insurance offers)

YellowPagesGoesGreen.org (to opt out of phone book delivery)

REUSE

BabyPlays, http://mybabyplays.com (the Netflix of toys)

BarterBee, www.barterbee.com

Bookmooch, http://bookmooch.com

Craigslist, www.craigslist.org

Dress for Success, www.dressforsuccess.org (gives disadvantaged women suitable clothes for job interviews)

eBay Green Team, www.ebaygreenteam.com

Freecycle, www.freecycle.org

Glass Slipper Project, www.glassslipperproject.org (recycle your prom dress!)

Habitat for Humanity, ReStore directory by state, www.habitat.org/cd/env/restore.aspx

LendList.org (lending network)

PaperBackSwap, www.paperbackswap.com

Swap-O-Rama-Rama, http://swaporamarama.org (clothes trading)

Swapstyle, www.swapstyle.com (clothes trading)

SwapTree, www.swaptree.com (trade books, DVDs, etc.)

Throwplace.com ("take what you need and throw what you don't")

The ULS Report, http://use-less-stuff.com

Zwaggle, www.zwaggle.com (swap and share stuff for kids)

RECYCLE

Basel Action Network, www.ban.org (lists responsible recyclers of electronics)

CollectiveGood, www.collectivegood.com (cell phone reuse/recycling)

Earth911, http://earth911.com (recycling for anything you can think of)

Gazelle, www.gazelle.com (electronics reuse/recycling)

LampRecycle.org (CFL recycling)

National Cristina Foundation, www.cristina.org (computer reuse/recycling)

Preserve Inc.'s Gimme 5 plastic recycling program, www.preserveproducts.com/recycling/gimme5.html

TechSoup, http://home.techsoup.org (computer reuse/recycling)

U.S. Environmental Protection Agency, "Mercury-Containing Light Bulb (Lamp) Collection and Recycling," www.epa.gov/epawaste/hazard/wastetypes/universal/lamps

U.S. Environmental Protection Agency, "Plug-In to eCycling Partners," www.epa.gov/epawaste/partnerships/plugin/partners.htm

GREEN BUILDING AND REMODELING

The Carbon-Free Home: 36 Remodeling Projects to Help Kick the Fossil-Fuel Habit, by Stephen and Rebekah Hren (Chelsea Green, 2008)

Green Decorating and Remodeling: Design Ideas and Sources for a Beautiful Eco-Friendly Home, by Heather Paper (Globe Pequot, 2008)

Green Remodeling: Changing the World One Room at a Time, by David Johnston and Kim Master (New Society, 2004)

Make Your Place: Affordable, Sustainable Nesting Skills, by Raleigh Briggs (Microcosm Publishing, 2008)

Your Green Home: A Guide to Planning a Healthy, Environmentally Friendly New Home, by Alex Wilson (New Society, 2006)

Alliance for Credible Forest Certification, http://credibleforestcertification.org/home/

Building Materials Reuse Association, www.bmra.org

Construction Materials Recycling Association, www.cdrecycling.org (building materials reuse/recycle)

Cradle to Cradle, www.c2ccertified.com (promotes environmentally intelligent design)

Forest Stewardship Council, www.fsc.org

Healthy Building Network, www.healthybuilding.net

Low Impact Living, www.lowimpactliving.com (includes directory of green contractors)

National Association of the Remodeling Industry, www.nari.org

National Fenestration Rating Council's Certified Products Directory, www.nfrc.org/getratings.aspx

ReBuilding Center, http://rebuildingcenter.org

ReDirect Guide, www.redirectguide.com (includes directory of green contractors)

Smartwood, www.smartwood.org

Sustainable Furnishings Council, www.sustainablefurnishings.org

U.S. Green Building Council's Green Home Guide, http://greenhomeguide.com

GREEN LIVING AND GREEN GOODS

Ecoholic: Your Guide to the Most Environmentally Friendly Information, Products, and Services, by Adria Vasil (W. W. Norton, 2009)

The Lazy Environmentalist: Your Guide to Easy, Stylish, Green Living, by Josh Dorfman (Stewart, Tabori & Chang, 2007)

Green Greener Greenest: A Practical Guide to Making Eco-Smart Choices a Part of Your Life, by Lori Bongiorno (Penguin, 2008)

Natural Capitalism: Creating the Next Industrial Revolution, by Paul Hawkin, Amory B. Lovins, and L. Hunter Lovins (Little, Brown and Company, 2000)

Consumer Reports, GreenerChoices website, www.greenerchoices.org

GreenRenter.com (searchable database of green rentals)

Green Your Apartment blog, http://greenyourapartment.com

Institute for Market Transformation to Sustainability, http://mts.sustainableproducts.com (promotes sustainable product choices)

Natural Home magazine, www.naturalhomemagazine.com

Sierra Club: GreenHome, www.sierraclubgreenhome.com

Walk Score, www.walkscore.com (rates neighborhoods on walkability)

ACKNOWLEDGMENTS

It takes a village to raise a child—the same could be said for writing a book. I've been lucky to have help with both. First of all, thanks to Don Snow for encouraging and fostering my career in words. Lou Bendrick and Dana Youlin planted the seeds—without them this book would not exist. Hal Clifford provided grounding and guidance at the beginning too. I've trusted and done well by his advice for many years. Hannah Fries and Erica Dorpalen added their keen insight. You two are amazing. Carole Gunter, Meg Miner, and Tes Reed buoyed me during my first months as a new mother. Without their patience and love for my daughter, I could never have found the time to sit and write. A special thanks goes to Tes for her green-cleaning expertise.

I'm also indebted to the folks who took time out of their busy lives to answer my questions: Jade Mortimer, Sandra Steingraber, Julia Brody, Sam Newman, Natalie Mims, and Raina Weber. Thank you. The wonderful ladies at Skipstone showed endless patience and understanding while I missed deadlines and struggled to balance a career, a baby, and a book—all the while sleep deprived. Many thanks to Kate Rogers, Mary Metz, and Julie Van Pelt for being easy on me. Austin, the best Australian shepherd on the planet, got me out for necessary head-clearing exercises like walking, running, hiking, and skiing. He takes his job seriously.

Signe was with me all the while I wrote—both inside and out. I didn't think it could be done, but she taught me that anything is possible.

Jason believed in this project from the beginning and was with me on it until the end. Without his cooking, babysitting, grocery shopping, house cleaning, encouragement, humor, endurance, vision, hours of research, and bountiful love, there would be no *Your Green Abode*. Thank you J. You are my foundation.

INDEX

ABOUT THE AUTHOR

Photo by Jamie Goldenberg

Tara Rae Miner has written about the environment for more than ten years, both as a freelancer and as an editor at *Camas, Chronicle of Community, Headwaters News*, and, most recently, as managing editor of *Orion* magazine. She has a master's degree in science from the Environmental Studies Program at the University of Montana. Tara's first eco-friendly home restoration, a former schoolhouse built in 1849, took place in New Marlborough, Massachusetts. Her new green abode is in Portland, Oregon, where she writes and lives with her husband, daughter, and remarkable Australian shepherd. This is her first book.

Urban Pantry: Tips & Recipes for a Thrifty, Sustainable & Seasonal Kitchen
Amy Pennington
Photography by Della Chen
A modern guide to stocking your kitchen and making the most out of food you buy or grow

Wake Up and Smell the Planet: The Non-Pompous, Non-Preachy Grist Guide to Greening Your Day
Grist Magazine; Edited by Brangien Davis
An irreverent and resourceful handbook for simplifying and greening your daily choices

Eco-Chic Home: Rethink, Reuse & Remake Your Way to Sustainable Style
Emily Anderson
Photography by Seth and Kendra Smoot
More than 60 easy design projects for an eco-friendly home

The Salvage Studio: Sustainable Home Comforts to Organize, Entertain, and Inspire
Amy Duncan, Beth Evans-Ramos, Lisa Hilderbrand
Photography by Kate Baldwin
Inspiration and do-it-yourself projects to create a warm and comforting home

Eat Where You Live: How to Find and Enjoy Local and Sustainable Food No Matter Where You Live
Lou Bendrick
A user-friendly field guide for eating healthy, locally grown foods

SKIPSTONE

www.skipstonebooks.org
www.mountaineersbooks.org
800-553-4453